What they said about mas Myler's previous books

Boxing's Hall of Shame

'Vell written and thoroughly researched by one of he best boxing writers in these islands. Myler has een eye for the story behind the story. A must read for all fight fans.'

Yorkshire Post

'xing scribe Thomas Myler shares with the reader a side seat for the sport's most controversial fights. an engaging read, one that feeds our fascination with the darker side of the sport.'

Bert Sugar, author and broadcaster

Ringside with the Celtic Warriors

'e latest offering from this highly respected boxing er is well up to the standard we expect from him.'

Boxing News

'Thomas Myler has come up with another gem. credentials and easy, readable style make this a must book for fight fans.'

The Sun

's a ring historian, Thomas Myler has few peers.'

Belfast Telegraph

Close Encounters with the Gloves Off

'ding like a beautiful love letter to the fight game's ous past, there's not a better boxing book on the shelves – anywhere.'

Irish Independent

'Admired and respected around the world, Thomas Myler has surpassed himself with this latest offering.'

Dublin Herald

Sugar Ray Robinson: The Inside Story

'It's all here, from Robinson's impoverished upb' ... New York, through his rise t ... ntual decline

Boxing News

NEW YORK
FIGHT NIGHTS
STATESIDE SCRAPS, SCRAPES AND SCUFFLES

THOMAS MYLER

First published by Pitch Publishing, 2017

Pitch Publishing
A2 Yeoman Gate
Yeoman Way
Worthing
Sussex
BN13 3QZ

www.pitchpublishing.co.uk
info@pitchpublishing.co.uk

A CIP catalogue record is available for this book
from the British Library.

ISBN 978-1-78531-299-1

Typesetting and origination by Pitch Publishing
Printed in the UK by Bell & Bain, Glasgow, Scotland

Contents

Thomas Myler is a well-known boxing historian, journalist, author and broadcaster. This is his eighth book. His most recent was *Close Encounters with the Gloves Off*, also published by Pitch, which includes interviews with famous boxing champions recalling the highs and lows of their careers. Thomas has spent a lifetime around boxers and boxing, and his work has appeared in many publications including *Boxing News*, *Boxing Illustrated*, *Boxing Digest* and *Fighting Fit*, plus Irish newspapers and magazines. He lives in Dublin.

Dedication

To Betty,
the undisputed champion

Acknowledgements

THIS book would not have been possible without the help of so many people too numerous to mention. But special note must be made of *Boxing News* and *Independent News and Media* for their always helpful assistance, as well as fine writers like Bob Mee and John Jarrett, two very good friends and true experts in the noble art. What they don't know about boxing is not worth knowing. My family, too, were always by my side, Jacqueline, Sinead, Ciaran, Colin and Vivian. Sadly, my wife Betty passed away after a short illness before I started writing this book, but she would have given it her full approval.

Many of the photographs are by kind permission of Associated Press, Press Association, *Boxing News, Ring, Irish Independent* and *Evening Herald*. The remainder are from the Thomas Myler Collection. Last but certainly not least, full credit must go to Pitch Publishing for having the foresight, dedication and care to get the book into print. Credit here must go to publishing executives Paul and Jane Camillin and their excellent team.

Thank you all.

Introduction

BOXING was first established in New York on 17 July 1882, when the newly opened Madison Square Garden at East 26th Street and Madison Avenue in Manhattan featured its first world champion, heavyweight John L Sullivan. Of Irish parentage, Sullivan was the man who used to walk into a bar in his native Boston, slam his huge right fist on the counter and declare, before ordering a large beer: 'My name is John L Sullivan and I can lick any sonofabitch in the house.' Not surprisingly, there were never any takers.

Sullivan had won the title five months earlier, when he knocked out Paddy Ryan in nine rounds in Mississippi. Boxing was at the time fought under London Prize Ring Rules with tight, unpadded gloves. Essentially, it was bare-knuckle fighting. For John L's Garden appearance, the occasion would be an exhibition over four rounds with an Englishman, Tug Wilson from Leicestershire, with no title at stake.

Wilson had begun his ring career in fairgrounds and built up a reputation as a tough, rugged battler. He expressed the view that he would return to England as Sullivan's conqueror and new champion. Wilson was managed by the publisher Richard K Fox, who had backed a succession of fighters to beat the 'Boston Strong Boy' with no success. This time, Wilson could well be the man to pull it off. A crowd of 12,000 witnessed a farce. Fox accepted John L's boast that if an opponent was still on his feet after four rounds, he could take the $1,000 forfeit as well as half the gate receipts. It didn't matter to Wilson that he was effectively an overgrown middleweight, having started his career as a featherweight. He was also 35 years of age while John L was in his prime, with his 24th birthday coming up.

All through the scheduled four rounds, with sweat rolling down his bulging torso, Sullivan relentlessly pursued his quarry in the stifling arena – and every time he came within striking distance, Wilson went down, usually before a blow was landed. In the opening round, the Leicester fighter hit the canvas seven times, each time staying down for a count of nine, which effectively meant he spent slightly more than a third of the round on the floor.

Grabbing, holding, wrestling and running at every opportunity, Wilson continued to drop regularly at the approach of the tiring champion and he was still technically on his feet when the final bell sounded. Sullivan was wild with rage, and he had reason to be, for not only had he failed, mainly through his own slowness and general lack of fitness, to knock out a third-rate opponent but he had lost the $1,000 forfeit and half the gate takings. 'You're a cheat,' he bellowed across the ring at Wilson. 'That was no fight. It was a farce. You disgraced my name in front of all these people, people who came to watch a fair fight and didn't get it. We'll have to fight again.'

They never did. Deep down, Wilson knew in his own heart he would stand little if any chance with Sullivan in a real fight, no matter how long it lasted. Returning to England he continued his career, trading on his newly acquired fame that he was still on his feet after taking on the great John L – and calling himself champion of the world. Nobody took him seriously. There was only one man entitled to that claim – Sullivan himself.

John L was back at the Garden on 14 May 1883, when he stopped Birmingham's Charlie Mitchell, the British Empire champion, in three rounds. Prizefighting was illegal in New York but the organisers would get around what they called 'that little problem' by listing the fights as 'sparring matches' or 'exhibitions in the manly art of self defence'. For the Sullivan–Mitchell fight, there were two local policemen at ringside to keep a sharp eye on proceedings. US sources list the result as a KO in the third round but it was officially stopped on orders from the cops, who motioned to Sullivan's corner that they bring the affair to a close. At this stage, the Englishman was hanging helpless and almost motionless on the ropes, with John L about to charge in and apply the finisher.

'Just one more crack at him,' pleaded Sullivan to his cornermen. 'Let me hit him just once more.' 'Do you want to kill him, John?' responded one of them. 'It's all over.' The 'Boston Strong Boy' was practically in tears as he left the ring. He had wanted a clean knockout and never got it.

Sullivan returned to the Garden on 19 January 1885 to meet his old rival, Irishman Paddy Ryan, who had lost the title to John L three years earlier in nine rounds. This time, the man from County Tipperary lasted just under a minute before the police intervened.

By now, Madison Square Garden was well established as a premier boxing venue, not only in New York but across America and the rest of the world. The building lasted four more years before needing repair but the owner, William Vanderbilt, decided to pull it down and rebuild it on the same site, at Madison Square on East 26th Street and Madison Avenue. MSG 2 opened with a flourish in June 1890 and over the next three decades many of the greatest boxers of all time would display their skills and punching power there, including James J Corbett, Mickey Walker, Harry Greb, Benny Leonard, Jack Dempsey and Gene Tunney.

The Frawley Law came into effect in 1911 and permitted boxing for the general public, although one of its conditions was that all contests must be billed as exhibitions with no decision given at the finish. Because of this, no man could officially win a bout except by a knockout or stoppage, and so the champions were comparatively safe as they avoided dangerous opponents who could claim their titles if impressive enough.

During this period of no-decision contests, there was what was referred to as 'popular verdicts', the winner being decided by a majority of the newspaper reporters. However, these verdicts did not carry enough weight to deprive a man of his title. All this changed in 1920 when the Walker Law came into effect and official decisions became the norm.

By 1925, the Garden required a facelift and the owners New York Life made up their minds to demolish it and create an entirely new structure. The last fight in the old arena was on 25 May 1925 between Italy's Johnny Dundee, the former world featherweight champion, and New York's Sid Terris, won by Terris on points. The new site was at Eighth Avenue between 49th and 50th Streets. MSG 3 was completed in just 249 days and could seat around 19,000 for boxing. One of the principal investors was the promoter Tex Rickard, the Don King of his day.

Rickard had promoted the first ever world championship fight at Madison Square Garden on 25 March 1916, when he persuaded big Jess Willard to defend his heavyweight title against Frank Moran, one of the White Hopes during the Jack Johnson era. Willard had won the title almost a year earlier when he knocked out the veteran Johnson in 26 rounds in Havana, Cuba. Willard won the newspaper decision after ten rounds and the fight attracted a new record gate of $152,000.

Rickard's major drawing card was the world heavyweight champion Jack Dempsey. Tex promoted five of Jack's big fights which topped $1 million – the second fight with Gene Tunney, the famous Battle of the Long Count in September 1927, reaching well over $2 million.

The new MSG opened on 11 December 1925 with much fanfare and would be known as The House That Tex Built. The first fight there was naturally a Rickard promotion and featured Paul Berlenbach, a New Yorker and former Olympic wrestling champion, successfully defending his world light-heavyweight title against the skilful Canadian Jack Delaney and winning a split decision over 15 rounds. Berlenbach had taken the title from Ireland's Mike McTigue on points seven months earlier but was considered lucky to beat Delaney. He was floored in the third round and was in bad trouble in the sixth and seventh but rallied in the later rounds to save his title.

By 1928, Dempsey, now retired, had been talking on and off to Rickard, who was president of the Madison Square Garden Corporation, about a big comeback. Tex was not sure about Dempsey's chances of a successful return to the ring. He had not fought since losing controversially to Tunney a year earlier in Chicago, though Dempsey himself insisted he still had a lot to offer. It's just that Rickard was not listening.

Dempsey never did return to the ring for serious combat. In any event, Rickard had plans for other big fights. Sadly, his dreams never came to pass. On 6 January 1929 Rickard, the man of vision, died in a Miami hospital of complications following an operation for acute appendicitis, four days after his 58th birthday. His body was taken to New York and lay in state at the Garden, the venue he helped to establish. Thousands filed into the arena to pay their final respects to the man who had done so much for New York boxing.

It would be six years before another major promoter would come on to the New York scene, and effectively run boxing not only at the Garden but in New York and the rest of the country. His name was Mike Jacobs.

A shrewd businessman who had once worked for Rickard, Jacobs promoted all of Joe Louis' 25 defences of his world heavyweight title in the 1930s and 1940s, including 17 in New York. He promoted fights at other weights too. 'Jacobs does all his business when most of the boys in the fight racket are either just going home or climbing out of the covers,' said the New York publicist Francis Albertanti. 'Put a ticket in his hand and Mike could squeeze three times as much money out of it than anybody else.'

If Jacobs was the dominant promoter in New York during the 1930s and 1940s, the 1950s were monopolised by the International Boxing Club (IBC) run by the millionaire businessman James D Norris. Unfortunately, Norris and the IBC allowed underworld figures such as Frankie Carbo and Frank 'Blinky' Palermo to infiltrate the organisation and permitted them to manipulate most of the champions and leading contenders to the detriment of the sport.

The IBC was disbanded in 1958 by the US Supreme Court in a nationwide boxing clean-up and several independent promoters came on to the New York scene. The fourth and current Madison Square Garden was located at 7th and 34th Streets, and was the first to be built above the platform of an active railway network, in this case Penn Station. The first boxing card there was on 4 March 1968. It was a double-header, with Nino Benvenuti regaining the world middleweight title by outpointing Emile Griffith over 15 rounds and Joe Frazier winning the New York version of the world heavyweight title by stopping Buster Mathis in 11 rounds. The card drew a crowd of 18,096, who paid $658,503, an indoor record at the time.

The Garden was back in the news three years later when two wealthy businessmen, Jerry Perenchio and Jack Kent Cooke, staged the Joe Frazier–Muhammad Ali world heavyweight championship fight on 8 March 1971. Billed as the Fight of the Century, it was won by Frazier on points and pulled in a crowd of 20,455, with receipts totalling $1,352,961.

As the 1970s wore on, two major promoters, Don King and Bob Arum, became central figures in the New York picture and are still promoting today. By the 1980s, Las Vegas was taking over from

New York, becoming the centrepoint of the sport, with casinos taking the place of the old open-air stadiums in the days when live gates were all-important. TV coverage would bring in the revenue, irrespective of the live attendance.

The old boxing venues in New York had become just memories. Madison Square Garden Bowl was effectively the Garden's outdoor arena and the scene of many historic fights. Also known as the Long Island Bowl, it opened in 1932 and was pulled down in 1945 to make way for a US Army mail depot. It is now a shopping mall and car dealership.

The Yankee Stadium first opened in April 1923 and its first fight a month later featured the former world heavyweight champion Jess Willard against Floyd Johnson, won by Willard in 11 rounds, before a crowd of 63,000. The stadium, which would stage over 30 world championship fights, was pulled down in 2010 and rebuilt two years later, primarily for baseball.

The Polo Grounds was built in 1876 and, as the name suggests, was used principally for polo but also for boxing, football and baseball. It was a landmark for big fights until it was demolished in December 1964, four years after Floyd Patterson knocked out Ingemar Johansson in five rounds. Another popular boxing location, Shea Stadium, the scene of much world title action, too, opened in April 1964 but was pulled down in February 2009 to provide additional parking for the adjacent Citi Field, current home of the New York Mets baseball club. Many big fights were held there.

The Coney Island Athletic Club, also known as the Coney Island Sporting Club, built in 1897, also played a significant role in New York boxing history. It was the location of several major world heavyweight championship fights around the turn of the 20th century. It is now the parking lot of the New York Aquarium.

Of the smaller venues, the St Nicholas Arena, known as St Nick's, would be best known. It staged many important fight cards and operated from 1906 to 1962. The ABC television studios now occupy the site. Another prominent venue was Ridgewood Grove. Built in 1921, many important fights were held there and it lasted until well into the 1980s.

Despite the inroads made by Las Vegas, New York has made something of a resurgence in the sport. Besides Madison Square Garden, there are several other boxing venues in operation such as the Manhattan Centre, the Paradise Theatre, the Roseland Ballroom, Aviator Sports, Turning Stone Casino and in particular, Barclays Center in Brooklyn.

Barclays Center is the focus of much attention today as a major boxing location. A multi-purpose indoor venue, it opened in September 2012 and continues to stage big fights. The people behind Barclays Center are looking to open more venues. It means that New York's long and rich tradition in boxing is in good, safe hands.

On 16 January 2016, two world heavyweight title fights were staged at Barclays Center when Deontay Wilder knocked out Artur Szpilka in the ninth round to successfully defend his World Boxing Council title and Charles Martin stopped Vyacheslav Glazkov in the third round to win the vacant International Boxing Federation belt.

The double-header was the first world heavyweight championship card held in Brooklyn for over 115 years, dating back to 11 May 1900, when James J Jeffries successfully defended his title by knocking out James J Corbett, 'Gentleman Jim', in 23 rounds at the Coney Island Athletic Club. Six months earlier, Jeffries had climbed into the same ring to face the challenge of Tom Sharkey, which is the opening chapter in this book. Enjoy the journey.

A J Liebling of the *New Yorker* got it right. Boxing is the sweet science. For me, it remains the greatest sport in the world.

Barry McGuigan

Chapter 1

Scorched scalps and a cauliflower ear

James J Jeffries v Tom Sharkey, Coney Island Athletic Club, New York, 3 November 1899

H E was not a big man as heavyweights go, certainly as far as the modern era is concerned, but Tom Sharkey was arguably the toughest fighter that boxing has ever seen, before or since. Standing only 5ft 8ins and generally weighing around 180lbs, not much over today's light-heavyweight limit, the Irishman was seemingly impervious to the heaviest punches as they bounced off him like hailstones off a corrugated roof.

Possessing a solid, square jaw that looked and seemed to be made of iron, with broad shoulders, a bull-like neck and power in his fists, Sharkey was described by boxing historian Tracy Callis as an earlier version of Rocky Marciano. 'Tom had the misfortune of fighting when boxing legends were at their best,' said Callis. 'Had he fought at any other time in history, he very likely would have been heavyweight champion of the world.'

The first striking feature Sharkey's opponents always noticed was that his massive 50-inch chest was decorated with tattoos of a four-mast sailing ship, a legacy of his days in the US Navy, and above it a large star. He used to boast that he would 'never give up the ship'. Crowning his overall rugged appearance towards the closing years of his career was a large cauliflower ear on the left side. Cauliflower ears are more associated with rugby players today but in the past, they were many fighters' trademarks. Most important of all, Sharkey could fight – and fight like hell. He never knew the meaning of the word 'quit', and if the truth be known, with his very limited education, could not even spell it.

This was the rough, tough, mean challenger that James J Jeffries from California was about to face in the first defence of his world heavyweight title since winning it from the freckled-faced, spindly-legged Cornishman Bob Fitzsimmons on a knockout in 11 rounds in the same ring five months earlier. Jeffries and his manager, William A Brady, the theatrical impresario, knew that this was going to be a war, and likely to go the full scheduled distance of 25 rounds, unless Jeffries could find the right spot at the right moment to finish off his man.

Born in Dundalk, County Louth on Ireland's north-east coast on 23 November 1873, the fifth child of a local railwayman and his wife, Sharkey had limited schooling but always had a sense of adventure, yearning to see as much of the world as he could. He went to work on the small merchant ships that plied their trade to Liverpool and Scotland. Later, he worked as a cabin boy on larger ships on the same routes before getting on vessels that took him around the world. 'I enjoyed my time at sea and had my share of excitement,' he recalled in later years. 'I often took my turn at the wheel and sailed all over the world – from London to Cape Town, Hong Kong to Sydney, San Francisco to the coast of China and into the Arctic, to Alaska, through the Indian Ocean and ports where no white man had ever set foot.'

While in New York harbour one day, he made his way to Brooklyn and enlisted in the US Navy. It was while watching boxing training sessions aboard ship every evening, with officers acting as referees, that he caught the boxing bug. Sharkey was soon invited to take part in the sessions, and enjoyed them so much that he made up his mind to become a boxer and soon established himself as a good fighter capable of handling himself against any of his shipmates in the roped square. He was as tough as old army boots.

'Tom was plenty smart inside the ring but not so smart out of it,' said Col Harvey L Miller, past president of the old National Boxing Association, now the World Boxing Association. 'I understood that Sailor Tom had very, very limited education but it didn't keep him out of the navy, and I once served with him. He was a ship's corporal, a rating now obsolete, a sort of ship's policeman. I remember one pay day on the ship, the paymaster ordered Tom to line the men up alphabetically.

'Tom looked down at his men and shouted: "If you fellas want to get paid, line up alphabetically." All would have been fine and dandy if he had left it at that, as all Adamses, Bakers, Conrads and such moved into position.

'But Tom had to show his authority. Pointing to one meek-looking guy looking for his place down near the end of the line, he snapped: "What's your name?" "Phillips," came the reply. "Phillips, is it?" roared Tom. "Well then, get the hell up among the F's!"'

Miller recalled another instance when Sharkey was going ashore with a landing party. His leggings had been slipped on in reverse, the laces on the inside. When challenged to explain, Sharkey said: 'Sure I had me legs crossed when I laced them up.'

Sharkey was a stickler too for obeying orders, literally. One of his superior officers was getting married and the best man, another officer, summoned Tom and ordered him to go into town and buy a couple of two-pound bags of rice. The instructions were explicit. When he got back, he was to hide under the gangway ladder and throw the rice at the bride when she came down the gangway ladder. 'Sure,' promised Sharkey.

As the bridal procession came into view, Tom cocked his arm and let fly one two-pound bag, and then the other, striking the bride full in the face and knocking her to the ground. The officer had not thought to tell Sharkey to first take the rice out of the bags before firing them. It was the first and only time a bride left for her honeymoon an hour later with a black eye and three missing teeth!

After he left the navy, Sharkey was managed by an Irishman, Tom McGrath from County Limerick, in San Francisco. One day, they got an offer to box in Australia. 'You don't want to go there, Tom,' said McGrath. 'It's thousands of miles away. There's nothing in Australia but a lot of kangaroos.' Sharkey stared at his manager: 'Sure I don't give a damn about nationality. A kangaroo's money is as good as anybody else's.'

Then there was the time shortly after Sharkey retired from boxing and opened a saloon on East 14th Street in Manhattan. One day James J Corbett, the former world heavyweight champion and an old foe of Sharkey's, dropped in and, after looking around, remarked: 'Nice place you have here, Tom, except of course you should have a chandelier.' Sharkey glared at James J suspiciously. 'Yeah,' he said finally, 'but who the hell would play it?'

Another evening, Sharkey was behind the bar when an old friend dropped in and teased the ex-fighter: 'You still can't read, Tom, isn't that right?' Sharkey answered: 'Of course I can.' Whereupon, the visitor went behind the bar to the wall mirror, which was clouded over with cigar smoke, wet his finger and wrote across the glass: 'THOMAS J SHARKEY'. He turned back to the former boxer and said: 'OK, read that.'

'That's easy,' Sharkey said. 'It says: NO SMOKIN.'

It is not clear when Sharkey had his first official fight, amateur or professional. Various historians have come up with different dates. Record compilers also differ, and not even his biographers, Greg Lewis and Moira Sharkey, a distant relation of the boxer, were able to shed any light on it in their book *I Fought Them All,* published in 2010. However, the publishers of the influential *Boxing Register,* regarded as the world's official record book, maintain they did some extensive research and lists his fight with the Englishman, Jack Gardner, on 17 March 1893 as being his first competitive fight when their ship, the USS *Philadelphia*, docked in Honolulu. Gardner claimed to be heavyweight champion of the British Navy. Sharkey knocked out his opponent in four rounds.

Whatever the full facts, Sharkey had 14 fights, winning 13, during the ship's 18-month stay in Honolulu. When the ship returned to the Mare Island yard in San Francisco, his naval service was coming to an end anyway. The Irishman continued his boxing in California, mainly in Colma and Vallejo, and these would certainly have been professional encounters. One of them was in Colma against Australian Billy Smith, a prominent professional who claimed he was the best heavyweight in San Francisco. Sharkey knocked him out in seven rounds.

Among the ringsiders was the aforementioned Tim McGrath, who was always looking out for promising talent. McGrath thought Sharkey could develop into a good fighter and signed him up. Under McGrath's guidance, Sharkey made good progress and he matched him with the formidable Joe Choynski, one of the world's leading heavyweights, at the People's Palace, San Francisco on 16 April 1896. Choynski had been in the ring with greats such as John L Sullivan, James J Corbett, Kid McCoy, Bob Fitzsimmons and others, and certainly knew what the noble art was all about. Sharkey won the decision over eight rounds – and on Choynski's home territory at that.

Among the crowd was Corbett and at the final bell he climbed into the ring in full dress attire, as befitting his 'Gentleman Jim' tag, and offered to take on Sharkey. McGrath, on behalf of Sharkey, agreed. The match was set for the Mechanics Pavilion, San Francisco for 24 June 1896. Corbett had been out of the ring, and consequently not in prime condition, since relinquishing his world heavyweight title a year earlier and was embarking on a comeback aimed at re-establishing himself as champion, even though everybody, including the boxing authorities, still regarded him as holder of the title.

As a safeguard, Corbett insisted the fight should be over four rounds, with little or any close-quarter work, and as it happened it was a fortunate agreement. While James J was able to outbox the unskilled if immensely strong Irishman in the opening round, he was beginning to run out of stamina in the second round, when Sharkey was able to rough him up with body shots and hooks to the head. It was the same in the third and fourth rounds and a weary Corbett flopped on his stool at the finish, gasping for breath. Referee Frank Carr called both fighters to the centre of the ring, held up their hands and declared the fight a draw. The decision was met with noisy disapproval from the fans, who clearly felt that Sharkey should have won. The exhausted Corbett could not leave his corner for nearly 30 minutes.

'The referee reminded us that there was to be no hitting in the clinches, as arranged by Corbett, but in the first round Corbett ignored these instructions, clinched, and landed a punch in my right eye,' recalled Sharkey in later years. 'It was the first black eye I ever had in my career. Corbett, a skilful boxer in his day, wanted to keep the fight at long range where he could jab, jab, jab, but when we got to close quarters all he did was hold. He was certainly no gentleman. I decided to play his game. I forgot all about him being a world champion and just put my head down and sailed in. Had the fight gone another round, I would surely have knocked him out and I would have been world heavyweight champion. He was a very, very lucky man that night.'

In a statement after the fight, Corbett said: 'When I say that Sharkey is a very strong man, I tell the whole story. I had no difficulty hitting him but he can stand more punishment than the ordinary fighter. I could have blinded him by hitting him in the right eye, which I nearly closed in the second round, but it would have done no good to hurt the fellow that much, so I refrained from doing so. If my seconds had made the claim, I would have secured the decision on fouls as he continually gave me the shoulder and the cross-buttock. But they had instructions to claim no fouls. I am ready for Sharkey in a longer fight. Finished fights are what I desire and not four-round contests in which a man cannot box scientifically but must slug and wrestle.'

Corbett was prepared to defend his title against Sharkey whenever and wherever the fight could be arranged but the Englishman, Bob Fitzsimmons, the former world middleweight champion who had now moved up to heavyweight, was claiming first call on Corbett's services. Meanwhile, Sharkey and McGrath visited New York and in Jimmy Wakely's popular saloon they were introduced to a man both had greatly admired, the legendary John L Sullivan. The former heavyweight champion of the world was down on his luck and plans were made to stage a benefit for him at Madison Square Garden. Sharkey offered his services and it was arranged to have him and John L box an exhibition over three rounds. The show proved a big success and took in $100,000 for Sullivan. 'Any help I could give my idol was no problem,' said Sharkey later. 'I was glad I could assist him in some way.'

Sharkey was still seeking a world title fight with Corbett but on 17 March 1897 James J lost his crown when he was knocked out by Bob Fitzsimmons in 14 rounds in Carson City, a gold rush town high in the Nevada mountains. Fitzsimmons was showing no interest in taking on Sharkey in a title bout and would subsequently drop the title in his first defence when he took on big James J Jeffries at the Coney Island Athletic Club on 9 June 1899. Jeffries was now Sharkey's main target. 'I know I can win the title and all I want is a chance to prove it,' he told friends.

James Jackson Jeffries was born on a farm in Carroll, southern Ohio on 15 April 1875. One of eight children of a farming family, he could trace his ancestry back to Normandy. When he was six, his family moved to farmland in California because one of the boys had a curved spine and they believed he would benefit from a warmer climate. James J would live in the Orange State all his life. After leaving school, he had various jobs as well as doing his stint on the farm. These included working as a meat packer and in a tin mine, as well as a riveter in the boiler house of the Santa Fe railroad in San Bernardino. It was there that he picked up one of his nicknames, the 'Californian Boilermaker', when he started boxing. Jeffries learned the rudiments of the sport at the East Side Athletic Club in Los Angeles. He was 6ft 2in tall and weighed 220lbs stripped when he was only 16.

James J had his first professional fight on 19 September 1895, when he knocked out Hank Griffin in 14 rounds in Los Angeles, but his parents disapproved as he was officially underage to box for pay at 20. He waited another year before restarting his career with full approval from home. Gaining several impressive wins, Jeffries was spotted in the gym one day by Billy Delaney, manager of world heavyweight champion Corbett, who was training for his title defence against Fitzsimmons. Delaney wanted someone who was big and husky and could take Corbett's punches without wilting, and Jeffries fitted the bill perfectly. He would become a regular sparmate for Corbett and would be managed by William A Brady, who was also Corbett's manager.

'Jeffries was a gruff, taciturn man whose ox-like strength gained for him great success in the ring,' Nat Fleischer of *Ring* magazine would recall. 'He lacked style, dash, boxing skill and other assets of an excellent fighter when he made the climb to the top but by the time he reached the heights, he gained international acclaim. In action he looked like a big bear, with his massive hairy chest, and he fought with the ferocity of one. His many nicknames included the "Iron Man of the Ring". He could batter an opponent into submission with his powerful wallops but could easily be hit and often took severe punishment until he perfected his crouch as a means of defence. Many giants of the ring tried to subdue him but without success until he made an ill-fated comeback after six years out of the ring and was heavily beaten by Jack Johnson.'

One of the big names Jeffries fought on the way to the title was the veteran Peter Jackson, but it was a fight James J did not want. Jackson was two weeks past his 37th birthday and his final retirement was only two more fights away. One of boxing's uncrowned champions, it was only racial prejudice that denied him his chance to win the world heavyweight title. A classy boxer-fighter from St Croix in the Virgin Islands, Jackson moved with his family to Australia when he was six years of age and lived there all his life.

Jackson would have difficulty in finding suitable opponents in Australia so he campaigned in the US but top boxers shunned him for racial and/or competitive reasons. John L Sullivan, the most famous heavyweight in America and the reigning world champion at the time, openly declared: 'I will not fight a n****. I never have and never will.' Although Sullivan had actually faced a black opponent previously, he would not change his stance regarding Jackson. 'N****es are inferior people,' he said.

Jackson, meanwhile, gained wins over leading American heavyweights, including Joe McAuliffe, Patsy Cardiff and George Godfrey, and had two fights in Europe, finishing off the Irish champion Peter Maher in the second round in Dublin and winning on a foul over the British title-holder Jem Smith to win the British Empire championship in three rounds in London. The West Indian dominated the fight and Smith was forced into a wrestling match to avoid a knockout. Jackson continued to fight and win. Back in the US, Corbett agreed to take on Jackson to further his own claims for a title fight with Sullivan and the match was set for the Californian Athletic Club for 21 May 1891.

The pair disliked each other intensely. Jackson considered Corbett 'a boaster' and one who belittled opponents, including his upcoming rival. Corbett, failing to live up to his 'Gentleman Jim' nickname, said the only reason he was taking on the fight was to further his own chances of proving to Sullivan that he was the best heavyweight contender in the world bar none and deserved a championship match. They refused to say one word to each other at functions leading up to the fight and the weigh-in. Jackson was the favourite at 2/1.

Both men were evenly matched, punching and parrying, with one and then the other gaining the advantage. Corbett's best punch was a left hook to the body while Jackson's right to the heart was very effective. Finally, with the 61st round just two minutes old, and having battled for over four hours, with many spectators getting restless and others falling asleep, referee Hiram Cook stepped between the two exhausted boxers, pulled them apart and sent them to their corners. Addressing the crowd, Cook declared: 'Gentlemen, this contest is becoming very unsatisfactory to you and the directors of the club. Both men have admitted that they cannot go on to a satisfactory conclusion. You have ample evidence that they cannot go on except as walkers. I therefore declare the entertainment ended and that it is a no-contest. All bets are therefore off.'

In his 1925 autobiography *The Roar of the Crowd*, Corbett said: 'The night I fought Peter Jackson, I thought he was a great fighter. Six months later I thought he was a great fighter. And today, after 33 years, I still maintain he was the greatest fighter I have ever seen.'

There were plans to re-match both men after Corbett won the world heavyweight championship but for one reason or another, the fight never materialised. In his later years, Jackson ran a boxing academy in London and took matches whenever he could but he knew the end was near when Jeffries beat him in three rounds in San Francisco. Within three years, he was dead from the tuberculosis that ravaged his body and he was buried in Queensland.

Jeffries went on to win the world title from Corbett's successor, Bob Fitzsimmons, and in his first defence agreed to defend it against Tom Sharkey. Each knew the other's style as they had fought shortly before, at a time when Jeff was the No 1 contender for Fitzsimmons. Their initial meeting was at the Mechanics Club, San Francisco on 6 May 1898. Interest in the scheduled 20-rounder was so great that Jim Coffroth, the first big-time boxing promoter, needed to find more seating accommodation urgently. He located a builder, who hastily erected bleachers on the main floor. On the afternoon of the bout, the stand holding the press box collapsed but it was quickly put together again. Then, during one of the preliminaries, a high section of seats holding about 500 fans crashed to the floor.

People were screaming and struggling to get out of the wreckage as ambulances raced to the scene. A number of people were injured, though not seriously, and it was a miracle that many were not killed. Spectators were moved to a different stand on the far side of the arena. A little later, and still during the preliminaries, a second stand on the far side of the arena collapsed, followed by a third. Several more people were rushed to hospital, again with no serious injuries, but by now there was panic in the hall. Spectators were screaming and dashing all over the place.

It was hoped that there would be no more disasters and there was an announcement that everything was now under control and calm could be restored. Many people had paid good money for seats and now they had to stand, with the air full of dust. Jeffries entered the ring a 10/9 favourite. 'Do y'see that sailing ship on Sharkey's body?' he remarked to his trainer Billy Delaney. 'Well, keep your eye on it because I'm going to sink it.'

When referee Alec Goggins, who had boxed a draw with Sharkey in his fighting days two years earlier, called both men together to the centre of the ring, it was very noticeable that they were in top condition, with each looking confident. From the first bell the Irishman was on the attack with jabs, hooks, uppercuts, swings, indeed everything that was in his repertoire. Jeffries was taken aback by Sharkey's fast start but would soon get his own punching going as the crowd roared their approval. Sharkey knew he would have to keep the pressure on his strong rival.

By the sixth round Sharkey had a marginal lead, roared on by a group of sailors from the USS *Olympia,* who had come to give some strong vocal support to the ex-sailor. 'There were at least 100 of them in the place,' Jeffries would remember, 'and every time Tom swung at me, they yelled like Red Indians. Whenever we got into a clinch, and there were many clinches, I'd give them a wink.'

As the rivals slugged it out in the sixth round, there was a loud crash. Both men stepped back and saw that a section of the temporary seats in the gallery had caved in and hundreds of people were sliding down and being wedged against the rail, despite assurances from ringside announcements earlier that everything was all right and there was nothing to worry about. After the boxers resumed fighting, another section of seating collapsed on the main floor. Would there be anything left of the hall by the finish?

The action in the ring continued as the rounds went by, and in a bruising ninth round Sharkey smashed Jeffries' nose and cut his upper lip. The burly Californian appeared to be running out of energy but he stormed back in the following rounds, crashing heavy left hooks into Sharkey's midsection and roughing him up. From the 12th to the 17th it was a slugfest, with neither man giving ground, though the American appeared a bit fresher. Jeffries' biographer, Jim Carney junior, described the final two rounds like this: 'Tom, fighting with renewed frenzy, charged in and more or less held his own. Announcing the verdict, the crowd cheered when referee Goggins raised Jim's hand and three of the four newspapermen present agreed with the verdict.'

Sharkey claimed he was entitled to the decision, or at least a draw, but he was not too vehement about it. When he went over to Jeffries' corner and asked for a rematch, James J said: 'Tom, you've given me my toughest fight and when I win the title, as I feel I will, you will be my first challenger.' Jeffries would keep his word.

Shortly after winning the title, Jeffries took off on an exhibition tour across Europe, where fans were impressed with his ability as a boxer and puncher, and he was hailed by kings, queens and princes. The final part of the tour took in cities in England, Scotland, Wales and Ireland. When his train stopped at Dundalk, Sharkey's birthplace, he told his promoter that he wanted to see if he could meet any of Tom's family, as Sharkey himself was living in America.

As he alighted from the train and headed for his car, a man rushed up to him and said: 'Mr Jeffries, there is somebody over here you would like to meet you.' The world champion was pleasantly surprised and asked who it was. 'It's little Jimmy Sharkey, Tom's dad,' said the man. A few minutes later, Sharkey senior and the world champion shook hands. As Jeffries remembered it in later years: 'Jimmy's looks and physical stature reminded me instantly of Tom, except that he was somewhat shorter than his famous son. We chatted amicably about our tough fight and of the great courage Tom had shown. I told Sharkey senior that I was fully prepared to give Tom first crack at my title and expected his manager to arrange it when I got back home.

'I clearly remember him looking me up and down and nodding. He said in that soft Irish brogue: "You look a fine, upstanding gentleman to me, Mr Jeffries, and I hope you give my son that chance. But let me tell you this. Now I don't want to scare the devil out of you, or wishing you any harm, but I hope he licks you." We both laughed, and as I headed for my car, I looked back and there he was, giving me a great wave of goodbye. A lovely little man.'

Jeffries kept to his word. The return fight was set for 3 November 1899 at the Coney Island Athletic Club in Brooklyn. Jeffries worked himself into top condition at his training camp at Elmhurst, New Jersey and had a variety of good sparring partners, including the talented Tommy Ryan, the reigning world middleweight champion and former welterweight king. Jeffries considered Ryan to be the greatest boxer at his weight in the world and if anybody could get him into top condition, and provide the sparring he needed, it was Ryan, who would also act as one of the trainers.

Ten days before the fight, one of Jeffries' sparmates threw a medicine ball at him and dislocated his left elbow. Jeff's acting chief trainer, Billy Delaney, promptly snapped the elbow back into place but the intense pain failed to go away and two days later, the champion decided to consult a specialist, who told him with a wry face: 'The bone is broken, Jim. You'll have to stay out of action for six months.'

When Jeffries insisted that he would have to go through with the fight as everything had been arranged, the specialist said, 'Do what you want but all I'm saying is that you are risking permanent injury if you do so.' The news caused a crisis in the camp. Jeffries' manager at the time was Bill Bradley, who had signed a two-year contract with James J in return for getting him the title fight with Fitzsimmons. Jeff's regular manager, Billy Delaney, stepped down for this period and, as already stated, acted as his main trainer.

Jeffries weighed 214lbs to Sharkey's 187lbs, and the Irishman was the shorter by five inches. The scheduled distance was 25 rounds. Jeffries was installed favourite at 10/7. 'The fight was a greater betting affair than any heavyweight contest ever fought in this country,' said the *New York Times*. 'For almost every man in the clubhouse had a choice and almost everyone was willing to back his opinion with his money.'

It would be the first fight to be filmed under artificial light and the Biograph Film Company, co-founded and run by the inventor and businessman Thomas Edison, wanted the ringside to be as bright as possible. It meant that the blazing glare of 400 lamps just 14ft over the ring took the temperature up to 100°C. Both boxers would later complain that the light from the lamps put blisters on their scalps, even though a large umbrella was placed over each corner as a shade during the intervals between rounds. Within a few weeks, all their hair would fall out. Conditions were not helped by the sultry November evening. Newspaper correspondents and telegraph operators were stripped to the waist, ready for the action which could well last for quite some time, considering the toughness and fitness of both gladiators.

The referee appointed was George Siler, one of America's leading officials, who combined his duties in the ring with his day job as chief boxing correspondent for the *Chicago Tribune*. He refused to climb into the ring unless a hat was provided, and this request was granted. Neither champion nor challenger asked for any favours and got none.

For a purse of $25,000, winner take all, this was the big one, boxing's greatest and richest prize, the heavyweight championship of the world, and they would give fans who paid between $5 and $25 their money's worth. When Siler called the two boxers together for their final instructions, he told them: 'I fully expect both you men to give us a good fight, and to be fair at all times. I won't stand for any nonsense. I never have and never will. Go back to your corners and await the bell.'

The crowd, estimated at close to 10,000, who paid almost $100,000 to see the slugfest, did not have to wait long for the action. Sharkey lunged from his corner and was met by Jeffries, both throwing punches that would surely have knocked out many other heavyweights. This was raw, savage stuff as one and then the other dug in tremendous blows from both hands. Jeffries had predicted that he would flatten his man in six or seven rounds and he had every intention of carrying that out.

Jeffries had to be careful, with his suspect left elbow injured in training, but so far it was not causing him any undue trouble. His trainer, Billy Delaney, had warned him before going out for the first round to spare his left as much as possible without allowing Sharkey or his corner to suspect anything and box in his familiar crouch. 'Everything's fine, Billy, don't worry about a thing,' said Jeffries.

It was the same in the second round, with both men fighting like battering rams. Jeffries was backing his man into a corner when suddenly he fired a solid right followed by a punishing left hook that caught Sharkey on the chin and sent him to the canvas. The Irishman had been partly off balance at the time and it was one of the few occasions he had ever visited the boards. He jumped up without a count and immediately went back into action. Just before the bell, Jeffries put him down again with a powerful left hook in a neutral corner, which brought cheers from his supporters scattered around the venue.

For a moment, Jeffries thought he had finished off the brawling Irishman. He didn't think *anybody* would get up after a blow like that as he considered it a harder punch than the first one that put Sharkey on the floor. But when the Irishman got up without taking a count, shook his head and came storming back into the attack, Jeffries knew that he himself was in deep trouble because in landing that second left hook, he had fractured his elbow again. But he knew he had to go on, defeat this persistent challenger and hold on to his prized world championship.

Jeffries bore his discomfort with a smile and never once let on to Sharkey or Tom's corner that he had only one hand. Forced to fight with just his right in round three, he tore at his opponent's belly, hoping to wear his man down. But Sharkey kept coming in and, after slipping near Jeffries' corner, jumped up and fired powerful lefts and rights to the head and body. Referee Siler warned the Irishman for holding.

Sharkey had particularly good rounds from the fourth through to the seventh, often taking four blows to land one, as he stormed into the attack. But Jeffries would not be denied. Despite the terrible pain from his fractured left elbow, he continued to use left hooks and jabs as the onrushing challenger fought as though his very life depended on it – and perhaps it did. Round after round, both men would flop on to their stools, pouring sweat under the burning lights, and allow their cornermen to quickly towel them down. One wilting fan passed out at ringside after shouting to the fighters: 'How can you fellows stand the heat? It's incredible even down here.'

In the tenth round, a detective was informed that an unauthorised camera had been spotted in the 15th row. The detective went to investigate but he had trouble reaching the culprit and the tightly packed crowd was blocking his way. They did not want anybody obstructing their view of the action in the ring. The lawman eventually succeeded in reaching the culprit, despite being punched in the face and kicked in the legs by the crowd, and took the camera away. When the cameraman protested, he was told: 'Look, do you want to start a riot among all these people? You'll get your camera back if you see me at ringside after the fight.' The cameraman was still protesting as the detective and his equipment vanished into the crowd.

Back in the ring, the action was fierce, with both men fighting like battering rams. First one and then the other would gain the advantage. Sharkey's left eye, cut in the tenth round by a fierce right from the Californian, was worrying him despite good work in the corner by his handlers. By the 14th round, everybody was wondering how the fighters managed to keep going at such a pace in the intense heat, but these were proud warriors. A heavy right in the 15th round broke Jeffries' nose but the bleeding American did not let it worry him. Sharkey seemed to be throwing more punches but it was difficult to know how much they hurt the big, powerful champion.

During the 15th round, Tommy Ryan yelled some advice from the Jeffries corner but Sharkey shouted back at him: 'Keep your mouth shut, Ryan, or I'll come over during the interval and shut it for you.' When Sharkey got back to his stool, Delaney told him: 'Don't mind what Ryan is yelling. He's only doing his job. Keep your mind focused on the man in front of you. That's all that matters, you hear me?' Sharkey nodded, and a second later the bell rang.

In a torrid 17th round, Jeffries started fast and broke two of Sharkey's ribs with a powerful right to the body, one of them penetrating the Irishman's skin. The injury forced Sharkey to lower his left hand to protect his ribs. He was also still able to guard his head by keeping his chin close to his chest. Jeffries was trying to wear down his man, but it was not easy. Sharkey would just shake his head and come storming back on to the attack. A sharp right cut Sharkey's left eye again and blood streamed down the side of his face.

The Irishman split Jeffries' forehead in the 18th round and another butt knocked out one of the champion's front teeth. Jeffries would later say very sportingly that he did not think the fouls were deliberate and that they were committed in the heat of the fierce battle. Even if they warranted disqualification, Jeffries did not want to win on a foul. This was a fight to the finish and that's the way he wanted it. Referee Siler would recall in later years that he did not see the butts but he did remember getting in the way of a mighty left hook on his shoulder from Sharkey, although he did not penalise Tom.

In the 19th round, Jeffries nailed his man repeatedly with heavy rights on Sharkey's left ear and it swelled up like a balloon. 'When I hit it, it was like hitting a big wet sponge,' Jeffries said later. 'The blood from his cut eye and the lacerated ear would splash in all directions and our tights were soaked with blood.' Though half blind with blood and with his eye cut, his ear swollen and one of his ribs sticking through his skin, Sharkey refused to quit and thus acknowledge that he had met a stronger man. Never.

In the interval between the 19th and 20th rounds, Delaney poured half a bottle of champagne down Jeffries' throat to keep him going and put a block of ice up against his head to cool him. At the bell Sharkey forced Jeffries into a neutral corner but missed with a right-hand swing. He followed up with three good punches with the left hand and a strong right uppercut, but the American merely smiled and answered with yet another right to Sharkey's aching ribs. Referee Siler had to work hard for his fee as he was continually pulling the fighters apart. General ringside opinion around the press benches at this stage was that Jeffries was ahead by three or four rounds, but the *New York Times* had the Irishman marginally in front.

The 21st round clearly went to Sharkey as he did the better work with both hands. Jeffries was now using his left jab quite a lot but it never stopped the Irishman from moving in, looking for that big opening that he hoped would bring about the American's downfall. A smashing left hook to Jeffries' head was so hard that Sharkey's body pivoted and he felt that the arm had completely turned round in its socket.

In the 22nd round, Jeffries went on the attack with pile-driving lefts and rights to the head and body and for the first time in the bruising battle, Sharkey looked decidedly groggy on several occasions. He would not give up, of course, and continued his aggression, though often holding on to his opponent, who was also showing signs of wear and tear. Towards the end of the round, Jeffries pounded the Irishman with hooks, jabs, crosses and uppercuts and Sharkey walked to his corner on shaky legs.

Surprisingly, Sharkey came out for the 23rd round looking fresh, no doubt having been given a pep talk by his corner. In one of the many clinches in this round, Jeffries pulled away his left hand, which was trapped under Sharkey's armpit, and his glove came off. Referee Siler waved the Irishman back as he tried to put the glove back on Jeffries' hand, but in the excitement Sharkey ignored Siler's instruction and swung at Jeffries' head. Jeffries replied by striking the Irishman in the face with his bare fist. Siler shouted, 'That's enough now, boys,' and ordered Sharkey to a neutral corner to await instructions while he got Jeffries' glove back on and laced it up.

In the 24th round, Sharkey concentrated on left and right shots, mainly to the head, but Jeffries was in full control by now, even though he was still feeling excruciating pain every time he connected with his broken left hand. He was using his right in the main and caught Sharkey with a solid right cross that would have put many other opponents to sleep. The challenger was still as full of fight as ever, despite his two broken ribs and facial cuts, but it was clearly the American's fight by now.

So to the 25th and last round of this epic encounter, a tribute to the courage and tenacity of two of the toughest battlers who ever stepped into a ring. Sharkey swung two fierce punches, a left that caught Jeffries on the side of the head and a right cross that landed on his chest. The Californian hooked a hard left to the chin and Sharkey backed away, only to storm back with lefts and rights. In a clinch, the Irishman slipped to the floor, partly pulling off Jeffries' right glove. Siler quickly readjusted it and the action continued.

In the closing minute, Jeffries sent his man to the boards with a sweeping right but the Irishman jumped up without a count. Jeffries hurt the challenger with a long, sweeping right just as the bell clanged. Referee Siler followed Jeffries to his corner and declared him 'winnah and still champeen of the world'. There were some boos, mainly from Sharkey supporters. Sharkey's manager felt his man should have been awarded the decision. 'Tom at least deserved a draw after such a heroic performance and many times had Jeffries in trouble,' said McGrath.

Jeffries always conceded that Sharkey had given him the toughest fight of his career, and the American press heaped praise on both men for their sterling performances. 'In no 25-round fight ever seen before was there such terrific punching from start to finish, combined with the ability to take it as fast as it came and go back for more,' said the *New York Times*. 'The sight of blood on Jeffries' face seemed to make a demon of Sharkey, who fought fiercely. That the fight went the full was evidence of the wonderful condition and vitality of both men, for during the hour and 40 minutes blows hard enough to have felled an ox were given frequently.

'When cheers greeted the announcement that Jeffries had earned the decision of referee Siler, three enthusiastic cheers were added for the sturdy ex-sailor, who had taken manfully such a terrible beating from an opponent who had height, reach and weight on his side. Siler's decision was satisfactory to the great majority of spectators.'

The *Brooklyn Eagle* said: 'It was a fight unparalleled in the history of journalism. No fight like it will be seen at Coney Island for many days, unless the principals in it are Jeffries and Sharkey. In the 20th and 21st rounds Sharkey did the better work, and the worse he made Jeffries look, the more the champion improved. Those around the ringside were predicting a draw after the 21st round. Jeffries' 25lb weight advantage counted for much. He leaned heavily and bore Sharkey into and almost over the ropes. But Sharkey will keep fighting until there is a breath of wind or spark of sensibility in him. There was no stage of the fight when Sharkey was not willing to take two blows to give one in return. He is the most pugnacious Irishman that ever donned gloves.'

Jeffries recalled in later years: 'The Sharkey fight was the toughest championship match in the heavyweight records. I am saying that and I know because I was in it. I'll boast that I was the only champion who had ever had to defend his title against Tom Sharkey when Sharkey was right – and he was right that night. They came no greater than Sharkey. With his ribs sticking out, his eye split open and his ear swollen as big as my fist, the human cyclone refused to stop, but kept coming. I hurt my left hand more than I had damaged Sharkey.'

Sharkey would remember: 'I figured I could knock Jeff off easy. My idol John L Sullivan told me I would be champion of the world some day and I believed everything John L said. I was cocksure and confident of winning the championship that night. I hit Jeff with everything I had. Honestly, I just itched before the first bell to clout him. I didn't think he could take my punches but he did. But I still thought I won. I felt I was robbed of a justly earned victory and the heavyweight championship of the world. I outpointed Jeffries in the majority of the rounds.'

Moira Sharkey, a distant relative of the boxer and co-author of the book *I Fought Them All,* remembered in 2010: 'From all accounts it was an epic fight, leaving both men badly hurt. Some thought Sharkey deserved to win but the referee favoured the champion. The pair were simply meant to trade blows and put on a show, but they went at each other like tigers. They both still had points to prove. Tom never really fully recovered from that bout, although he continued on with his career, but he would never fight for the title again.'

Five months after the Sharkey fight, Jeffries took on Jack Finnegan in Detroit and knocked his man out in 55 seconds. Some record historians do not recognise it as a championship bout but research shows it was indeed for the title and is one of the shortest world heavyweight championship fights on record. Jeffries went on to successfully defend his title five more times, including two classic fights with the former champion James J Corbett, who had once employed Jeffries as a sparring partner and had treated him harshly in training sessions. It was something Jeffries never forgot and he got his revenge by knocking out 'Gentleman Jim' in the 23rd round in New York in 1900 and three years later in ten rounds in San Francisco.

Jeffries retired undefeated in 1905 with an impressive 18-0-2 record at a time when it was getting harder and harder to find suitable challengers. But he was persuaded to return to the ring on 4 July 1910, when he was 35 years of age and settled as a farmer, to take on the unpopular new champion, Jack Johnson, in Reno, Nevada. Jack London, the novelist, had infamously called out in the *New York Sun* for Jeffries to come back to the ring 'and wipe the smile off the n*****'s face'. Johnson administered a painful beating to the old champion and stopped him in the 15th round.

In retirement, Jeffries operated a bar, trained boxers and ran a farm, where he bred prize cattle. He also took part in boxing exhibitions and acted in movies, although a series of poor investments forced him to declare bankruptcy in the 1920s. He always referred to Sharkey as 'my toughest ever opponent'. Jeffries died in Burbank, California on 3 March 1953 at the age of 77.

As for Sharkey, he continued to take on top fighters and stopped Joe Choynski in two rounds in May 1900. Three months later, a two-round knockout loss to former champion Bob Fitzsimmons sent him down the ratings. Another old rival, Gus Ruhlin, finished him in 11 rounds in June 1902 and he finally called it quits after being outpointed by the clumsy Jack Monroe in February 1904, ending the bout barely able to see through swollen eyes.

In the Ruhlin fight, Sharkey had stopped the majority of the American's punches with the top of his head or his left ear. When he left the ring that night, his ear had been transformed into something like a large orange, and blue in colour. Within a few days, the swelling went down and the horrible blue colour gave way to a normal flesh colour. But it did not return to its normal shape. Sharkey had adopted a cauliflower ear which, in the words of a contemporary boxing writer, was 'a ghastly mass of flesh that jutted out from the side of his head like the gas lantern on the flank of a coach'. Undoubtedly, his punishing 25-round battle with Jeffries in 1899 also contributed in no small way to the deformity.

Sharkey was not afraid of any fighter alive but he was very sensitive about 'this one blemish on my anatomy, my left ear'. Nevertheless, he felt that the ear would remain as it was, and that he could learn to live with it. But each time he fought after that, the continued poundings enlarged the organ. After he knocked out Fred Russell in four rounds in Denver, Colorado in 1901, he complained to a local reporter: 'If the ear keeps this way, I'll have to pin it back.' In time, Sharkey felt more and more self-conscious about his deformity and tried to hide it with an oversize cowboy hat, but the ear always managed to show itself. 'I am not ashamed of being a fighter,' he told a family friend, 'but I am distressed that people who don't even recognise me can tell at once what profession I'm in... just by looking at my left ear.'

It distressed the Irish battler so much that he placed an advert in a New York newspaper which read: 'I will pay the sum of $5,000 to the person who can provide me with a new ear, or do a sensible job on the one I have.' It might have been Sharkey's idea of a publicity gimmick, since he was well past his prime at the time and fights were getting harder to come by.

Several doctors, including some with wide reputations, answered his appeal. They invited him to their surgeries to be examined but Tom always insisted that they come to his rooms at the Carlton hotel on Broadway. He set aside three full days, making himself available to any doctor willing to accept the challenge. On the first day, no fewer than 12 medical practitioners pulled, pinched, tapped and scraped away at the world's most famous cauliflower ear. In the succeeding two days, a total of 27 doctors got their chance. When the examinations were completed, only six of the 39 doctors who examined the boxer were willing to attempt corrective measures.

Dr Richard Muller, a New York surgeon, reported: 'The ear can be treated by either tapping, dissection to remove any false growth, by bleeding or by outward applications to reduce infection. I do not consider any of these methods to be especially dangerous. The trouble is entirely external and has nothing to do with the internal anatomy of the ear.'

Dr Joseph Bell, a noted eye, ear and nose specialist, remarked: 'I have treated several persons to correct what is commonly called "cauliflower ear". The surest method is by lancing and I have prepared a sketch of the operation to show its simplicity. I shall be delighted to treat your ear and I believe I can guarantee success. The operation is not very painful.'

Sharkey liked Dr Bell's analysis of the situation best of all, and he agreed to allow the surgeon to operate. Arrangements were made by Tom to be in Dr Bell's surgery promptly at 9am one morning. He was to pay half of the $5,000 stipulated fee before the operation and the balance 'when I'm satisfied when I see for myself that he did the job right', Sharkey recalled. But as the day drew near, the old fighter started to have other ideas.

He was beginning to have doubts about the whole thing and asked Bob Armstrong, his friend and sparring partner: 'Bob, does this ear make me look ugly?' Armstrong replied: 'No, Tom. I don't think so. It makes you look exactly what you are – a fighter.' 'Yes,' agreed Tom. 'It's an honour when people look at me on the street and say: "There goes Tom Sharkey, the famous fighter." Bob, you are very right,' replied the Irishman.

On the appointed morning, Dr Bell had his surgery all bright and shining, ready to accept his famous patient. Reporters had gathered outside and Dr Bell was explaining exactly how he was going to make Tom Sharkey 'the handsomest fighter in the world'. What Dr Bell didn't know was that while he was waiting for the fighter to come to his surgery, Sharkey was more than 200 miles away, sleeping soundly on the night train he had boarded the previous evening for Chicago. For the rest of his life, no medical person would ever put a knife to the famous ear.

In retirement, the old battler purchased a palatial house in Brooklyn, ran a saloon in Manhattan and bought a stable of trotting horses. He also boxed exhibitions with Jeffries at carnivals and fairs. Within a few years, however, he found himself down on his luck, not helped by a costly divorce and investments that went disastrously wrong. Sharkey managed to get a few character roles in movies after moving back to California, where his ring career began all those years ago. 'When he retired, Tom had a

$500,000 fortune, which would be worth about $10 million by today's standards, but within a little over a decade it was all gone,' recalled Moira Sharkey.

Sharkey died penniless in San Francisco on 17 April 1953, seven months short of his 80th birthday. His old friend and most famous foe, James J Jeffries, had passed away just six weeks earlier. On hearing of Jeffries' death, Sharkey, then in hospital and gravely ill himself, remarked: 'It took a long time but I finally beat the bugger in the end.'

Chapter 2

Madison mayhem on a night of shame

Riddick Bowe v Andrew Golota, Madison Square Garden, 11 July 1996

I T'S not always the championship fights that make the newspaper headlines and occupy pages in boxing magazines. Sometimes it's the contests with no titles on the line except prestige, and perhaps a rating, that do it, and often for the wrong reasons, such as the Riddick Bowe v Andrew Golota fight. Not only was it marred by fouls but the finish caused a riot which was condemned worldwide. The Associated Press news agency reported on 'sickening scenes of violence which turned the legendary MSG venue into a battleground'.

To examine the background of the fight, it is important to note that the enigmatic Bowe, a native New Yorker from Brooklyn, was unquestionably the dominant figure in world heavyweight boxing during the three years of Mike Tyson's absence from the ring following his rape trial and subsequent incarceration. Jack Dempsey dominated the 1920s and Joe Louis ruled in the late 1930s and throughout the 1940s. Rocky Marciano was on top in the 1950s but the 1960s and 1970s belonged to Muhammad Ali. Mike Tyson brought a new excitement to boxing in the 1980s but the pin-up boy of the 1990s was Riddick Bowe. He was known as 'Big Daddy', not because of his considerable bulk – although he was

6ft 5in and usually around 240–250lbs – but because of his large family. Bowe and his wife Judith had five children.

Let it be said that there is no attempt here to class Bowe alongside the legendary figures of the ring, or even near them, but there is no denying that he brought a new excitement to the sport when it needed it. He became undisputed heavyweight champion of the world and that's the supreme achievement in boxing. He overcame poverty and a deprived childhood to achieve success. Bowe's three thrilling fights with Evander Holyfield, two of which he won, were among the most exciting ring battles ever, and in an era when, unlike today, Americans dominated the heavyweight scene. But he lacked that vital ingredient that divides the good from the great.

'It's hard to talk about "Big Daddy" without a sense of pathos,' wrote Gavin Evans in his book *Kings of the Ring*. 'What might have been is never far away. Bowe was a boxer of superior talent – serious power, impressive punch variety and an ability to fight inside or at a distance. A flawed fighter, perhaps, and a dirty one certainly, but he could have been a contender for greatness.

'What he lacked was the mind of a champion. He was the anti-Tyson, proof that even the worst ghettos have their Cinderellas. And yet he also came with niggling doubts about whether he had the discipline and strength of character to prevail. There were also doubts about his abrasive, thin-skinned manager Rock Newman, although everyone loved his wizened old trainer Eddie Futch.'

Futch, who guided 21 boxers to world titles, including heavyweights Joe Frazier, Larry Holmes, Ken Norton and Michael Spinks, would later tell the author that Bowe had more potential than any other boxer he had ever trained. 'Sadly, the problem, the big problem, with Riddick was that while he was a brilliant prospect and could well have been one of the greatest heavyweights of all time, he lacked the will, and he hated training,' explained Futch.

'There were many times Riddick's weight ballooned up and up and I had a hell of a job getting it down to fitness levels. When he was in good shape, he looked a world beater, and was a world beater, but the will to win, and the physical ability to back it up, unfortunately let him down. A tragedy, really.'

Bowe was born in the tough Brownsville district of Brooklyn on 10 August 1967. He was his mother Dorothy's 12th child and she raised him after her husband walked out. His brother Henry died of Aids and his sister Brenda was stabbed to death by a drug addict during an attempted robbery.

Despite the turmoil of his private life, Bowe was able to turn to boxing, which probably saved him. He had an impressive amateur career as a heavyweight and super-heavyweight, winning four Golden Gloves titles and the US Junior Championships. He was also a finalist in the Pan-American Games in Bucharest in 1985 and won a silver medal in the 1988 Seoul Olympics, getting stopped in two rounds by Lennox Lewis, the Londoner who was boxing for Canada. Bowe's overall amateur record was 104-18. A professional career now seemed inevitable, and he opted for Rock Newman as his manager.

Newman, a former champion athlete, was a brash promoter who dabbled in politics and radio talk shows. When he heard about Bowe through a friend, he went to Brownsville and met up with the boxer and his family in their dilapidated, two-roomed apartment in a six-storey housing block. The windows were broken and the lift rarely worked. The block was known as Gunsmoke City. Newman promised to take Bowe to the top and the highly regarded Eddie Futch took on the job of developing him. In Bowe's debut in Reno, Nevada on 6 March 1989, he knocked out Lionel Butler in two rounds. By the end of the year, he had picked up 14 wins and eight more by the end of his second.

More importantly, Bowe was gradually moving up the ratings with victories over contenders such as Tyrell Biggs, Tony Tubbs, Bruce Seldon and Pierre Coetzer, the fight which led to a shot at the undisputed world heavyweight title held by Evander Holyfield. The contest was held on 14 November 1992 in Las Vegas and in a thriller Bowe put Holyfield on the canvas in the 11th round to win the decision over 12 and the unified championship. *Ring* magazine voted it Fight of the Year.

Boxing had a new golden boy, a big, powerful hitter with a strong chin, good infighting ability and a solid left jab. At 25, and with $7 million in his bank account, Bowe's adventures, or sometimes misadventures, had just begun. Bowe had said that when he became champion, he would 'make the world a better place'. Now that he was the king, he meant to carry out his promise. He embarked on a world tour, with no boxing, by stopping off to shake hands with Pope John Paul II in Rome, chatting with Nelson

Mandela in South Africa, visiting a Somalia torn by famine and civil war and back in the US continuing his support for President Clinton.

When Futch took him aside on his return to give him some advice, Bowe shook his head in disagreement. 'Look, you're doing too much travelling, too much running round,' the trainer said. 'Remember, you're the champion now, the best, and you'll have to put boxing first to stay that way. I've seen too many good fighters in my time fall by the wayside.'

Meanwhile, the World Boxing Council were putting pressure on Bowe to defend his title against their leading contender Lennox Lewis, but neither Riddick nor his manager were anxious to accommodate the Londoner, who had ruined Bowe's Olympic dreams. They were also at war with promoter Don King and his control and monopoly of the WBC. The organisation threatened to strip Bowe of the title but when the boxer and his entourage were in London for the BBC's Sports Personality of the Year awards in December 1992, Riddick and Newman beat the WBC to the punch by announcing they were giving up the title.

With that, Bowe walked out of the hotel by a back entrance, and with photographers and reporters in hot pursuit, promptly dumped his belt into a rubbish bin. Embarrassed WBC officials quickly retrieved the belt and promptly announced they were withdrawing recognition of Bowe. A few weeks later, they proclaimed Lewis as the new champion.

Bowe told *Ring* magazine's Bernard Fernandez in August 2015: 'Throwing the belt into the trash can was Rock Newman's idea. I wish I had never done that. I really wanted to fight Lennox. I wanted to fight him so bad I could taste it. I wanted to fight him more than anything.'

Bowe and Newman agreed to a return fight with Holyfield, who had previously lost the title to Riddick. The match was set for Las Vegas on 6 November 1993 and this time Holyfield reversed the decision with a points win. Bowe had been champion seven days short of a full year, although he would reign again 16 months later by knocking out Herbie Hide, a Nigerian raised in Norfolk, in the sixth round of a match in Las Vegas that was recognised by the World Boxing Organisation. After the Hide fight, Bowe visited Mike Tyson in prison and told him he could have a title fight on his release. When Tyson was freed after serving a three-year sentence which had been reduced from ten, he said he wanted a few more fights under his belt before taking on any of the top contenders. But the Bowe–Tyson fight never happened.

In between the Holyfield return and the Hide fight, Bowe was involved in two controversial incidents. After flooring the unbeaten Buster Mathis Jr in the fourth round of their August 1994 fight, Riddick struck his opponent with a powerful right while Mathis was on one knee. It seemed disqualification was inevitable but referee Arthur Mercante ruled the blow 'an unintentional foul' and the New Jersey Boxing Commission called it a no-contest.

Four months later in Las Vegas, Bowe struck his opponent Larry Donald with a left-right combination at the pre-fight press conference after Donald made some uncomplimentary remarks. Bowe won a dull fight on points but mayhem erupted again at the post-fight conference when a court official attempted to serve Riddick with a lawsuit, charging him with assault and battery. Bowe refused to sign the papers and in the melee that followed, both camps traded insults, with Bowe having to be pulled out of the door by police.

More trouble was to follow in June 1995 when, at the pre-fight conference ahead of his fight with Jorge Luis Gonzalez in Las Vegas, he threw a glass at the big Cuban. As Gonzalez attempted to attack Bowe, order was restored. As a result, both boxers were given a restraining order by the Nevada State Athletic Commission which forbade them from appearing together at any press conference in the build-up to the fight. This rule also extended to the weigh-in. When the pair eventually met in the ring, Bowe won by a knockout in the sixth round.

Meanwhile, a Polish heavyweight based in Chicago was getting a lot of attention as a promising prospect. A poor kid from the streets of Warsaw, Andrew Golota grew up in the care of a foster mother after his parents went their separate ways. Interested in boxing as a youngster, he would go on to win a silver medal at the 1985 World Junior Championships in Bucharest, a gold at the 1986 European Juniors in Copenhagen, and a bronze at both the 1988 Seoul Olympics and the 1989 European Senior Championships in Athens. He was also a four-time Polish champion.

Golota fled Poland in 1990 after being involved in a pub brawl and made his way to Chicago, where he had friends and continued with his amateur boxing. At 6ft 4in and weighing around 250lbs, he reckoned he could go places as a professional. He looked up Lou Duva, of the New York promotional group Main Events, and signed up with the veteran trainer, who he felt could take him to the top. Ironically, Bowe had asked Duva to handle him when he was starting out. Duva trained him for several weeks at the Starrett City Boxing Club in Brooklyn but claimed he quickly lost interest in the boxer on the grounds that while Riddick was undoubtedly talented, he was bone lazy.

Duva had a different view of Golota, who was always in the gym, although he felt that after the Pole had completed half a dozen fights he would have to curb his natural impetuousness, which included butting, low punching, using his elbows and shoulders in clinches and the occasional bite on the blind side of the referee. 'Besides all that,' he said with a straight face, 'he's as clean as a whistle.'

Golota justified Duva's confidence in him by winning all his first 27 fights, 25 inside the scheduled distance, mainly brawls, before he got his big chance against one of the best heavyweights in the world, Bowe. Riddick was no longer the heavyweight champion – Tyson had regained that honour, at least in the eyes of the WBC – but he was still a formidable contender with a 39-1-1 record. Bowe climbed into the Garden ring on 11 July 1996 a solid 10/1 favourite. As a result, Bowe did not take Golota seriously and paid scant attention to his training despite Eddie Futch's protestations: 'Don't underestimate this guy. He could be dangerous.'

On the afternoon of the fight, it all came close to being cancelled. Golota said he understood that the fight was to be held over the normal non-title ten rounds, but he was informed it would be over 12, the championship distance. The wording of the contract gave Bowe's manager Rock Newman the option to make it a 12-round contest, which he had done that morning without informing Golota or his team.

Golota was furious when he heard he would have to box an extra two rounds as he had trained for ten. He shouted at his handlers before officials from Spencer Promotions and Main Events, the co-promoters, were summoned. They tried to calm him down but he refused to back down and started to pack his bags. He intended going straight home to Chicago, fight or no fight, ignoring or forgetting the fact that an extra six minutes of action would presumably benefit him as he was in much better condition than Bowe for the longer haul. Spencer Promotions insisted he would have to go through with the fight as per contract but he would not be swayed. It was not until Main Events agreed to add an extra $50,000 to his $600,000 purse that he backed down.

The weigh-in passed without incident, with Bowe scaling a career-high 256lbs and Golota coming in at 243lbs. Both were aged 28. On fight night, a crowd of 11,252 passed through the turnstiles. When referee Wayne Kelly called the two boxers to the centre of the ring for last-minute instructions, the tension was heavy. This could be a war, even if it was one-sided. Bowe was a strong favourite. The Pole was expected to come out brawling but instead showed good boxing ability and was able to outjab and outspeed his opponent, who was flat-footed and showed no real head movement. Golota was effectively able to duck under Bowe's punches and dance away. The American did get through with some sharp left jabs and a few sharp rights but it was Golota's round, even if several of his punches were borderline shots.

Referee Kelly had been concerned before the fight about the Pole's reputation for dirty fighting, including biting. 'If this guy bites Bowe, I've got a plan on what to do,' he said without any elaboration, although it was clear that he had disqualification in mind.

After a quiet opening round, with both boxers sizing each other up, Golota made good use of his jab in the second and was making the former champion miss with counter punches by moving his head back. Bowe was simply marching after his man, looking for that one big shot that was a long time coming. Even when Bowe did land with jabs and hooks, Golota took the punches well and did not seem to be in any great danger. With about 50 seconds remaining in the round Bowe finally got through with some meaningful blows, two good left hooks to the jaw. The stunned Pole backed off as Bowe moved in but Golota unleashed a fast two-handed flurry that had the New Yorker holding on. Bowe then punched back wildly and at the bell just missed the referee with a sweeping left hook as Kelly danced swiftly out of the way.

In was noticeable that Bowe's left eye was starting to swell as the bell rang for round three, and he began the session determined to take control. Stiff jabs pushed his rival back a few paces. The Warsaw warrior, however, soon got the upper hand and landed a smashing left hook to Bowe's head before the bell. In the fourth, it seemed as if Bowe was tiring fast, leading to the belief that he was not as fit as he should have been. His punches were becoming wild and sloppy and the Pole was showing superior hand speed.

A solid right staggered Bowe and he fell into the ropes in some distress. Suddenly, like a bomb going off, the fight exploded into action. Golota landed a vicious left to the groin and Bowe sank to the canvas, his face a mask of pain. Kelly immediately called 'Stop' and deducted a point from the Pole. He also informed Bowe that he would be given five minutes to recover or he would be disqualified. He took close to two minutes before resuming. There was a little less than 30 seconds remaining in the round and the action was uneventful.

Things began to go further downhill for Bowe in the fifth while Golota seemed to be improving. Riddick made a promising start by punching with both hands but the Pole hurt him against the ropes as he raked him with hard, accurate blows. Looking in bad shape at this stage, Bowe punched back wildly but Golota saw the shots coming and was able to score with hard, accurate punches. At the bell, and coming out of a clinch, a frustrated Bowe pushed off his man, who replied with a scowl. It was now developing into a hate fight.

In the sixth round, Golota got a second warning from Kelly to 'keep your punches up' but whether he heard the referee or simply ignored him was not clear. He was keeping after Bowe all the time and midway through the round landed a borderline right uppercut, which caused a point to be deducted. Although the punch did not land in the groin area, the American doubled up, grimacing in pain, and was given an additional 60 seconds to recuperate.

In the seventh, Golota really took over. He punched hard and accurately with hardly a reply from the tired and dispirited New Yorker before getting a third point deducted when landing a very low right uppercut. Bowe grimaced with pain but did not ask for a rest. While Riddick was the victim of low punches, he himself was not blameless. He used rabbit punches throughout, though Golota was by far the worse offender. The Pole continued on the attack and hammered away with both gloves, putting Bowe in real trouble. He was shaken, tired and mentally discouraged and it looked like he was only a few punches away from a stoppage defeat.

Golota, having had those three points taken away and on the cusp of disqualification himself, needed only to bide his time and watch his punches to pull off a sensational victory. Then, inexplicably, he unleashed a powerful left hook which landed smack in Bowe's groin. The American sank down on his back like a sack of potatoes dumped from a truck. Kelly quickly moved in to signal he was disqualifying the Pole, resulting in his first loss as a professional. Twenty-seven seconds remained in the round.

As Bowe writhed on the canvas, his entourage, consisting of manager Newman, two associates, Jason Harris and Bernard Brooks, and the boxer's cousin Stephen Bowe, climbed through the ropes and rushed towards Golota's corner. As Brooks shoved Golota away, the boxer retaliated with a left hook that put his attacker on the canvas. Brooks then whacked Golota on the head with a mobile phone, which were considerably bigger and heavier than they are today, 20 years on. It opened a gash on the big Pole's head, which would require 13 stitches.

By now, the whole scene was one of sheer chaos and turmoil. Several fans who had been waving Polish flags and had come to support the Warsaw boxer also tried to storm the ring, but were beaten back by stern police officers wielding batons. From then on, the trouble escalated. Heavy folding chairs, drink cans and any other objects not nailed down were thrown, and the ring was filled with people punching, kicking and shouting. The *New York Times* said it resembled a battlefield. After Golota was struck by the mobile phone, Lou Duva, his 74-year-old trainer, climbed into the ring 'to pull my fighter out of there'. Earlier in the day, Duva had relinquished his role as chief cornerman after his implanted cardiac stimulator had failed him. Once in the ring, he was pushed to the canvas, where he lay flat on his back before being rushed to New York Medical Center for observation, due to fears that he had suffered a heart attack.

Meanwhile Golota, the back of his head covered in blood, had managed to climb out on to the apron of the ring, jump to the floor, stare down a young spectator who had confronted him and hurry through the crowded aisle to his dressing room. By this stage, the ring was filled with police officers, security guards and spectators punching, pushing, stomping, shoving and yelling, with much of it covered by Home Box Office, which was televising the fight live in America. As the melee spread into the arena, some spectators tossed more folding chairs towards the ring, with many ringside fans hastily retreating to the relative safety of the upper seats.

A short time passed before the announcement 'All security to ringside' by Michael Buffer blared over the public address system. Moments later, it was followed by a further announcement: 'All New York City police report to ringside.' This left the rest of the arena unsupervised, with more fights breaking out. A standard staff of 76 uniformed security men had been assigned for the fight and 18 police officers were designated for duty outside the Garden. However, this number was totally inadequate to handle what had now become a full-scale riot, the likes of which had never been witnessed at a boxing match before, in New York or anywhere else in the US.

An extra 150 police officers were rushed to the scene, as was the city's chief citizen Mayor Rudolph Giuliani. Five years later, Giuliani's dust-streaked face would be seen on television screens and newspapers all around the world, memorably embodying the grief of New Yorkers and their determination not to be beaten down by the terrorist attacks on the Twin Towers on 9/11. Police wearing riot helmets set up flares on 33rd Street and Seventh Avenue as they directed traffic away from the Garden's main entrance and hundreds of onlookers continued to mill about, many visibly shaken. In the previous Garden, three riots occurred in the mid-1960s, each involving spectators throwing bottles and cartons towards the ring following unpopular decisions, but nothing on such a massive scale as this one.

The mayhem continued inside the arena, with fist fights breaking out all over and people shouting and screaming. Because of the ethnic differences between the two boxers – one a black man who had clawed his way up from poor beginnings in a Brooklyn slum and the other an equally impoverished white man from a Warsaw ghetto – much of the melee was fought along racial lines. The ringside reporters had long hurried to dressing rooms, pulling Mayor Giuliani along with them. Moments later, when it seemed that the situation was improving, it all erupted again, with fights breaking out between African Americans and Polish Americans.

Waving batons, the police, reputedly the toughest in the world, eventually got the situation under some semblance of control, although it took over half an hour as Garden officials ordered everybody to vacate the building. Twenty-two people, including eight police officers, were taken to St Vincent's Hospital for treatment. There were 16 arrests. 'This was the product of a few people who acted like criminals,' said Mayor Giuliani.

Ironically Madison Square Garden, the traditional home of US boxing for well over a century and an independent sports promotion outfit in its own right, had closed its doors to boxing three years earlier when it was taken over by the giant Paramount Communications organisation. The new owners had apparently been scared off by yet another US Senate investigation into irregularities in the fight game and wanted to give the place a new image. Inside a year, however, they had second thoughts and opened the doors to the sport again following pressure from boxing people not only in New York but across the US. Now they had been confronted by a full-scale riot.

Not surprisingly, there was condemnation of the disgraceful scenes from all quarters, with politicians and people in high places calling for a complete ban on boxing, not only in New York City but in the state. The *New York Times* came out strongest in attacking the riot. 'Four low blows produced an even lower blow for boxing last night,' said Dave Anderson, who strongly criticised the Garden authorities' slowness in controlling 'the ugly incident'. He went on: 'The sport incurred another major injury to its dwindling image.' Gerald Eskenazi in the same paper wrote: 'The bout that dissolved into a frightening brawl evoked the darkest evening of boxing's controversial past.'

Under the heading 'What A Riot', *Ring* magazine's Steve Farhood wrote: 'Those who care about boxing could only shake their heads in frustration and disgust.' Farhood not only blamed Bowe's manager Rock Newman for his inability to control his cornermen but also felt 'the Garden's security was grossly ineffective'. Jack Hirsch in *Boxing News* said: 'In all my years of attending shows, I have never felt threatened to such an extent. People were attacking one another for no apparent reason, not only at ringside but in other parts of the arena as well. We waited for the Garden's security force to get things under control. When it became apparent that they were understaffed, the criminal element inside the arena took over.'

Glyn Leach wrote in *Boxing Monthly*: 'As a veteran of a few of these disturbances now, I can easily say that this was the worst violence I have witnessed at ringside. As for the police, where were they? It was 15 minutes into the riot before I saw any police presence, and there was none of any value until nearly half an hour of fighting had passed – and they were ham-fisted when they did arrive. I saw one man, who must have been at least 65, pushed through a crash-barrier by one of New York's finest.'

As for the action inside the ring, the scorecards of the three judges were not available in the sheer mayhem that unfolded but the ringside boxing writers all had Golota well ahead, even allowing for the three points deducted for low blows. The majority of reporters gave Bowe only one of the six completed rounds. Bowe was fined $1 million, a fifth of his purse, and the licences of Newman and Duva were suspended indefinitely.

As it happened, Bowe and his team, including Newman, were back for the return fight but without Eddie Futch. The veteran trainer, who had been with Riddick from the start, had resigned because of 'irreconcilable differences'. Futch told me in later years: 'To be honest, Thomas, I was shocked the way Bowe looked in that first fight. He lost focus and everything else became more important than being the best fighter around. He might have been the best heavyweight of all time. He was big, strong, had a good left hand and could fight inside. But he was never the same after knocking out Jesse Ferguson in 1993, shortly before he fought the return with Evander Holyfield, which he lost.

'He had lost the plot by then. The final nail in the coffin was the first fight with Golota. I could have walked away before the fight but I said: "Maybe I can get one more good fight out of him so as he can extend his career." But after that, I said to him: "I'm not going to waste my time if you're not going to work." Bowe had a lot of ability but his people didn't follow through.'

The return fight was held on 14 December 1996 at the Convention Center, Atlantic City after Madison Square Garden officials, to the surprise of nobody, wanted nothing to do with it. Incredibly, Golota self-destructed again and was disqualified in the ninth round by referee Eddie Cotton after the Pole sent Bowe writhing on his back in agony following three deliberately aimed low blows. The erratic Golota had earlier been deducted two points for a low blow and a headbutt.

Happily, there was no trouble this time except for a few minor disturbances which broke out among the highly charged crowd of 12,013. The trouble was quickly brought under control by the tight security, which had been put in place to avoid a recurrence of the July shambles. Bowe–Golota II had been a thriller, and the Pole had looked a certain winner before remarkably throwing it all away again. He had Bowe repeatedly on the verge of a knockout. As one ringside reporter remarked: 'Some guys never learn.'

Golota, meanwhile, continued with his career but in October 1997 he was blasted out by Lennox Lewis in 95 seconds. Over the following years, he had an inconsistent record with some good wins but also some major losses. He finally hung up his gloves in 2013 after three successive defeats in his native Poland, having compiled a record of 41-9-1 with two no-contests.

After the Golota fights, Bowe retired from boxing and joined the US Marine Corps. But after three days of training with his platoon at Parris Island, South Carolina, he walked out, 'sick of the hard training regime'. His estranged wife, Judy, had already fled their home in Maryland with their five children and moved to North Carolina but he located them, forced them into a truck and set off for his home in Fort Washington, Maryland. During the kidnapping, Bowe stabbed his wife in the chest.

Police captured him in South Hill, Virginia and freed his family. Bowe appeared in court and pleaded guilty to 'interstate domestic violence', and was sentenced to 18 months in prison. Despite the agreed sentence, the judge later reduced it to only 30 days, due to a claim of brain damage by Bowe's defence. This sentence was later overturned and Bowe served 17 months behind bars. Shortly after his release, he was arrested in Long Island after a domestic dispute with his new wife, Terri, who alleged that he hit her, their two children and a family friend, but he was acquitted when the witness failed to appear in court. That marriage also fell apart.

After being declared bankrupt in 2005, Bowe signed up with a new manager, Bob Bain, and returned to boxing after seven and a half years away. Bowe scored two wins over journeymen but, not satisfied with his form, he retired again, only to make a third comeback in Germany just before Christmas 2008 after an absence of more than three years. He won but lost interest again and hung up his gloves for the last time at the age of 41. Bowe reappeared on the sports scene in June 2013 when he tried kick boxing, but he lost heavily in the second round of a Muay Thai fight. In 2015, he was inducted into the International Boxing Hall of Fame in Canastota, New York.

Bowe's boxing record stands at 43-1 with 33 knockouts or stoppages. *Ring* magazine writer Bernard Fernandez feels that while the Brooklyn fighter went to hell and back with Evander Holyfield three times and faced credible opponents in his career, he could have done better. 'Considering the talent-enriched period in which he competed, where is the name Lennox Lewis? Or Mike Tyson?' asked Fernandez. 'Not to mention Michael Moorer, George Foreman, Larry Holmes, Ray Mercer, Buster Douglas, Tommy Morrison, Razor Ruddock and David Tua.'

In his autobiography *Let's Get It On*, famed referee Mills Lane, who had officiated at some of Bowe's fights, castigated him. Lane said that Bowe could have been one of boxing's greatest fighters but foolishly squandered the opportunity through immaturity and lack of discipline.

Bowe himself is philosophical about his boxing career. 'Besides the trash can incident, I really don't have any regrets, except that I wish I had been more into the financial part of the game,' he said. 'The fact that I fought Evander Holyfield three times, winning two, pretty much made up for everything else. I think those other guys, Lennox Lewis and Mike Tyson, realise that they couldn't have done anything any better than I did against Holyfield when I beat him in Las Vegas in November 1992 and won the undisputed heavyweight championship of the world. They couldn't even have done it so good. When they saw what I did to Holyfield, they had to know they couldn't have beaten me anyhow.'

Chapter 3

Atom drops on the flys

Jimmy Wilde v Pancho Villa, Polo Grounds, 18 June 1923

ON this hot summer's evening in New York under a cloudless sky, America was well into the Roaring 20s, an uninhibited era of bathtub gin and speakeasies and gangsters and swingers too, before the word came into popular usage. Jack Dempsey ruled the heavyweight division and Benny Leonard was king of the lightweights. Down among the flyweights was a little Welshman with the power of Dempsey and the skill of Leonard, a rare combination. His name was Jimmy Wilde and he was undisputed king of the 112-pounders.

Today you can buy atomic cocktails and atomic ice cream in cafes, restaurants, bars or wherever. But back then, long before two atomic bombs were dropped on Japan to end America's war in the Pacific, the atom to sporting fans meant only one thing – the 'Mighty Atom' himself, the 'Ghost with a Hammer in his Hand', the 'Tylorstown Terror', Jimmy Wilde.

Wilde was in town for a defence of his title against the dynamic Filipino puncher Pancho Villa at the Polo Grounds. With America determined to end Britain's domination of the championship and bring the title to their side of the Atlantic for the first time in 11 years, and Britain equally determined to hang on to it, the city was buzzing with excitement.

The flyweight division was the last of the traditional eight weight classes to be established. It was created in London by the

National Sporting Club, predecessor of the current British Boxing Board of Control, in 1912, when Sid Smith defeated Curley Walker on points over 20 rounds in London.

It was not until 1916 that America accepted a legitimate flyweight champion when Wilde, as British champion, fought and knocked out the US representative Giuseppe Di Melfi, known as Young Zulu Kid, in 11 rounds in London. Boxing now had a flyweight champion and a new division, both recognised universally for the first time.

At 5ft 2in, frail-looking with skinny limbs and protruding ribs that belied the power of his punches, Wilde never weighed more than 108lbs, four pounds below the flyweight limit. He looked too frail, even sickly, to be allowed to enter a boxing ring. Yet in an age of outstanding flyweights, Wilde was world champion for seven years and four months, a record that still stands today, over 100 years on. He lost only three and drew two of his 149 bouts spread over 12 years, with two of those losses coming at the tail end of his career.

Gene Tunney, the former heavyweight champion of the world, called Wilde 'the greatest fighter he had ever seen' and it is universally acknowledged by boxing writers and historians today that he remains the No 1 flyweight in boxing history. In the 100 Greatest Boxers of All Time list compiled by *Boxing News*, Wilde is the highest-rated British boxer at No 8, directly behind, in descending order, Sugar Ray Robinson, Muhammad Ali, Henry Armstrong, Joe Louis, Sugar Ray Leonard, Roberto Duran and Harry Greb.

'Wilde's vigorous aggression made him very popular and gained him many victories,' said the author and historian Gilbert Odd. 'Always on the attack, gloves held at hip level, body swaying, head moving, he was a difficult target to pinpoint with a decisive punch, while his own blows came from all angles and with unexpected explosive power. He delighted in trapping an opponent on the ropes or in a corner when he would release a bombardment of shock punches without fear of return as the other man would be too busy defending himself.'

Wilde was born into a coal mining family at Quakers Yard, near Merthyr Tydfil, south Wales on 15 May 1892 at a time when working in the pits meant little money for hazardous work and hard labour. The men toiled long hours and lived in identical, shabby wooden shacks, and their humble abodes were always covered with everlasting soot and grime.

On leaving school at 14, Wilde worked in the pits himself. He was small enough to crawl face down through gullies impassable to most of his colleagues. He hacked away, developing the back and shoulder muscles that were to give him the punching power in later years to knock out all types of rivals. The family later moved to the village of Tylorstown in the Rhondda Valley, hence one of his nicknames, the 'Tylorstown Terror'.

To augment his earnings, Wilde boxed for pennies among his workmates and coming up to his 18th birthday in 1910, his landlord, an old bare-knuckle fighter named Dai Davies, encouraged him to join Jack Scarrott's travelling boxing booth, which was visiting the town. Davies convinced Wilde he had a future in boxing and that joining the booth as it travelled around the country would give him good experience. It would also take him out of the mines. Crowds were amazed at his toughness and ability to knock down much larger opponents, most of whom were local tough men weighing around 200lbs.

Davies used to give Wilde lessons in the noble art, teaching him the tricks and manoeuvres he had learned in over 100 bloody battles. They would work out in the most unexpected places – the miners' mobile schoolroom, in the pit itself, on top of heaps of coal slag and even in the Davies' bedroom, with the furniture pushed aside. During this period Wilde got to know Davies' daughter, Elizabeth, the woman who would later become his wife.

When they first met, Elizabeth disapproved of Jimmy's boxing ambitions, having from early childhood seen her father come home with split lips and black eyes. When they decided to get married, Wilde actually gave up his boxing ambitions for a while. But eventually he convinced her that professional boxing would take him out of the mines and into a new life with the promise of better pay. Elizabeth would play a major role in Jimmy's ring career. Very often, while doing his roadwork, she would act as his pacemaker on her bicycle. He often sparred with her in their bedroom, fitting her out with a breastplate for a few rounds as he perfected his footwork while she threw haymakers at his bobbing head.

Wilde officially turned professional on, appropriately enough, Boxing Day 1910. Managed by Teddy Lewis, reserve captain of local rugby club Pontypridd RFC, he made fast progress, learning as he went along. In 1911 he had 28 fights, winning 27 and drawing one. In 1912 he had nine bouts, all wins, eight by either knockout or stoppage. In 1913, he increased it to 30 fights without taking too much out of himself because so few of his fights went the scheduled distance. Having become the best in Wales and the northern cities of England and Scotland, Wilde was anxious to become better known by going to London.

Wilde and Lewis pestered Dick Burge, the promoter at one of London's most famous boxing venues, the Ring, at Blackfriars, and Burge matched him with a promising 112-pounder known as Matt Wells' Nipper. When Burge's wife Bella saw Wilde working out in the gym, she told her husband alongside her: 'You ought to be ashamed of yourself for putting a little skinny kid like this into the ring. He'll be murdered and we'll be thrown into jail.' Overhearing Bella's remarks, Wilde turned to her and said: 'You've nothing to worry about, ma'am. I've fought in the pits and I've fought in the booths and now I'm a professional. I can look after myself.' Bella need not have worried because Wilde knocked out his man in 45 seconds.

A second appearance at Blackfriars was not forthcoming so Wilde and Lewis looked to the National Sporting Club in Covent Garden. The prestigious club was founded in March 1891 as a private club and was run under very strict rules regarding both the boxers and the members. Bouts would take place after dinner, before about 1,300 members and guests. The bouts would be fought in absolute silence as no talking was permitted during the rounds. The NSC built up a great tradition of sportsmanship and fair play. In 1909, the club's president, the 5th Earl of Lonsdale, had introduced the Lonsdale Belt as a prize to be awarded to the British champion at each weight. The belts were made from porcelain and 22-carat gold.

When Wilde and his manager approached Lord Lonsdale about an appearance there, he was turned down, with no reason given. Undaunted, they returned to Wales, where Wilde continued to fight and win. When Lewis suggested rather optimistically they try London once again, the pair set off and went back to the NSC, but were met with another refusal. It was then that the truth finally came out. NSC matchmaker Peggy Bettinson explained: 'Look, Wilde is too small and puny, and there would be too many complaints from members about bad matchmaking if we allowed him into the ring.'

Knowing that the boxer and his manager would not be put off by banning Wilde, Bettinson reluctantly found a French flyweight for him, Eugene Husson, who was even lighter than Wilde. They both weighed under 100lbs for the fight, scheduled for 30 March 1914 at the NSC. 'While Wilde probably could have knocked out Husson quickly, he chose instead to put on an exhibition of the full range of his boxing skills before disposing of his opponent in the sixth,' said Harry Mullan in his book, *The Ultimate Encyclopaedia of Boxing.*

Having finally convinced the game's most powerful figures that he was the goods, Wilde completed 1914 with 20 wins from January to December, including nine by knockouts. Anytime he appeared at the NSC, he always got a big reception. In his first fight in the New Year, he was paired with Scotland's talented Tancy Lee for the vacant British and European flyweight titles at the NSC over 20 rounds on 25 January. Wilde was suffering from a bout of flu going into the ring but Lee, from the seaside town of Leith, near Edinburgh, proved a tough opponent with a powerful right hand, which repeatedly crashed into the Welshman's face and body.

Wilde kept going but by the 14th round it was a wild goose chase, to borrow a phrase from Shakespeare's *Romeo and Juliet.* Lee took all Wilde's best shots and finally stopped the Welshman in the 17th round, when Jimmy's corner threw in the towel. In the dressing room afterwards, he was furious with Lewis' action. 'Don't ever do that again,' he commanded. It was an order that almost cost Wilde his life in his last battle.

Instead of being discouraged by the Lee defeat, it spurred him on, and a year later he won the British title by stopping Joe Symonds in the 12th round. He defended the championship against his lone conqueror Tancy Lee in London on 26 June 1916 and, this time fully fit, stopped the Scot in 11 rounds. Wilde was already being regarded as the unofficial world flyweight champion, certainly in Britain, especially after knocking out Johnny Rosner in 11 rounds in Liverpool earlier in the year and virtually cleaning up the flyweight division. The American authorities agreed to recognise the winner of a 20-round fight at the newly built Holborn Stadium, London between Wilde and Young Zulu Kid, born in Italy but a naturalised American, on 18 December 1916.

The Kid, who claimed he got his ring name from his golliwog mascot, a black-faced rag doll which he carried around with him, was also known as the 'Fighting Newsboy'. On arrival in London brimful of confidence, he told waiting newspapermen at Southampton: 'Your Jimmy Wilde is calling himself the uncrowned flyweight champion of the world but he's in for the shock of his life. He won't be able to stand up to my constant bombardment for more than a few rounds.' When this information was relayed to Wilde in London, the Welshman smiled and said: 'It's all talk. The real test comes when we get into the ring but speaking for myself, I'm fully confident I can keep the title in Britain.'

The Kid, totally indifferent to Wilde's reputation as a destructive puncher, danced out of his corner at the first bell as if he wanted to get it over with as quickly as possible. He bobbed up and down like a rubber ball on an elastic cord and Wilde was quite bewildered. A 20/1 favourite, Jimmy took a few pot shots at the lively challenger, missed badly and had to take a few stinging shots to the head. But in the second round, Wilde got through with his heavy punches and a powerful right to the chin sent the Kid to the canvas, the bell saving him.

If Wilde thought it was all over bar the shouting, he was in for a surprise. For the next few rounds, the American tossed plenty of hard punches that often drove Wilde back under their sheer force. But Jimmy was gradually getting on top and slowly the chunky challenger began to wilt, his punches becoming slower and noticeably weaker. In the 11th round, a smashing left hook screwed the Kid's head right around and a follow-through right knocked him against the ropes. Wilde knew he had his man and a combination left-right sent the Kid staggering back against the ropes. Another right sent him down as the towel came soaring over the ropes. It was all over. Jimmy Wilde was undisputed flyweight champion of the world and the Holborn Stadium had come into being. It remained a notable boxing hall until the middle of the Second World War, when it was flattened by a German bomb.

By now, Wilde was called up for army service in the First World War and found himself based in Aldershot as a PT instructor, later promoted to sergeant. Frequently on tour, he promoted morale and raised funds for various charity and military funds. Duties restricted his professional boxing activity but the authorities permitted him to have occasional contests and box exhibitions. One of Wilde's big wins was over Joe Conn, a challenger for the British featherweight title, on Chelsea Football Club's ground at

Stamford Bridge on 31 August 1916. Outweighed by 18 pounds and up against a classy opponent, Wilde swarmed all over his man and stopped him in the 11th round. Because he was serving in the army, Jimmy could not accept payment for the fight but his wife Elizabeth received a present of a package of diamonds valued at £3,000, which would have been his purse had it not been for the war.

When hostilities ended, Wilde set off on an American and Canadian tour in July 1919 and stayed for six months, winning all his 12 fights, five either by knockouts or stoppages. He came home after Christmas 1920 to accept an offer to meet the talented American Pete Herman at the Royal Albert Hall, London's equivalent of Madison Square Garden, on 13 January. Herman, from New Orleans, was a smart boxer and a great puncher. It was an overweight fight as Herman was a fully fledged bantamweight and had surprisingly just lost his world title three weeks earlier to the Irish-American Joe Lynch, amid allegations that he threw the fight in return for 'the right money'. He would subsequently regain the title with an easy win over Lynch.

Both camps agreed that Herman would not weigh more than 118lbs, the bantamweight limit, but when Wilde's manager discovered that the American had weighed in privately rather than officially as normal, which would be a few hours before the fight, he was enraged. 'It's a public weigh-in or the fight is off,' Lewis told Herman's manager Sam Goldman, who insisted no agreement ever existed. With the dispute still unresolved up to the time the boxers were due to enter the ring, Wilde said he would not leave his dressing room until Herman weighed in.

To add to the tense situation, the crowd outside was in an angry mood. The scheduled preliminary bout between Bombardier Billy Wells, the former British heavyweight champion, and America's Battling Levinsky had fallen through because of a hand injury sustained by Levinsky. Also, arrangements had been made to film the fights for newsreel coverage.

Events may have taken a nastier turn had somebody not gone into Wilde's dressing room and said that the Prince of Wales was in a ringside seat. 'I see,' said the little Welshman. 'In that case, to hell with contracts, agreements, weights, I can't keep him waiting,' he declared. He left the dressing room with his handlers and went out to the ring.

The big fight was saved but it turned out to be a horrible mismatch. Herman actually weighed a good 121lbs, three pounds over the agreed weight, while Wilde scaled 103lbs. The 18lbs advantage was too much, providing the American with extra strength and vitality. No matter how hard the Welshman's punches to head and body, the American's were stronger. Wilde was down three times before the referee intervened. Taking the flyweight champion to his corner, he said: 'It's the best thing, Jimmy. I can't let you take any more.' Despite the heavy defeat, Wilde was sporting enough to admit he had met a superior opponent. 'I can say that Herman beat me because he was a better boxer,' he said through bruised lips, with his face showing signs of the battering.

Denzil Bachelor, the British boxing writer and author, wrote later: 'Rather than disappoint his Prince, the future King of England, Wilde accepted an invitation to professional suicide. He fought tigerishly, bravely, but it was not enough.'

Wilde announced his retirement after the fight with no regrets. He was happily married, had money in the bank and had won and retained the flyweight championship of the world. What more could anyone ask? In any event, there were no worthy challengers around. But two and a half years later, the scene changed dramatically. The American promoter Tex Rickard made him an attractive offer of $65,000, a flyweight record at the time, to come to New York and defend his title against the younger and dangerous Filipino Pancho Villa. It would be a big outdoor show at the Polo Grounds, New York and set for 18 June 1923 – with all expenses paid for the British party.

Wilde was certainly not short of cash as he and his wife had lived a quiet life despite his fame and the heavy demands on his time, but this was good money to contribute to his life savings. Despite the cash offer, neither Wilde's wife nor his manager Teddy Lewis wanted him to accept, but the boxer was adamant. 'I'm still the undefeated flyweight champion of the world and it's up to me to defend my title,' he insisted. With that, the party prepared to set off for the New World. Wilde had fought all over America in the past but this would be his New York debut and he looked forward to impressing the fans, even up against such a formidable opponent.

As the crowd of 23,000 filed into the ballpark, there was time to reflect on the career of Pancho Villa. Considered by many experts as the greatest Asian boxer in ring history, he was explosive and relentless when the bell sounded. Even smaller than Wilde, he stood a fraction over five feet. Born Francisco Guilledo on the island of Panay in the Philippines on 1 August 1901, he was the son of a local cowhand who abandoned his family when Guilledo was only six, and grew up helping his mother raise goats she tended on the farm. At the age of 11, he befriended a local boxer and together they migrated to Manila, settling in the north-western town of Tondo, with its teeming slums and underdeveloped land.

Guilledo would often fight with other kids in the street and boxers in the local gym, and soon attracted the attention of local boxing regulars. A talent scout spotted him and encouraged him to fight for cash. Francisco had his first paid fight at the age of 18 against Alberto 'Kid' Castro in 1919 and won with a knockout in three rounds. Within two years, he was the Philippine flyweight champion and later won the bantamweight title, but he gave up the sport when the woman he was courting suddenly broke off their relationship. Discouraged and homesick, he returned to Panay with a plan to retire and take up some other occupation, but the clamour of Filipino fight fans encouraged him to give boxing another try.

In the gym one day, he caught the attention of an American promoter, Frank Churchill, who was visiting the town from his base in Manila. Impressed by the lad's aggressive style and heavy punching, Churchill signed him to a contract and promised to guide him to a world title – but not before changing his name to Pancho Villa, the famous Mexican bandit. Villa fought exclusively in the Philippines from 1919 through to April 1922, often defeating men much heavier. In this period, he compiled an impressive record of 48 wins, one loss, three draws and two no-decisions.

By now, promoter Tex Rickard had heard glowing reports of Villa's work in the Philippines and invited him and Churchill to try their luck in the US. 'Villa has to be a big draw Stateside, Frank, and the small men are great attractions here,' cabled Rickard. Calling a press conference on the day before they sailed, Churchill said to the newspapermen gathered at the docks: 'We're sailing to the US and we will return with the world championship or not return at all. That's a promise.' The promoter's encouraging and direct comments brought a round of applause from the writers.

As it happened, Villa got off to a bad and disappointing start in the US. Making his debut in Jersey City on 7 June 1922, he dropped a decision to Abe Goldstein over 12 rounds. Fight number two a month later, also in Jersey City, ended in his second loss when Frankie Genaro defeated him in another ten-rounder, although the verdict was disputed. Churchill put the defeats down to his boxer not being fully acclimatised but the American press and public were thinking otherwise. Damon Runyon of the *New York Journal-American* was among several writers very disappointed with Villa's performances, with one saying that the Filipino was 'a damp squib' and advised him to 'head back where he came from'.

Churchill was now experiencing trouble in arranging fights in major venues. With money running out fast, he approached Rickard to feature his boxer on one of his cards. After all, it was Rickard who encouraged them to come to the US in the first place. 'Let's wait until Pancho establishes himself, Frank, then we'll see,' promised Tex.

Villa soon found his true form. On a card at Ebbets Field, home of the Brooklyn Dodgers Baseball Club, on 14 September 1922, he sensationally knocked out the former world bantamweight champion Johnny Buff in 11 rounds to win the American flyweight title. Damon Runyon at ringside turned to a colleague and remarked: 'You know, I picked Buff but I'm glad Villa won. I hear Jimmy Wilde is talking about a comeback and he still holds the world flyweight title. It's high time we had a challenger to bring the championship back to the US.'

Feelers were put out to Wilde to come out of his two-year retirement 'for one last fight' against the American champion Frankie Genaro, who held a disputed points win over the No 2 contender, Villa. The fight was set for early 1923 in New York, to be promoted by Tom O'Rourke, Rickard's rival, but Genaro's manager Phil Bernstein made demands that O'Rourke was not prepared to meet and the fight was called off. On hearing the news, Churchill went over to Rickard's office. 'Don't do any business with Bernstein at all, Tex,' he pleaded. 'Villa is your best bet to fight Wilde. Everybody knows that Villa was robbed against Genaro anyway. Besides, Genaro wouldn't draw flies. Give us the Wilde fight and if we don't sell out, take the difference out of our purse.'

The next day, Rickard called a press conference to announce that Wilde was returning to the US to defend his world flyweight title against Villa at the Polo Grounds on 18 June 1923. It promised to be an action-packed fight with two heavy punchers in opposition, and on fight night a crowd of 35,000 passed through the turnstiles on a sweltering evening. At the weigh-in earlier in the day, Wilde had scaled at 109lbs and Villa one pound heavier. The major disadvantage for Wilde was the age gap. The Welshman was 31, nine years older than the Filipino. But he said he was not unduly worried on that score.

'I expect a tough fight,' he told newspapermen after stepping off the scales. 'I appreciate the fact that in Villa, I'm going to meet one of the toughest little men in boxing. I realise too that I'm going to be put to a real test and that is what I've prepared for.' Villa said: 'I'm in the best condition of my career and, once in condition, my worries are over. I don't intend to give Wilde a minute's rest while we are in the ring.'

Wilde described the scene in his autobiography *Fighting Was My Business*: 'I remember seeing Villa in his corner. Dark, swarthy, a little round-shouldered, his eyes summing me up, the way mine were regarding him. He exuded confidence, but up to that moment I was equally confident. Blame it on all those fights I had over the years but I honestly did not think that Pancho would beat me. I looked down at my wife at ringside, lifted my glove to her and saw her smile. That gave me extra confidence.'

After announcer Joe Humphries made the formal announcements, referee Patsy Haley brought the two boxers together in the centre of the ring to give them their final instructions before they returned to their corners to await the first bell.

Both men came out fast, with Wilde using his left jabs and long rights to score effectively as Villa sought an opening for his big punches. As the round progressed, the Filipino managed to get through with left hooks, right crosses and uppercuts. 'Villa was coming at me like a tiger and he almost overwhelmed me in that first round, but I knew his method of fighting and I wasn't worried,' recalled Wilde. But writers saw it differently. 'There was little method and no beauty in Villa's attacks as he rushed pell-mell into the champion, churning away with both fists,' said the boxing writer and historian Robert J Thornton. 'A right landed with trip-hammer force in the pit of Wilde's stomach, causing the Briton to gasp like a gaffed fish.'

If the first round was fairly even, depending on which way you looked at it – Wilde's superior boxing or Villa's powerful aggression – the second round quite clearly belonged to the Filipino. He kept up a constant bombardment of hooks, uppercuts and swings that drove the champion back and had him holding at every opportunity. Towards the end of the round, Villa landed a powerful left hook to the face which made Jimmy blink. He followed it up with more big punches and just before the end of the round Wilde looked like he was going down but he boxed his way out of immediate trouble and seemed glad to hear the bell.

Nor was there any respite for Wilde in the third round. The rapidly weakening champion was losing strength by the minute, with only his courage keeping him upright. But the shot that obliterated any hope he had of remaining champion came just seconds before the end of the round. As Bob Edgren of the *New York Evening World* saw it: 'They were mixing it when the bell rang. Wilde dropped his hands and partly turned to go to his corner. Pancho had drawn his right back to swing. I saw him stop and hold the blow for an instant. But there was Wilde, hands down, head turned away, an easy target. Either the temptation was too great or instinct too strong. Villa let the swing go with everything behind it, landing square on Wilde's chin. He went down and his seconds dragged him to his corner, worked over him for nearly a minute before he stirred.'

That was the turning point. Perhaps more importantly, it was also an incident that would normally have merited immediate disqualification. Haley said he had had turned away from the boxers at the bell and did not see the punch. 'Maybe Villa started the punch as the bell rang, I just don't know,' he would explain. Thirty-five years later, Robert J Thornton wrote in *Boxing and Wrestling* magazine: 'It seems likely that Villa would have won the fight even if that unfortunate blow after the bell had not landed. The sands of time had run out on Wilde.'

Fighting purely on instinct in the fourth round, the world champion jabbed and moved as he fended off most of Villa's blows. But those that Pancho landed, particularly to the body, had the wispy champion lurching like a ship in a perfect storm. Wilde's seconds worked feverishly on him in the corner but at this stage it looked a lost cause.

In the fifth and part of the sixth, Wilde drew deep from some secret reservoir, rallied and at times actually outfought the challenger. But the reprieve ended for him in the waning moments of the sixth, when Villa picked up the tempo again and unleashed another attack that drove Wilde back across the ring. At the bell, he reeled back to his corner and was in such bad shape that referee Haley told him he was going to stop the fight, or rather the slaughter. 'Don't you dare,' said the gallant champion. 'He'll have to knock me down and out first.'

Wilde staggered out for round seven with both eyes almost closed, bleeding from the nose and with several nicks on his face. Instinctively pawing out a left hand in an effort to hold Villa off, the Filipino brushed it aside and cracked across heavy lefts and rights as Wilde fell into a clinch. With the round less than two minutes old, Pancho shot over a left and right to Wilde's jaw. Jimmy's whole body went stiff and he pitched over on his face like a chopped tree. His face hit the canvas first and those close to the ring saw a white puff of resin dust rise slowly around his head. Wilde's illustrious career was finally over. The time was 1:46 of round seven.

Hype Igoe of the *New York World* wrote: 'Wilde's remarkable reign as the greatest of world champions came to a sickening end, for the brave little man went face down into the resin after taking a cruel beating. Wilde, it seemed, never had a chance. He was beaten from the first round on. Lacking all of his sure-footed speed and killing punch of yore, Wilde walked into the cannon's mouth, a sad, most defiant smile on his face, made unsightly by the spiteful fists of the great little Filipino. Age was horribly spiked and gaffed, youth strutting from the fight unmarked, a vast crowd shrieking the praise of a strange little man just crowned king.'

Wilde was carried to his dressing room and within minutes all kinds of rumours flew around like seagulls over a fishing boat. That Wilde was dying. That he had lost his speech and his sight. No, he only lost his title after one of the most gallant performances ever seen in a New York ring.

'I just lost to a better man,' said the Welshman in the dressing room as his wife consoled him. 'Pancho is a worthy champion and I wish him all the luck in the world for the future. I think he'll hold the title for a long time.' Villa would soon enter the packed room and shake Wilde's hand. 'You're the greatest man I've ever fought,' he said before leaving with tears in his eyes.

Wilde never fought again and put his earnings into several businesses, including a cinema chain and a cafe he called The Mighty Atom. With a record of 131-3-2 and 13 no-decisions, he maintained his interest in boxing. For several years, he wrote a widely read column in the *Sunday Empire News* and often graced the ringside on big fight nights in London. In 1965, he was mugged at Cardiff railway station and never fully recovered from the beating, lingering on for four more years in hospital. Wilde died on 10 March 1969 at the age of 76.

Villa returned to Manila after his championship win and received a hero's welcome, feted with a parade and a lavish reception at Malacanan Palace. He made two defences of his title in the US and returned to Manila for a third. After that, it was back to stateside for a non-title fight against the Irishman Jimmy McLarnin, scheduled for Ewing Field, San Francisco on 4 July 1925. Several days before the fight, Villa's face became swollen and he had a dental surgeon remove one of his wisdom teeth.

Against the advice of his physician and dentist, who both recommended bed rest, Villa climbed through the ropes with a swollen jaw that was plainly discernible to the ringsiders. He had managed to convince the Californian State Athletic Commission that he was fine. Lighter by seven pounds, he ended up spending most of the fight using one hand to protect his afflicted face. McLarnin, pacing himself well, was much quicker and Pancho weathered the ten rounds but lost the decision.

Villa and his large entourage spent the next few days and nights touring the local clubs and bars, wining and dining as though he had won. But feeling unwell, he was rushed to hospital, where it was discovered that the infection had spread to his throat. He was rushed into surgery but lapsed into a coma while on the operating table and died the following day, 14 July 1925, a little over a week before his 24th birthday. In 1999, with a record of 75-5-4 and 23 no-decisions, Villa was voted by the Associated Press as the world's best flyweight of the 20th century.

Chapter 4

The 'Man Mountain' and the Mob

Primo Carnera v Jack Sharkey, Long Island Bowl, 29 June 1933

ALL roads were leading to the Long Island Bowl for the world heavyweight title fight between the champion Jack Sharkey, from Boston, and his big Italian challenger Primo Carnera, billed as the 'Man Mountain'. From early afternoon, the police presence around the venue was strong, with 600 officers from the borough of Queens brought in to control the crowds and an extra 150 assigned to duty inside the arena when the gates opened at 4pm. The first of four preliminaries was timed to start at 8.15pm, with the big fight scheduled for 10pm. The weather forecasters predicted showers but in the event of a postponement the contest would be held the following day.

Tickets, with prices starting from $2.30 in the bleachers down to $15 at ringside, could still be purchased either at the box office or at several ticket agencies in the area. The Bowl could accommodate 71,000 fans but promoter James J Johnston, born in Liverpool but reared in the tough Hell's Kitchen area of New York, said he was expecting a crowd of around 50,000 and a gate of $300,000. A share of the proceeds would go to the Free Milk Fund for Babies, set up 12 years earlier by the wife of the millionaire media tycoon William Randolph Hearst to aid the poor of New York.

Sharkey, known as the 'Boston Gob', had won the title from Germany's Max Schmeling on a controversial points decision over 15 rounds, also at the Bowl, almost exactly a year earlier. He was expected to enter the ring a slight favourite, according to the newspapers. The thing about Sharkey was his unpredictability. He won fights he was expected to lose and lost fights he was expected to win. You never knew what to expect when Sharkey climbed through the ropes, especially in fights where the stakes were high.

As John Kieran, a feature writer on the *New York Times*, wrote on the day of the fight: 'What Sharkey will do in defence of his title this time is a mystery. He cried after losing to Jack Dempsey and the fans went asleep during his fight with Young Stribling. He moaned and screeched when he was disqualified against Phil Scott and he became hysterical and almost fell down in a faint when he knocked out Jack Delaney in one round. He ko'd Tommy Loughran with one solid punch. That's Jack Sharkey, coming or going. He may be dull or dashing, a slashing hitter or a bored boxer, a free swinger or a clinging vine. What he will do this time is a mystery. He may fight like a fury or he may fold up like an accordion. Possibly he will put on something special this time.'

Good or bad, Sharkey was a well-respected boxer with fine ring skills and an arsenal of punches. Promoter Tex Rickard said of him: 'I've seen 'em all, big and little, and Jack Sharkey stands out because he was the fastest heavyweight of all, with a left like a piston and a right straight and hard as a ramrod.' During Sharkey's reign as champion and remembering his inconsistencies, William Muldoon, the New York State Commissioner, called Jack 'the best fighter in the world – from the neck down'. Still, on his good days and his bad days, over the years, he would face 11 opponents who were either world champions or former champions, and he would be the only man to face both Jack Dempsey and Joe Louis.

Sharkey had already beaten Carnera on a 15-round decision two years earlier but the big Italian had shown much improvement since then. Primo would provide sterner opposition this time. At the same time, Sharkey was supremely confident he could turn back the big Italian's challenge and leave the ring still heavyweight champion of the world.

Sharkey was born Josef Paul Cukoschay, sometimes spelt Zukauskas, on 26 October 1902 in Binghampton, a small town in upstate New York. His parents, Benjamin and Agnes, were Lithuanian immigrants and there was a community of Lithuanians in Binghampton. The town was known as the Valley of Opportunity because of the abundance of jobs in several factories, most notably making shoes and cigars. Benjamin got a job in a shoe factory and Agnes took in boarders to earn a little extra money. When Benjamin became ill and could not work for a while, young Josef left school in the eighth grade and looked around for work to help the family finances.

'While I realised that education was a vital part of growing up, I had no choice but to quit school and go out to work,' he recalled in later years. 'I was working in a shoe factory when I was 12, and by the time I was 14 I was part of a construction gang building a dam. I used to mix the cement by hand. It was hard work and it paid well and it kept me outdoors, which I liked. After that, I did other jobs such as working as a brakeman on the local railroad and I spent some time as a glassblower. You name it. I did it. Growing up, though, I avoided fights. When the Lithuanians fought, they fought to kill, and my favourite occupation was breathing.'

At 15, he left home as he wasn't getting along with his father and tried to enlist in the US Navy 'for a bit of adventure', but was turned down because of his age. He crossed the Brooklyn Bridge by foot and lived rough in New York City, once again picking up any jobs he could find. Deciding to have another try at enlisting in the navy, he was accepted this time and was consigned to the USS *South Carolina,* which patrolled the Caribbean. 'We called it the Banana Fleet,' he remembered. 'We used to go ashore with another company of US Marines, and a cannon, and break up any uprisings.'

His superiors used to organise boxing tournaments on board and when he offered to take part, he was accepted. Winning his first fight in 30 seconds, he went on to box 39 times, losing only once, and vowed to become a full-time boxer on his discharge. Landing in Boston, he sought out the local promoter and offered to box on his next bill. The promoter agreed to pay him $100, as long as he changed his name. 'Nobody will be able to pronounce that Lithuanian name of yours so you'll have to change it,' said the promoter. Josef Paul Cukoschay was now simply Jack Sharkey. 'I borrowed Jack from my favourite heavyweight at the time, Jack Dempsey, and Sharkey from the great old Irish fighter Tom Sharkey,' he said in an interview.

As Jack Sharkey, and basing himself in Boston, he won his first professional fight by knocking out Billy Muldoon in the first round on 24 January 1924. By the end of the year, and now a married man settled in the Chestnut Hill area of Boston, his record stood at 8-3 with one no-decision. At the close of 1925, it was 16-5 with one no-decision, a record which included his first professional title, the American Legion heavyweight championship. By now Sharkey had got himself a manager, Johnny Buckley, an influential boxing man with many connections. He was also getting good notices in newspapers as well as *Ring* magazine. A ten-round points victory over the fearsome 220lb contender George Godfrey at the Mechanics Building in Boston on 21 September 1926 put him at the forefront and the fight made headlines both in the Boston and New York papers.

Godfrey, from Mobile, Alabama, was ranked No 6 by *Ring* magazine at the time and was regarded as one of the best heavyweights in America. He claimed he was denied a chance to fight for the title due to the colour of his skin and the best he could do was to fight for and win the 'coloured heavyweight championship of the world', which was not recognised officially. Godfrey was a 10-8 favourite but Sharkey won an easy decision with his better boxing and sharper hitting.

Sharkey and his manager immediately issued a formal challenge to Dempsey for a title shot, but the next day the boxing world was turned upside down when Dempsey became the victim of a massive upset when he lost his title to the New Yorker Gene Tunney on a rainy night in Philadelphia. Tunney outboxed and outfought the 'Manassa Mauler' and won the decision after ten rounds. When Sharkey heard the result, he told Buckley: 'Get me Tunney.'

When Tunney said he was not ready just yet to discuss his first challenger, Sharkey and Buckley accepted a fight with Harry Wills, a front-ranking contender weighing 220lbs of lean muscle and standing 6ft 3in in his socks. Like Godfrey and several other greats such as Sam Langford, Joe Jenette and Sam McVey, Wills was handicapped because he was of black skin. It was no secret that the infamous colour bar provided a convenient way for many white boxers to avoid meeting dangerous opponents.

In 1924, promoter Tex Rickard did get the signatures of champion Dempsey and his perennial challenger Wills for a title fight, but it was merely a front. They never met in actual combat.

Floyd Fitzsimmons, a rival promoter, had also tried to set up a Dempsey–Wills fight but Rickard intervened, claiming he was Dempsey's official promoter.

It was now felt that the winner of the Sharkey–Wills match would be the No 1 contender. They met at Ebbets Field, Brooklyn on 12 October 1926. When referee Patsy Haley called the two men to the centre of the ring for their instructions, Wills noticed an excessive amount of Vaseline on Jack's hair. 'Rub that grease off,' yelled Wills. Sharkey, never lost for an answer, moved close to the favoured heavyweight, stuck his head under Harry's chin and said: 'Rub it off yourself, Wills.' When Wills refused, Sharkey said: 'Then go put some on your own head because you'll need it before this thing is over.' Wills was dumbfounded and all he could do was turn away and head for his corner. Sharkey admitted afterwards that he had the fight won there and then.

The contest itself was one-sided, with Sharkey doing all the punching. Wills held repeatedly and tried to clinch at every opportunity. The referee threatened to disqualify Wills on several occasions if he didn't stop stalling and start fighting. Finally, in the 13th round, with Wills a well-beaten man and continually holding, as well as slapping with the inside of the glove, Haley, red with rage, stepped between the two boxers and announced he was disqualifying Wills. Harry knew he had no chance and took the easy way out.

Two more impressive wins, a stoppage in 12 rounds over the former world light-heavyweight champion Mike McTigue and a victory in five rounds against the highly rated contender Jimmy Maloney, earned Sharkey a match with Jack Dempsey for the right to challenge Gene Tunney. They met on 21 July 1927 before a crowd close to 100,000 at the Yankee Stadium. Dempsey had lost his title to Tunney nearly a year earlier and felt a good win over Sharkey would qualify him for a rematch with Gene.

For six rounds, it was all Sharkey as he battered the old champion at will. Only Dempsey's great courage and ability to take a good punch saved him from a knockout in the early rounds. The Boston ex-sailor looked a sure winner. In the seventh, with Sharkey still way ahead on points, he made the fatal mistake of turning his head to complain to referee Jack O'Sullivan that he had been hit low. Sharkey was ignoring the golden rule that a boxer must defend himself at all times during a contest. His inconsistency was coming to the fore. Seizing his big opportunity, Dempsey landed three rights to the body and a smashing left hook to Sharkey's unprotected jaw that sent the Boston contender down and very much out.

Sharkey and Buckley roared their disapproval and claimed 'Foul! Foul!' but the verdict stood. Buckley demanded a return but it never happened. Dempsey went on to get his rematch with Tunney in Chicago a year later in what became known as the 'Battle of the Long Count', with Tunney floored for 14 seconds before rising and beating Dempsey on points over ten rounds. Sharkey took a six-month rest after the Dempsey fight but seemed to lose form on his return, gaining a lucky draw against the New Zealander Tom Heeney and losing a decision to Cleveland's rugged Johnny Risko. He was fighting like a man without any incentive and spent less and less time in the gym, preferring to go fishing.

When Tunney retired as undefeated champion in July 1928, he left the division in utter confusion, with every heavyweight in the world trying to get into the proposed tournament to find his successor. Buckley encouraged Sharkey to get back into shape as soon as possible and get into a qualifying position for a title fight. With a fresh incentive, Jack looked the Sharkey of old by winning his next five fights. They included a decisive points victory over the talented Young Stribling, known as the 'Georgia Peach', and an impressive stoppage in three rounds over Tommy Loughran, the Philadelphian boxing master who had just relinquished his world light-heavyweight title to campaign as a heavyweight.

While Sharkey was doing so well on his 'comeback', though he never officially retired, a German heavyweight named Max Schmeling had loomed on the fistic scene. Max, a powerful hitter, particularly with his right, was so impressive in his US appearances that the two controlling bodies, the New York State Athletic Commission and the National Boxing Association, agreed that Schmeling would meet the winner of a final eliminator between Sharkey and the London heavyweight Phil Scott. A better boxer than many of his critics would admit, Scott still failed under pressure and was known in America as 'Phainting Phil' because he won some of his contests by claiming that he had been fouled by body shots.

Sharkey and Scott met in Florida on 27 February 1930. Under the 1929 rules of the NYSAC and agreed to by the NBA, the contest would be conducted under the no-foul rule, which meant that a contestant could not win a fight on a foul blow but would be penalised by losing points. Both boxers accepted this. From the very start of the fight Sharkey, a 5/1 favourite, centred his attacks on the Englishman's body and floored Scott with a low left hook for a count of six in the second round. Still feeling the effects of the punch, Scott managed to retreat and hold off the aggressive American with long left jabs for the remainder of the round.

But the 60-second interval was not long enough for him to recover. Sharkey opened the third round aggressively and midway through the session put Scott on the floor for the second time with two body shots and a grazing left hook to the head. The Londoner scrambled to his feet and held before being told by referee Lou Magnolia to break. Scott was finding it difficult to keep the rampaging Sharkey at arm's length and was put down again from a heavy right hook to the body. Clutching his right hip, Scott rose at seven but Sharkey would not be denied and dropped Phil with a pile-driving left hook to the body. In obvious pain, Scott managed to make it to his feet at five before collapsing to the canvas, rolling over in agony. Scott's handlers were screaming 'Foul'.

The situation was now critical for Sharkey. A lucrative world title fight hung in the balance and everyone wondered whether his erratic emotions would once again rob him of his big chance. Fortunately for Jack, the referee refused to recognise Scott's corner claiming foul and insisted he get up. When the Englishman continued to roll around the floor, Magnolia disqualified him under the rule and declared Sharkey the winner. The result is now listed as a knockout. Undoubtedly Scott's reputation for crying foul – and Phil would claim he had been hit low six times – influenced the referee's actions and worked to Sharkey's advantage. With the elimination of Scott, the way was now clear for the Boston boxer's first shot at the heavyweight title.

On 12 June 1930, a perfectly trained Sharkey climbed into the ring at the Yankee Stadium to meet Max Schmeling for the heavyweight championship before a crowd of 80,000 eager fans. Schmeling had cleaned up the opposition in Europe but he knew that if he wanted to achieve his ambition of being world champion, he would have to conquer America. Having arrived in New York for the first time in 1928, he was still considered just another 'stiff' European fighter who had never fought anyone of note, but in his favour was a powerful right-hand punch. His dark hair and good looks gave him a striking resemblance to his idol Jack Dempsey but as far as American fans were concerned the similarities ended there, even though they had never seen him in action. The fact that Max was heavyweight champion of Germany meant nothing in US rings.

Schmeling won his first two fights on American soil without attracting any notice, except a few lines in the New York newspapers. It was not until he linked up with one Joe Jacobs, a Jewish fight manager and matchmaker with a long, fat cigar forever between his teeth, that things started to happen. Jacobs was known in boxing circles as 'Yussel the Muscle', Yussel being the Jewish name for Joseph. Jacobs, who grew up in a New York tenement, became Schmeling's manager and matched him with the world-rated Johnny Risko. Max knocked the Clevelander out in nine rounds. A 15-round decision over the Spaniard Paulino Uzcudun followed and qualified Schmeling for a fight with Sharkey for the vacant world heavyweight championship. The bout was scheduled for 12 June 1930 at the Yankee Stadium.

Before a crowd of 79,222 fans Sharkey took an early lead in the scheduled 15-rounder, outboxing the slower German and tying him up in the clinches. Schmeling was always trying to get through with his heavy punches, particularly his famed right, but Sharkey was always a little too fast. Early in the fourth round Max rallied somewhat, and while Sharkey had been concentrating on the head up to the tenth, he switched to his rival's midsection. Midway through the round, a wild left hook from Sharkey landed well below the belt and down went Max clutching his stomach.

'Foul! Foul,' yelled Schmeling's manager as he jumped into the ring with his boxer squirming on the canvas. Referee Jim Crowley had already begun counting but was looking around bewildered and seeking some clarity. Arthur Brisbane, editor-in-chief of the *Hearst Newspaper Syndicate*, the single most prominent and influential newspaperman of his day, stood up in his press seat and shouted: 'I will kill boxing in New York State if you don't disqualify that man for fouling!' Crowley knew Brisbane would do that. He looked at judge Harold Barnes, who confirmed the low blow. It was all Crowley needed. He pointed to Schmeling, who had been dragged to his corner by his seconds and Joe Jacobs, and declared him heavyweight champion of the world.

Just over a year later, Schmeling made the first defence of his title when he stopped Young Stribling in the 15th round in Ohio before agreeing to give Sharkey a return fight. This time, the setting was Madison Square Garden Bowl on 21 June 1932 before a crowd of 61,865. It went the full 15 rounds and as strange as it may seem, it was the loser who emerged as the real winner. Schmeling put on a fine exhibition of boxing and punching and in the opinion of the majority present, had won the fight with plenty to spare. But it was not to be. Referee Gunboat Smith gave it to Sharkey 7-3 and five even, while judge George F Kelly voted 8-7 for Sharkey. Judge Charles Matison went for Schmeling by 10-5.

Schmeling's manager, Joe Jacobs, seized the opportunity and grabbing announcer Clem McCarthy's radio microphone shouted the immortal words: 'We wuz robbed. We shoulda stood in bed!' Jacobs would make a formal complaint to the New York State Athletic Commission demanding that they change the verdict and proclaim Schmeling as champion. They refused and a third fight never materialised. In any event, Sharkey's connections were making arrangements for their man to defend his title against the giant Italian Primo Carnera in a big outdoor fight in New York the following summer. After protracted negotiations, the date and venue were set for 29 June 1933 at Long Island Bowl, the Garden's outdoor venue.

A massive publicity campaign got under way, with much of it set around Carnera 'the giant', the heaviest man to fight for boxing's biggest and richest prize. Primo, who was 6ft 5in and generally weighed between 240lbs and 260lbs, often 275lbs, would not be considered massive by today's standards, with large heavyweights now considered the norm. Back in the 1930s, it was a different story. Thus Carnera enjoyed a sizeable advantage over most of his opponents, who were generally around 60lbs lighter and six or seven inches shorter.

One publicity release leading up to the Sharkey title fight read: 'For breakfast, Primo has a quart of orange juice, two quarters of milk, 19 pieces of toast, 14 eggs, a loaf of bread and a half pound of Virginia ham.' His size earned him the nickname the 'Ambling Alp' and *Time* magazine called him 'The Monster'. Unfortunately, Carnera's legacy is tainted because of his close associations with mobsters, although Primo, a modest and unassuming man, would admit on many occasions that while he knew of his underworld connections, rightly or wrongly he felt that they would further his career and bring him into the big money. He was an honest and brave fighter, and much better than history would have us believe. It would be fair to say that, on ability, Primo would be on a par with the current crop of world heavyweights, an opinion generally agreed on by boxing writers.

The first son of a woodcutter, Carnera was born on 26 October 1906 in Sequals, a picturesque little town in the foothills of the Alps in northern Italy and full of white-painted buildings with red- and orange-tiled roofs. It was set among lush pastures and forested foothills. Not surprisingly, Carnera was large at birth, weighing 15lbs. He continued to grow at a fast rate, standing more than 5ft tall at the age of nine and achieving his full 6ft 5in in his mid-teens. As tall as Primo was, he was never lanky or thin. Instead, he was always large, muscular and strong.

Growing up, Primo harboured no intentions of becoming a boxer and was content to go his own quiet way. His boyhood friends would remember him as always being considerate of others and he developed into a kind of guardian angel to the small and the weak. While in his teens, he showed a natural aptitude towards sketching and painting. He was so good that a local artist who examined his work expressed a willingness to tutor the lad free of charge, but Carnera was restless. He wanted to travel and leave the poverty of Sequals behind. 'There must be a place in this wide world for me,' he was quoted as saying.

Primo showed no desire to be a stonecutter like his father but decided to try his hand at carpentry and became an apprentice to his uncle, an experienced woodcutter. But the job did not pay well and Carnera made up his mind to leave his home village and travel to Le Mans in France, where he heard that there were plenty of jobs. He stayed with an aunt and looked around for work. Surprisingly, after what he had been led to believe, work was scarce. As it happened, a travelling circus was passing through the town, and on enquiring, he was taken on, where his size and strength proved useful in erecting and dismantling the big top. The pay was reasonably good too, and it was an opportunity to see the country as well as make new friends. Later on, and still with the circus, Primo became part of the show as a wrestler, boxer and weightlifter, and was billed as 'Jan the Unconquerable Spaniard'.

Carnera enjoyed the life, visiting different towns and cities, and when the circus reached a resort near Bordeaux, he was spotted by Paul Journee, a former heavyweight champion of France and now a boxing manager and matchmaker, who was always on the lookout for promising new talent. Journee saw Primo lifting some heavy equipment and was impressed by the Italian's size and strength. Introducing himself, Journee wasted no time on small matters. He told Primo that there was natural ability in his large frame and that he could go places in the fight game once he learned the sport's basics.

On meeting up the next day, Journee produced a contract, binding for 15 years, with a commission of 35 per cent to the management. It was a simple enough document but Carnera had difficulty reading it because of his limited education. However, he did question the 15-year issue and Journee, unusually for a manager, agreed to a fight-by-fight arrangement, with an option of cancelling the contact if the boxer was not happy with any aspects of it. To advance Primo's career, Journee wrote to his own former mentor, Leon See, who had a training camp outside Paris, and suggested See, an Oxford graduate, could manage Primo, and Journee would look after the training side of things. Agreement was reached.

Carnera, along with Journee, left for Paris, having been with the circus for two years, and met up with See, who arranged for Primo to work out at a local gym 'just to get the feel of the ring and pick up the rudiments of the sport', as See put it. 'You don't need to go into the amateurs. Straight into the pros and make some money.' Carnera made his ring debut as a professional against Leon Sebillo at the Salle Wagram in Paris on 12 September 1928. It was a preliminary fight on a card by the American promoter Jeff Dickson, who was domiciled in Paris.

Though clumsy and awkward, Primo knocked out the moderate Sebillo in the second round with a right to the chin. See had been worried about Sebillo as he reputedly carried a heavy punch, but according to a book he wrote later, he visited Sebillo's dressing room half an hour before the boxers were due to enter the ring and handed the fighter an envelope containing 500 francs to throw the fight.

'Having already gasped in amazement at the sight of the towering Carnera at the weigh-in, Sebillo, 72lbs lighter, needed no heavy persuasion,' wrote Primo's biographer Frederic Mullally. 'He could do without taking a lethal sucker punch from this unknown but formidably muscled titan.'

See did a remarkable job of publicising the giant and promoters all over Europe, including Britain, were eager for him to headline their shows. Over the next year, Carnera fought in Berlin, Leipzig, San Sebastian, Marseille, Dieppe, Paris and London, all without a single defeat. While most of his opponents were carefully selected, there were several established heavyweights among his victims. With 15 bouts on his impressive record, Primo was matched with the talented American Young Stribling at the Albert Hall, London on 18 November 1929. Carnera fought doggedly and his bull-like strength made things uncomfortable for Stribling. The American was concentrating on body punching and in the fourth round one of his left hooks crashed into Primo's groin. The Italian collapsed in agony and Stribling was promptly disqualified.

The unsatisfactory finish led to a return fight three weeks later in Paris. This meeting was also to end up in a disqualification, and this time Carnera was the culprit. Stribling was ahead on points when the bell rang to end the seventh round. The American dropped his arms and turned towards his corner just as Carnera started a ponderous right. The blow caught the unsuspecting Stribling on the back of the head and he went down. Carnera was immediately disqualified. There were allegations that both fights were fixed, with a pre-arranged win for each boxer and a third fight on the level, but the claims were never proven. In any event, Stribling returned to the US soon afterwards.

By the end of 1929, Carnera had learned some ringcraft and how to punch correctly, and See decided it was the time for an American invasion. 'The Yanks will love the big guy,' See told Maurice Eudeline, who had edged out Journee as Primo's new coach. Walter Friedman, a veteran New York boxing manager who had seen Carnera in the two Stribling fights, agreed to handle Carnera's affairs in the US. It was no coincidence that Friedman, a big spender known as 'Good Time Charley', was a close friend of Bill Duffy, a Broadway nightclub owner and racketeer who dabbled in boxers as a sideline, and Owney Madden, a bootlegger, numbers racketeer and Public Enemy No 1 who would soon go to jail for killing a rival mobster. Duffy was soon to join the Carnera entourage as an 'adviser'.

'Primo was given ample opportunity further to satisfy his craving for travel,' said Nat Fleischer in his book *The Heavyweight Championship*. 'In nine months he made no less than 24 appearances in American rings, his tour being conducted with all the giddy fanfare of a four-ring circus and carrying him all over the US. In most of his contests, the set-up was of the kind that made it almost impossible for Carnera not to win.'

There was the occasional defeat when Primo's opponent would 'forget' the arranged agreement and paid a price to the mobsters but generally it was win, win, win. Despite the gangsters' influence on Primo's opponents, the Italian was learning and improving in the ring, developing a powerful left hook and strong right. Returning briefly to Europe, he outpointed the tough Paulino Uzcudun in Barcelona and stopped the promising Reggie Meen, a future British heavyweight champion, in two rounds in London.

Back in the US, it was another barnstorming tour, with the Italian showing such a big improvement in his boxing, and helped by his opponents taking the occasional dive to boost his record, that his handlers matched him with the leading heavyweight contender Jack Sharkey at Ebbets Field, New York, scheduled for 12 October 1931. Though beaten by the skilful and more experienced Bostonian and dropped in the fourth round, Carnera impressed the critics, including Damon Runyon of the *New York American*.

Within two years, and more victories mixed with the odd defeat, Primo qualified for a world title fight with Sharkey, who had won the championship by defeating Max Schmeling on a controversial decision. The match that clinched the Sharkey fight was his win in 13 rounds over the legitimate contender Ernie Schaaf at Madison Square Garden on 10 February 1933. Schaaf had an impressive 59-13-2 record against Carnera's 74-6-0 sheet. From New Jersey, Schaaf had been in tough wars earlier, notably against brawler 'Two-Ton' Tony Galento and big-punching future heavyweight champion Max Baer. Eighteen days before the Carnera bout, Schaaf had been released from a week's stay in hospital suffering from flu and did not feel well at all.

For 12 rounds, Schaaf fought listlessly while Carnera landed solid blows from long range. In the 13th Primo landed a solid left jab that snapped Schaaf's head back and he went down on his left side. He tried to rise at four but fell back and at five referee Billy Cavanaugh waved it all over. As the decision was announced, many in the crowd yelled 'Fake, fake' and booed lustily. Schaaf's seconds hauled him to his corner, still unconscious, and he was rushed to the Polyclinic hospital across the street, where he regained consciousness. However, overnight his condition worsened and he underwent a three-and-a-half-hour operation for bleeding on the brain. He died the following morning.

Carnera was charged with manslaughter but acquitted on the basis that Schaaf had entered the ring with a blood clot on his brain. Rather than the stoppage against Carnera, the hammering he had taken from Baer, when he lay unconscious in his dressing room for four hours before being removed to hospital, was considered the main cause of the fatality. In any event, the Sharkey–Carnera title fight would go ahead. The match was set for 29 June 1933 at Long Island Bowl and attracted interest across the world. The Liverpool-born promoter James J Johnston forecast receipts of $300,000 and an attendance of 50,000 in the venue which could accommodate 71,000. A portion of the proceeds would go to the Free Milk Fund for Babies, which was chaired by Mrs Millicent Hearst, at the time the estranged wife of newspaper magnate William Randolph Hearst.

Forty-eight hours before the fight, Sharkey had driven from Gus Wilson's training camp at Orangeburg, New Jersey to New York City for the weigh-in. Before leaving, he met newspapermen and expressed full confidence in being able to repel the European challenger. 'Carnera had better be in good shape because I am sure to beat him,' he said. 'I'm in the best condition of my career, and my team at Orangeburg for the past two months can attest to that. I can easily go the full 15-round route if necessary but I won't need to do that because I won't be around after 15 rounds. I intend to go after him in the first round and try for an early knockout. That's my plan, so watch out Primo. I'm coming to get you.'

Sharkey's manager Johnny Buckley said: 'I've never known Jack to be in better shape, mentally and physically. He's punching harder than ever and I certainly don't expect Carnera to be able to stand up for 15 rounds under the force of Jack's heavy hitting. Some might forget that Jack beat him two years ago, knocking him down in the fourth round and having him wobbly on several occasions after that.'

Carnera had worked out at Pompton Lakes, New Jersey and he too was brimful of confidence. On his final day at the camp before driving to New York City, he told reporters: 'Yes, I am supremely confident I will win and return to Italy with the heavyweight championship, the first from my country to win the title. I lasted 15 rounds with Sharkey two years ago, when I knew very little about boxing. I have improved a great lot since then. If this champion is no better than he was when he fought me before, he won't be the champion after this title fight.'

Luigi Soresi was Primo's financial adviser, brought in because the boxer felt happy about having someone from Italy take care of his cash matters, but as things turned out, he did not make a good job of it. He was also Primo's 'publicity officer'. When asked on the last day of the camp how he felt about Carnera's chances, he said confidently: 'I see no reason whatsoever why Primo cannot win this title fight and become the next heavyweight champion of the world. I have watched him train day after day and know that he has the qualifications to bring him victory over Sharkey.

'He is the heavier puncher and the better boxer, and these two prime assets will carry him to victory. Yes, I know Sharkey beat him before on points but that was two years ago. Primo has learned from that defeat and he will prove it this time, whether the fight ends on a knockout, a stoppage or goes the full 15 rounds, though personally I cannot see it lasting the distance.'

Tommy Burns, the former world heavyweight champion from Canada, said he had watched both fighters in training and came away with the view that Carnera looked the likely winner. 'This big Italian is the most amazing fighter I've ever seen and I feel he is certain to take the title to Italy,' said Burns, who lost his title to Jack Johnson in 14 bloody rounds in 1908. 'I would advise anybody to put their money on Carnera because he is going to walk out of that ring as the new champion.'

US newspapermen were split on their forecasts. Most tipped Sharkey to hold on to his title but Carnera had strong support too. Ed Frayne of the *New York American* felt that Carnera would win on points but declined to say how long it would take Primo to do the job. 'Take your pick, round one to 15, but it's got to be Carnera for me.' Damon Runyon, also of the *New York American,* declined to make a definite prediction but leaned towards the Italian. 'Carnera is not an instinctive fighter,' said Runyon. 'He has no ferocity but he has amazing speed for such a big man. When upwards of 250lbs is merely shoving a ham of a hand encased in leather against a human object, that object is apt to be damaged.' Wilton S Farnsworth, the paper's sports editor, went for Carnera on a decision. 'He will be too strong for Sharkey,' wrote Farnsworth.

Joe Williams of the *New York World-Telegram* declined to cover the fight for two reasons – Carnera's connections with gangsters and Sharkey's inconsistent form. 'Put on the hot seat I would have to admit that I would not trust either one of these guys as far as I can throw the Empire State Building with my left hand,' he wrote. 'It's another way of saying that in this fight you can make your own choice. I don't want any part of it.'

When the champion and challenger came face to face at the weigh-in at the offices of the New York State Athletic Commission, Sharkey looked Carnera up and down and asked: 'Are you in shape, big boy?' Carnera, taken by surprise, became flustered and fumbling for words said finally: 'Yes, I am, you can bet I am.' Sharkey had already gone across the room to see some family friends and did not hear Primo's reply. When Sharkey stepped on the scales, the bar balanced at 201lbs. When Carnera did likewise, he scaled 260lbs, giving him an advantage of 59lbs, a new record in boxing history. Carnera, at 6ft 5ins, was also taller by five inches.

Cloudy conditions and a threat of rain by evening kept the attendance down to 42,000 but as it happened, by the time the two boxers had entered the ring, the skies had cleared. Sharkey had been favourite at 11/10 earlier in the afternoon in Times Square but shortly before climbing into the ring Carnera came in at 6/5, in some quarters 7/5, to become the second European of the 1930s to wear the heavyweight crown. Three former world heavyweight champions in Jack Dempsey, Gene Tunney and Tommy Burns, as well as ex-world light-heavyweight king Tommy Loughran and one-time world lightweight champion Benny Leonard, mingled at ringside with political leaders, stars of stage and screen, industrial and sporting celebrities and women prominent in society.

One familiar face on big fight night was missing. Joe Humphries, the veteran announcer who had introduced the contestants in most of New York's big championship fights, had been taken ill several weeks earlier and not recovered sufficiently to work this time. His place was taken by Harry Balough, who had officiated in small clubs for several years. Balough, sometimes spelt Balogh or Ballogh, set a new dress standard for announcers, appearing in a dinner jacket, stiff shirt front and braided trousers. He would become a familiar face in the ring for many years.

Seconds after referee Arthur Donovan called the two fighters together for their final instructions, they went back to their corners to await the bell. Sharkey was the first to score with long left hooks to the head and body before Carnera ripped in a right uppercut to the chin. They sparred at long range for a few seconds before Sharkey rushed in and scored with a left hook to the body as Primo considered the next move. A left-right from Carnera sent Sharkey back to the ropes but the American moved away to ring centre before firing a long left that missed by at least 12 inches, causing him to slip and nearly fall headlong through the ropes.

Sharkey was being surprised by his opponent's speed and manoeuvrability and in the second round he became more cautious in his approach. A long left found Carnera's face but he missed with a right to the head before the pair clinched. On breaking, Sharkey caught his man with a solid right to the head that drove the big Italian to the ropes. Carnera came back with heavy lefts and rights and used his longer reach to keep the lighter man at bay, but it was noticeable that Sharkey was better at close quarters, where he was able to tie up the challenger.

Sharkey started round three by boxing out of a crouch. Slipping under Carnera's long arms, he bobbed and weaved as Primo's shots missed their targets. Carnera was warned by referee Donovan for not stepping back after a clinch. Sharkey was getting through with long left jabs and hooks, and evaded Carnera's counter-lunge. Sharkey seemed to be ahead by now. This is how Alan Gould of the Associated Press saw it: 'The American was fighting one of the greatest battles of his career at this stage. Bobbing, feinting, his lips in a thin snarl, eyes flashing between narrowed lids, the Boston sailor ripped into battle in flashes. He moved the giant Italian around, found his openings, then lashed his punches – long rights to the head, left hooks to the body, straight to the mark.'

Sharkey came out fast in the fourth round and, rushing Carnera to the ropes, caught his man with a long left hook to the chin. Primo missed badly with a counter right and grabbed his opponent, pulled him in and scored with a right uppercut but received his second warning from Donovan for holding. Sharkey hooked a left to the body and grazed the Italian's jaw with a wide right cross. Primo connected with a stiff right that shook Sharkey and Jack's corner were shouting: 'Keep moving, keep moving.'

Carnera was using his long left jab a little better in the fifth round after instructions from his seconds to keep the pressure on the lighter man and wear him down. But it was not going to be easy. A powerful right hook to the temple staggered Carnera half a minute into the round and for a moment it looked like he would go to the canvas. But he shook off the effects of the blow, although he was finding Sharkey difficult to hit. Jack continued to pepper Primo with snapping left jabs and the occasional left hook and it was a slightly tired and confused Carnera who went to his corner at the bell.

Sharkey came out fast for the sixth round, attacking his man with left hooks and uppercuts as Primo grabbed and held. A short right on the inside made Carnera wobble like a drunk on his way home after a hard night but he had sufficient strength to come back and drive the Boston ex-sailor back across the ring. Primo seemed to have a great reserve of strength and sent Sharkey to his knees at the ropes and almost out of the ring but he was up before a count could be started. Sharkey went back on to the attack but the Italian was ready for him. Pushing Sharkey away, he unleashed a terrific right uppercut that caught the American square on the jaw.

Jack reeled and crashed down, landing on his stomach. According to *Time* magazine, the power of the punch raised Sharkey's feet off the ground. The Associated Press reported: 'An inside right uppercut, brought up swiftly as the giant came to grips along the ropes with his foe, felled Sharkey as though he had been a tree hit by the woodman's final blow.' Donovan tolled the count of ten and raised Carnera's right hand as the winner and new heavyweight champion of the world. The time was 2.27 of the sixth round.

As Sharkey was lifted to his corner, still dazed, his manager Johnny Buckley called for Carnera's gloves to be checked, not believing that Primo could hit that hard. Amid scenes of considerable excitement at the crowning of a new champion, Bill Duffy, Carnera's 'adviser', invited referee Donovan and members of the New York State Athletic Commission to examine the new champion's gloves. No irregularities were found.

Sharkey's first words to his manager when he had recovered sufficiently in his corner were: 'Well, it's a long time since something like this happened to me, Johnny. Now that he's the new champion, he can take on all the hard work and the headaches that go with the title. So good luck to him.' In his dressing room, he repeated Jack Dempsey's famous reply to his wife's query after he lost his title to Gene Tunney. 'I forgot to duck,' said Sharkey. When Sharkey was asked if he would look for a return with Carnera, he said: 'Sure, if it can be arranged. I thought Carnera had improved since I beat him two years ago but only in self defence. I just got careless out there and he caught me with that right uppercut. I guess the old blade needs sharpening.'

In Carnera's dressing room, there was jubilation. Almost at a loss for words, Primo said: 'I thought he fought better than he did the last time, and he hurt me much more than he did then. But he didn't reach me as often, and when I discovered that fact early on, I knew I could win.' Bill Duffy said: 'I knew Sharkey was tough but I also was sure that he wouldn't be able to hurt Primo. Our man has shown more improvement than anybody can imagine, and he has certainly learned how to hit, and hit hard.'

As time went, there were allegations that Sharkey took a dive on the instructions of Carnera's connections, and that the knockout punch never landed. It is a controversy that has never gone away. In his book *The Heavyweight Championship*, Nat Fleischer ridiculed the theory that an 'invisible' punch put Sharkey on the canvas for the full count. The general feeling today, over 80 years on, is that there was no fix and that a genuine punch, with all Carnera's 260lbs behind it, won him the title. A look at clips of the fight today should convince any doubters.

In 1974, Sharkey told Peter Heller for his book *In This Corner*: 'I still can't convince anybody, and even my own wife has her doubts, that it was a genuine knockout. Carnera handled me with ease. Those arms were like the limbs of a tree and when he put them in front of me, there was nothing I could hit. The doubters figured that as most of Carnera's bouts were dubious, so was his title fight. How would losing have benefited me? The prestige and the honour there is in the heavyweight championship of the world. What could I get by losing? I've got everything I want financially and all that, so what good is any more?'

Carnera made two successful defences of his title.

In October 1933, he outpointed the Spaniard Paulino Uzcudun in Rome and five months later defeated the former world light-heavyweight champion Tommy Loughran in Miami, both over 15 rounds. The Loughran fight is noteworthy in that the 86lbs difference in weight – Carnera at 270lbs and Loughran at 184lbs – was a world record that stood for 73 years until the Nikolay Valuev–Monte Barrett fight in October 2006, when the weight gap was 105lbs. Loughran, who had beaten three past or future heavyweight champions in James J Braddock, Max Baer and Jack Sharkey, could not handle Carnera's size and claimed that Primo's size 16 boots were continually trampling on his feet.

Carnera lost the title in his third defence when he was stopped by Max Baer at Long Island Bowl on 14 June 1934. His career went downhill from then on and he turned to wrestling, promoting, personal appearances and made several movies featuring stars such as Marlon Brando, Rod Steiger, Bon Hope, Joan Fontaine, Terry Moore, James Mason, Robert Wagner, Janet Leigh and Diana Dors. A well-respected ex-champion, he became an American citizen and lived in Los Angeles for several years before returning to his old hometown of Sequals in Italy, where he died on 29 June 1967, aged 61. Primo's ring record was 88-14 with one no-decision.

Sharkey never got another shot at the heavyweight title and he retired following two points losses to King Levinsky and Tommy Loughran immediately after the Carnera defeat. In 1935, he made a comeback and knocked out the appropriately named Unknown Wilson in two rounds, but after a loss, a draw and a win, he was outclassed and stopped in three rounds by the young Joe Louis in three rounds at the Yankee Stadium in August 1936. It was Sharkey's last fight and he finished 38-14-3. In retirement, he refereed fights, ran a bar, made personal appearances and spent three months touring Africa and Italy with the US armed forces during the Second World War, covering 25,000 miles. He also indulged in his lifelong passion for fly-fishing. The 'Boston Gob' died of respiratory failure at the age of 91 on 17 August 1994.

Chapter 5

Tale of the Unexpected

Max Baer v James J Braddock, Long Island Bowl, 13 June 1935

BOXING has had many familiar scenarios – the cocky, young challenger determined to grab the title and the veteran champion grimly intent on retaining it. Only on this occasion the roles were reversed, the old challenger desperately wanting the title and the brash, younger champion sure in the belief that he could hang on to it. It was champion Max Baer against challenger James J Braddock for the heavyweight championship of the world.

Baer had more nicknames than any other boxer in history. While sportswriters, in the US rather than the UK and elsewhere, have always had a habit of putting tags on fighters, Baer would have to top the list. At various times in his busy career, and often at the same time, Baer was referred to as the 'Magnificent Madcap', the 'Magnificent Screwball', the 'Livermore Larruper', 'Clown Prince of the Ring', 'The Playboy Puncher', 'Merry Maxie', 'Mad Maxie' and simply the 'Joker'.

Max was one of boxing's most colourful characters. He loved to clown and wisecrack, and while his persona may have endeared him to the fans, it almost certainly prevented him from achieving his full potential. Even when he collapsed from a heart attack in his hotel room while shaving, and was asked by the porter who was immediately summoned if he wanted a house doctor, he said: 'No, I want a people doctor.' But when he was in the mood, Baer could really fight – and fight well. His record is littered with star names and he finished up with a tally of 72-12-0.

Nat Fleischer, who founded and edited *Ring* magazine, said: 'Baer was over 6ft tall, weighed around 195lbs and had the finest physical equipment a boxer could want. He had massive shoulders, long and supple muscular arms, slim waist, strong legs and a deadly right hand. Unfortunately he never took boxing seriously, always clowning and depending upon his right hand to end matters, unlike James J Braddock, for instance, who always took his sport seriously.'

Jimmy Cannon of the *New York Post* felt that Baer's heart was not really in boxing. 'Sure, he was shaped to be a fighter but I don't think his heart belonged in that immense and thrilling body,' said Cannon. 'It was a clown's heart, a heart that must have been hurt by terror and fear in the years that Baer was forced to pretend he was a fighter. I'm positive Baer disliked punching another man.'

Harry Mullan, the author and boxing historian, felt that Baer missed out on true greatness. 'Had Baer been able to take himself seriously, his ferocious hitting could have made him an outstanding world heavyweight champion,' said Mullan, who was editor of *Boxing News* for 19 years.

Maximilian Adelbert Baer was born in Omaha, Nebraska on 11 February 1909, the second of five children. His father Jacob was German-Jewish and his mother Nora Scottish-Irish. When Max was four years of age, the family moved to Denver, Colorado, where his father was manager of a slaughterhouse. Several years later they relocated to Livermore, California, where Jacob set up business, operating his own plant and butchering cattle. He also rented a ranch.

Max quit school at 13 and went to work alongside his younger brother and future heavyweight contender Buddy in his father's plant and on the ranch, swinging his axe with power and vigour, showing endurance qualities that even amazed Jacob. Like a previous heavyweight champion, Bob Fitzsimmons, who attributed his punching power to working as a blacksmith in his early days, Max would put his great physical strength and knockout force as a boxer down to those years when lugging sides of beef around. At the age of 20, Max weighed 190lbs and was 6ft tall.

He paid little attention to boxing in the early days but one night, during the interval at a local dance, Max and four of his buddies discovered a demijohn of wine in a truck alongside the hall. The five of them decided to steal the wine and drink it around the back. As they were about halfway through the drinking session, the owner discovered them and waded in, swinging lefts and rights. The others managed to break away and ran off, leaving Max, much the bigger and stronger, to take care of matters. As the would-be avenger rushed forward to hurl another big punch at Max, he was not quite fast enough. Max let go a terrific right all the way from his hip, caught his man on the chin and sent him down and out on the grass.

At that moment, a new Max Baer was born. For the first time in his life, he realised he could punch, and punch hard. What's more, he enjoyed the sensation. The fighting instinct was awake. The lure of the boxing ring beckoned. 'At that moment, I knew what I wanted to be, a fighter,' he would recall in later years. 'But I had to get away from the farm. I explained to mom and dad what I wanted to do with my life and they gave me full support. Dad said I was big and strong and could always handle myself in the ring.'

Baer moved to Oakland, California, where he got a job at a diesel engine plant. One evening after work, he wandered into the local gym patronised by professional boxers. He loved the feel of the place and talked boxing with the hangers-on, worked on the punch bags and sometimes got an opportunity to pull on the gloves if some heavyweight was in need on a workout. One day, he got chatting to a former boxer named Ray Pelky and they agreed to go a few rounds with each other. Pelky was impressed with the youngster's power and fine physique, and suggested Max should talk to their boss, J Hamilton Lorimer, a fight fan, about pursuing a boxing career.

'Max was a wonderful guy, who was always talking boxing,' Lorimer would recall. 'When he came to me, I listened, and when he began to train in an amateur sort of way, even though he was working out in a professional gym, he used to ask me to hold the stopwatch for him. He was big and powerful but I thought him too good looking to go in for boxing. I wanted to cure him of all that nonsense so I matched him with Chief Caribou, an Indian heavyweight out of Stockholm, the toughest guy around, in a four-rounder. I remember it well, 16 May 1929.

'From the opening bell Baer danced around his opponent, yelling threats, but doing little. That is until the fourth round, when he swung a right hand that had all his power behind it and Caribou went down for the full count. He earned $35 and he was now officially a professional boxer. I learned after the fight that Baer had drunk five bottles of soda pop in the dressing room, presumably to give him courage to climb between the ropes. After his impressive win, Baer was convinced he could go places in boxing so we teamed up, Max doing the fighting and me the managing.'

Baer had 16 fights in that first year, losing just one on a foul. In his second year, he was pulling in $15,000 in the California area. Max was so adored by the fans that he began to develop the playboy, devil-may-care personality that he would always be associated with, but one that would eventually bring about his downfall.

By this time, Lorimer was at his wits' end trying to curb Baer's shenanigans and wild ways, and decided to let Ancil Hoffman, a well-known local manager, matchmaker and promoter, take him over. Hoffman matched Baer with Frankie Campbell, a promising heavyweight campaigning on the West Coast. Campbell was better than any other fighter Baer had faced to date. A fast, skilful boxer who knew all the moves, and used them, he had seen Baer fight and wisely decided not to trade punches with the hard-hitting Californian, electing instead to box him at long range. He followed this plan successfully in the opening round. Several times Baer let go that powerful right but Campbell either got inside it or backed away, making Max miss repeatedly.

Baer began to force the pace and gradually connect with heavy blows. As the fifth round opened, Max seemed headed for victory as Campbell tired. Two solid rights to the head sent Campbell reeling to the ropes. In went Baer and pounded away at his opponent's body and jaw with both hands as Campbell slumped to the canvas. Six hours later, he died in the local hospital of brain injuries. Baer was arrested, charged with manslaughter and handed a year's suspension by the Californian State Athletic Commission.

What made Baer's position all the more unpleasant was the attitude of some of the newspapers, which made a sensational issue out of the incident, with headlines such as 'Butcher', 'Murderer' and 'Ban This Killer From The Ring'. The tragedy plunged Baer into prolonged grief and remorse, and for a time he wondered if he ever would be his old self again. 'I was being branded as a bloodthirsty criminal, and God knows I was innocent of any wrong-doing,' he recalled. 'Ancil put up the bail and got me released.

'The surgeons announced that Frankie had died of a brain-concussion and it was a tremendous relief when the court ruled that was an accident and cleared me of the manslaughter charge. But for the time being, I felt as if I never wanted to see a boxing glove or enter a ring again. My enthusiasm for the game had gone. All I wanted to do was to get away from California, go somewhere else, anywhere, and try to forget.'

On top of all this, Baer was flat broke. The house he had bought for his parents was only partially paid for and his personal debts were mounting. He had never saved and either gave people loans or just gave money away. Hoffman finally convinced Max that he should not blame himself for the tragedy and that a change of scene might help him. He took Baer on a long trip which wound up in New York. While there, Max made up his mind to return to the ring but not before boxing a benefit show for Campbell's widow.

Baer was out of action for four months before resuming against heavyweight contender Ernie Schaaf at Madison Square Garden, New York on 19 December 1930. Max was reluctant to let his punches go and lost the decision over ten rounds. It was not the old Baer. Instead he was lackadaisical and over-cautious, and was so disappointed with his performance that he threatened to quit boxing for good. In any event, there were other attractions in the city, in the shape of beautiful, high society women. The handsome Max had no trouble finding them. With his fine physique, sunny personality and flashing smile, he soon won them over, squiring them around the Broadway hot spots, with the ladies naturally picking up the tabs, seeing that Baer had no money himself.

It was while he was in New York that Max met the beautiful Dorothy Dunbar – 'the loveliest woman I had ever seen' was how he described Dorothy later. She was a wealthy divorcee and they fell instantly in love. Before long, they wound up in Las Vegas and got married. The first thing Hoffman knew of the event was when he read about it in one of the gossip columns. Getting in touch with his boxer, he warned Baer that if he wanted to get back into shape, physically and mentally, he would have to get down to some serious training and forget his 'love life'. The manager was clearly ignoring the fact that Max was a married man with certain responsibilities to his new wife. Baer laughed: 'Life is for living, Ancil, old man.'

Back in New York, Baer's life was getting completely out of control. He was seeing other women constantly and when Dorothy first found out, they had a fierce row. It would be a common scenario, with Max promising to mend his erring ways and Dorothy forgiving him. But the marriage was already going downhill fast and they were divorced inside a year. Meanwhile Baer, running short of ready cash, had returned to the ring in January 1931. He won seven fights but lost three important ones, to former world light-heavyweight champion Tommy Loughran and heavyweight contenders Johnny Risko and Paulino Uzcudun. With money running out, and to fund his lavish lifestyle, Max managed to sell shares in himself to rich buyers. When Hoffman finally discovered what had happened, he found that various sponsors owned 113 per cent of Max Baer, with various people getting a chunk of him for sums ranging from $500 to $10,000.

Baer's record in 1932 was an improvement but there were still big gaps in his defence. It was not until he had breakfast one morning on Broadway with Jack Dempsey, the former heavyweight champion of the world, that things started to improve. Mind you, Dempsey found lots of flaws with the unpredictable Livermore fighter but he had an unshakeable faith in Max to deliver the goods when required, despite Baer's reputation as a ladies' man who detested training.

Baer had just one fight in 1933 but it was the most important one of his career to date. It was on 8 June at the Yankee Stadium against Germany's Max Schmeling, who was still seething with anger over losing his world heavyweight title to the Boston man Jack Sharkey the previous June on a very controversial decision over 15 rounds. The German now knew that an impressive win over Baer would give him a great chance of regaining the title and ringside odds were 3/1 in his favour.

The German, a sharpshooter with lots of endurance, boxed in an upright manner whereas Baer adopted a slightly crouching style. Schmeling justified his favouritism for the first five rounds by beating Baer to the punch with that unerring left jab and following through with his best punch, a powerful right delivered with all his power. Baer was hurting Schmeling with long looping rights and roughing his man up, prompting Schmeling to complain to referee Arthur Donovan about Baer hitting low and using the open glove. Still, by the ninth round the German's better all-round work had him ahead, though just before the bell he was caught by a terrific right to the head that hurt him.

The fight changed dramatically in the tenth when Baer went after his man, swinging and hooking blows to Schmeling's face and body. Some missed but the majority reached the target, topped off by a powerful right that sent the German to the floor for a count of nine. On resuming, Schmeling looked like a drunk trying to skip rope as Baer held back and appealed to the referee to intervene. Donovan did just that and signalled that it was all over at 1:51. This was Max Baer at his very best.

As Baer climbed out of the ring, he blew kisses to several women he spotted at ringside, including one of his regular companions, the beautiful June Knight, a graceful singer/dancer who was charming audiences on Broadway. Max's life of wine, women and song was now impeding his boxing career. Known as the 'Playboy Puncher', his divorce from Dorothy Dunbar was still pending and a former girlfriend, Olive Beck, had filed a breach of promise suit against him. There were reports, too, of liaisons with unmarried and married movie stars but he assured manager Hoffman there was nothing to worry about. 'Boxing is my business,' he said.

Baer was now the legitimate contender for the heavyweight championship of the world held by the 'Boston Gob', Jack Sharkey, who was scheduled to defend his title three weeks later against the 6ft 5in Italian Primo Carnera. In a major upset, Carnera became the new champion with a controversial knockout in six rounds at Madison Square Garden's outdoor venue, the Long Island Bowl. For Max Baer, it was now 'exit Sharkey and come in Carnera'. Max was supremely confident of beating the big Italian and was prepared to bet heavily on himself to become the new champion. As it happened, Louis B Mayer, head of Metro-Goldwyn-Mayer studios in Hollywood, was looking around for new movie projects and felt that a boxing picture would do well, especially one starring the handsome, masculine Baer and the heavyweight champion of the world Carnera. It was called *The Prizefighter and the Lady*.

The leading lady was Myrna Loy, one of the top stars of the day. She played a gangster's moll and Baer, in the lead role, falls for her. In one sequence, Max does a soft-shoe routine while singing, accompanied by a bevy of beauties. He was in his element, art imitating life.

Carnera was not fully at ease with the glitz and glamour of the Hollywood set. The first son of a poor stonecutter from the northern Italian town of Sequals, Primo was bashful by nature, the total opposite of the gregarious Baer, who revelled in the world of Tinseltown. Max did not make it any easier for Primo by forever playing practical jokes on him, teasing him good-naturedly. Studio hands had to do all they could to prevent the two fighters from going to the floor in a rough-and-tumble skirmish. Baer also deviated from the script, much to the annoyance of director/producer W S Van Dyke.

Baer and Carnera were scheduled to go ten rounds, with Jack Dempsey acting as referee, and the story was to show Primo knocked out by his opponent. This did not suit Carnera's people, who felt it would be bad for their man's image, as might be expected. After much discussion, a compromise was reached. It was agreed that Primo would be floored a few times and the bout would end in a draw.

MGM paid Baer $30,000 for the shoot, but money was not the prime reason he accepted the role. The movie would give him a line on Carnera's style if and when they met. With all his clowning, practical joking and seemingly careless attitude, he had studied the Italian and discovered his weak spots. Max found that Carnera could be hit with a long overhand right as well as a right uppercut, particularly from long range.

With the movie completed, Baer would put all this knowledge to good use when the real thing happened. On 14 June 1934 at Long Island Bowl, Max squared off with the Italian for the heavyweight championship of the world. At the weigh-in, Baer was up to his usual antics. Leaning over to Carnera's massive chest, he began plucking out hairs, chanting mournfully: 'He loves me, he loves me not!' and so on. Primo exploded: 'Hey, you make me a damn fool. Wise guy, eh?' much to the amusement of the room. Baer entered the ring wearing a robe with the name 'Steve Morgan' on the back, the same one he wore in the movie. Some observers claimed that if Max lost, he could always say that it was 'Steve Morgan' who was beaten and not himself.

The fight was pitifully one-sided. Not long after the first bell, Baer dropped the Italian with a hard right to the jaw in what would be the first of 12 counts. When Primo got up, his eyes glazed, Max rushed in again and put him down for the second time. In the following rounds it was all Baer, and the only reason Carnera lasted so long was that Max saw fit to swagger around the ring and laugh at his opponent. On one occasion, when both tumbled to the canvas, Baer quipped: 'Last man up is a sissy!' The fight was finally halted by referee Arthur Donovan at 2.16 of the 11th round after Baer floored Primo twice more with heavy rights to the head. Max's movie work with Carnera on *The Prizefighter and the Lady* had paid off handsomely.

Over the following months, the new heavyweight champion of the world went on nationwide exhibition tours and made personal appearances, often in nightclubs. Max was always prepared as well to sign autographs and pick up ladies' phone numbers while he was at it. On his travels, the women either chased him or he pursued them. One reportedly tried to kidnap him. This was the life, Max Baer's life. He also got his own radio show in California.

On one of his exhibition tours, Max caught up with his old rival King Levinsky. As a rule, the genial, easy-going Baer did not take advantage of his opponents in exhibition matches and was satisfied to clown his way through. But Levinsky, a rugged heavyweight from Chicago, decided to pull a fast one and make a real fight of it. He started to fire his heaviest punches in the opening round and Baer did not like it. In round two, the world champion went to work. Driving Levinsky across the ring with a two-handed attack, he caught his man with a powerful left hook to the chin that sent him down and very much out. By the time Levinsky woke up asking 'What happened? Where's Baer?' Max was back in the dressing room, laughing and joking.

It would be a full year almost to the day before Baer got around to putting his title on the line. The challenger was the veteran and No 1 contender James J Braddock. The match was set for 13 June 1935 at Madison Square Garden Bowl.

Braddock's story is one of the most remarkable in boxing history. One of seven children, he was born James Walter Braddock on 7 June 1905 in Hell's Kitchen on New York's tough West Side. His parents were of Irish extraction from Manchester who had set sail for America to seek a better life with more opportunities. It is thought that his father Joe, a one-time booth fighter, tagged on the 'James J' to his son's name as something of an in-joke, following in the tradition of great champions like James J Corbett and James J Jeffries, both of which Braddock Sr admired.

Braddock was only nine months old when his father moved the family across the Hudson River and settled in Hoboken, New Jersey. Joe was at various times a furniture mover, a railway guard and a pier watchman. Money was scarce but he made sure there was always enough food on the table and warm clothes and good footwear in the winter months for them.

The young Braddock quit school at 14 when he was in eighth grade and got a job in a printing shop to help family finances. He swam and fished, played baseball, and got into lots of street fights, like most kids in the area. Like many other boys too, he used to dream of being a fireman or a train driver. He also saved those small coloured pictures of boxers, football players, warships and various birds which could be purchased in cigarette packages.

'I was never really interested in boxing growing up, even into most of my teens,' James J recalled in later years. 'But I did have a few scraps at St Joseph of the Palisades grammar school. There were about 30 or 35 boys in our class and while they could all fight a bit, I often had to defend myself in fights in the schoolyard. One kid was my nemesis, Jimmy Morris. He was older and bigger but we had some real punch-ups. Morris kid was one tough lad. No matter how hard you hit him, he kept coming back for more. He just wouldn't go away. He was also the first one that ever hurt me. He may have been the first to break my nose, too, though I couldn't be sure about that.

'My brother Joe, who was four years older than me, often had to come to my rescue. I remember Joe had 19 fights as a professional boxer and he used to say that if I ever wanted to be a boxer that he would teach me the rudiments of the sport.'

Braddock's father was passionate about boxing and he used to claim that he sailed to America on the same ship as two famous bare-knuckle fighters, Jake Kilrain and Charlie Mitchell, as if that contributed in any way to his son's proficiency with boxing gloves in later years. It seemed only natural, though, that boxing would eventually come into James J's life, listening to stories of famous fights and fighters at home.

At 19, Braddock worked as a messenger boy for Western Union, where one of his most vivid memories was of standing outside the offices of the *Hudson Dispatch* newspaper on Independence Day, 4 July 1919, holding a batch of telegrams to be delivered, and listening to a vivid round-by-round commentary of the Jack

Dempsey–Jess Willard world heavyweight championship fight in Toledo, Ohio being broadcast through a megaphone.

Encouraged by elder brother Joe, James J dropped into the local gym to watch the boxers going through their paces as they worked out in the ring, pounding the punch bags, striking the speed ball and doing floor exercises. He enjoyed the experience and would confess in later years: 'In that gym, I found myself bitten by the boxing bug. This was what I wanted to be, a boxer.'

Braddock decided to launch his amateur career at the age of 17 in 1922 as a middleweight and made steady progress. Inside two years, he had impressed observers by winning prestigious titles in two weight divisions. At 6ft 2in with a strong left jab, a particularly solid right and surprisingly good knowledge of the art of boxing considering his youthfulness, he captured the New Jersey light-heavyweight and heavyweight titles. The victories turned James J into something of a local hero and local sportswriters predicted a bright future for him.

Four years after climbing into a ring for his first amateur contest, Braddock made up his mind to turn professional with brother Joe as his manager. He made his debut in a four-rounder on 14 April 1926 against Al Settle in Hoboken and the bout ended in a no-decision verdict. A New Jersey law at the time made illegal the rendering of official decisions in boxing matches, apparently in the belief that gambling would be discouraged if no official verdict was given. Except for fights ending by foul or a knockout, they would be officially listed as no decision. Eight days later, in Ridgefield Park, New Jersey, Braddock stopped George Deschner, a German of much promise, in two rounds after having him on the boards three times. The career of James J Braddock was well and truly under way.

Braddock was now training at a professional gym in the city run by a famous Afro-American fighter Joe Jenette, who had retired seven years earlier without ever getting a long-deserved opportunity of fighting for the world heavyweight title. His problem was the colour of his skin. Jenette, often spelt Jeanette (although the former spelling is on his gravestone and is used in a new biography) could box, move, fight or brawl as the situation demanded.

But racism, promoters' fear of riots and racial considerations made it nearly impossible for black boxers to get bouts against leading whites. As a result, black heavyweights were repeatedly matched against each other. Jenette fought Sam Langford 15 times, Battling Jim Johnson nine times, Sam McVey five times and Harry Wills three times. He lamented the fact that Jack Johnson never gave him a title fight. 'Jack forgot all about his old friends when he won the title and drew the colour line,' he said. *The Boxing Register*, the record book published by the International Hall of Fame in New York, lists Jenette as having 157 fights but other sources claim it was nearer 170. Jenette himself believed the figure was close to 400.

Jenette expressed an interest in managing Braddock with brother Joe's full approval. Other managers were also interested but it was Joe Gould who got James J's signature on a contract. A New Yorker with a fat cigar always clenched between his teeth, Gould had a very promising middleweight called Harry Galfund. Looking for investors to help promote Galfund's career, Gould managed to entice some wealthy New Jersey businessmen into Jenette's gym to watch Galfund work out. He was looking for $2,000 from each backer for a share in his boxer's contract. Noticing Braddock working on the bag, he approached James J and said he would give him five dollars to spar with Galfund, adding with a whisper: 'Just make my boy look good. OK?'

'That was my lucky, lucky day,' Gould would recall. 'Here were some potential backers to run the rule over my prospect and what happens? After two rounds, this guy Braddock tosses over a right hand to the jaw and Galfund goes down and out. I guess Braddock couldn't resist it. The backers just turned around and walked out of the gym. I paid off Galfund and signed up Braddock there and then. His brother would train him until we found somebody else, and I would do the managing and arranging the fight schedule. It worked, as the history books confirm.'

W C Heinz wrote in *True* magazine: 'That's the way it started for them. It developed into one of the great partnerships of boxing. Jim was 21 at the time and Gould was 30. They looked like Mutt and Jeff. Joe was a little guy out of Poughkeepsie, New York, the son of a rabbi. He was a dapper, smooth-faced talker and schemer, and served as a captain in the army in the Second World War. Gould was great for Braddock. He stuck by his fighter, no matter who tried to move in on him, not even big Frenchy DeMange, who was Owney Madden's sidekick in the rackets.'

In his first year, 1926, and campaigning as a light-heavyweight – although he often took on heavyweights if no 175-pounders were available – Braddock had 16 fights, with 14 wins and two no-decisions. He made his Madison Square Garden debut in 1927 with a knockout in the first round over George LaRocco and got on the cover of *Ring* magazine. Impressive victories over leading contenders earned him a shot at the world light-heavyweight title against Tommy Loughran at the Yankee Stadium on 18 July 1929. Although Braddock was a solid boxer-puncher, the classy Philadelphian stylist proved too smart and won an easy decision over 15 rounds. Consolation for Braddock was that he collected his biggest purse to date, $17,000.

Increasing weight prompted Braddock to move up to the heavyweight division but he was having trouble with his hands, particularly his right, which was causing him considerable pain whenever he punched with it. Medical attention only temporarily solved the problem and he was losing fights he could have won. He was even considering retirement from the ring. Worse was to follow in October 1929 with the Wall Street Crash, which wiped out his savings and several solid investments. James J and the whole of America were on the floor – and the referee was counting. The Great Depression had arrived.

Now a married man with three young children, and losing more fights than he won, Braddock told Gould he was retiring. He was completely discouraged – and flat broke. He began looking around for a job, any job, but the going was tough. Occasionally, he found work on the New Jersey docks but not enough to keep the family in groceries, and he found it necessary to join the long dole queues.

One day in June 1934, Gould got a call from James J Johnston, matchmaker at the Long Island Bowl, offering Braddock a spot on the undercard of the upcoming Primo Carnera–Max Baer world heavyweight championship fight. The opponent would be a promising heavyweight named John 'Corn' Griffin. When Gould told Johnston that his boxer had retired, the matchmaker said: 'I'm stuck Joe. I can't find anybody else at a few days' notice. You gotta help me out, even if there's only a purse of $250 in it.' Gould accepted, and went straight to Braddock's home and handed him the cash. It beat the $5 a day working on the docks or the $24 monthly he got from the welfare department.

Given little chance against Griffin, who had designs on big things in boxing, Braddock climbed off the canvas in the second round to floor the Georgia puncher twice in the third with right-hand shots to the head just before the referee intervened to save Griffin from a certain knockout. Impressive points wins over strong favourites such as the talented John Henry Lewis and the dangerous Art Lasky earned Braddock the No 2 contender's spot for Max Baer's heavyweight title. Max Schmeling was the No 1 contender but he refused a final eliminator match with Braddock, so Johnston paired James J with Baer for the championship. The date: 13 June 1935. The venue: the Long Island Bowl.

Baer trained at Asbury Park on the New Jersey shore, convinced he would take care of the challenger in double quick time. 'Jimmy's a swell guy,' he told reporters at his camp, 'but I guess I'll have to take him to the cleaners. I'm sorry, Jimmy boy.' He confided to Nat Fleischer of *Ring* magazine: 'Look, Braddock is a shot fighter. He's old, he's past it and he knows deep down in his heart that he can't take the title off me. I guess I'll stop him in about six rounds. I'd be surprised if it goes much longer than that. You'll find out on the night and that's a promise.' When Fleischer reminded Baer that he should pay more attention to his training as reports were coming through that he was preparing in a very slapdash way, often neglecting sparring and partying into the early hours with lady friends and Hollywood celebrities, Max replied: 'Don't you worry, Nat. I'll be in top shape.'

When Trevor Wignall of the *Daily Express* visited Baer's camp three days before the fight, he found Max singing in the shower and drinking from a bottle of beer. When the world champion emerged, he told Wignall: 'You English guys all doubt my fitness. I need this drink to put back what energy I've lost in some hard sparring sessions out there.' Expanding his chest and flexing his muscles, he added: 'But look at me. Be honest, have you ever seen anybody in better condition?' Wignall agreed he hadn't, and wrote later: 'I caused Baer to frown a little when I mentioned that the shine on his body and the rippling of his muscles were no evidence that his stamina and judgement were all they could be.'

Braddock, on the contrary, was training with scrupulous care and attention at his camp in the Catskills in Upper New York State. He looked in fine shape when pressmen visited his quarters. Sitting on a rubbing table between sessions one afternoon, he commented: 'My confidence is strong and I'm totally convinced that I'll be the new champion at the finish. I won't be standing still like Primo Carnera did. I'll be moving around and Baer will have to go looking for me. I know I'm a better technical boxer than he is and that will show on the night. I've too much to lose in this fight.'

The boxing writers, however, did not share that optimism despite reports from the Baer camp that he was not training as hard as he should, with the world heavyweight championship in the balance.

'I'm telling you,' wrote Paul Gallico in the *New York Daily News*, 'that Baer will knock Braddock out inside of three rounds, and the referee will have to look sharp because Jimmy is game and gets up, and if Baer hits him when he is groggy and can't get his hands up, Baer may injure him fatally.'

Dave Walsh, writing for the International News Service, said: 'It will be surprising to me if we don't all end up in a police court. But there happens to be a theory that Baer, being a puncher from long range, the thing is to move in on him, and Braddock's manager Joe Gould subscribes to this. Personally, I'd just as move inside on an incoming train with a cowcatcher in front.'

Damon Runyon, the author and boxing columnist for the *New York American*, did not see it that way at all. One of the very few writers who felt that Braddock had a chance to pull off a big upset because of his dedication and Baer's alleged lack of fitness, Runyon wrote: 'There is a possibility that Braddock could cause a shock. It comes down to tactics. A fast, clever boxer could always make Jim look futile but Baer hardly rates as either fast or clever. Braddock is more difficult to hit than many observers think, and he has a style all of his own that is somewhat deceiving.'

On the morning of the fight, the offices of the New York State Athletic Commission were packed with newspapermen, officials, champions, ex-champions, would-be champions and all kinds of fight people for the official weigh-in. A rather serious and slightly dour Braddock stepped on the scales and weighed 182lbs. Moments later, a typically smiling, wisecracking Baer, very tanned compared to the pale-skinned challenger, came forward and scaled 209lbs, giving him a weight advantage of 17 pounds. After Harry Walker, long-time commission doctor, gave both boxers their pre-medical, Baer and Braddock shook hands.

On fight night, a flaming red sunset greeted the large crowd as they filed into the open air arena, where no champion had ever defended his title successfully. The venue was jokingly referred to as 'the Jinx Bowl'. As the venue filled up, around the ringside were representatives from all communities, stars of stage and screen, politics, the business community and the arts, a cross-section of American life. Boxing too was well represented, and it was not difficult to spot familiar faces such as Jack Dempsey and Gene Tunney, two former world heavyweight champions, as well as the new sensation, Joe Louis.

When Braddock entered the brightly lit ring, he got rounds of cheers but Baer's arrival was greeted by boos. Did the crowd, estimated at 35,000, suspect that Max had not taken this fight seriously enough? In any event, Baer was a 15/1 favourite and don't fight fans always support the underdog, especially one like James J Braddock?

On their respective records, Baer came out on top, 40-7-0 against Braddock on 44-23-4. To the very end, Max totally dismissed Braddock's chances but James J was in the condition of his career. He had made a close study of Baer's fighting tactics and figured out a way to beat him. His plan was steady, straight jabbing, refusal to mix it at close quarters and dependence on his endurance and ability to withstand punishment.

Arthur Donovan was originally named as the referee but Baer had rejected him 'for personal reasons' and Jack McAvoy was called in. After the official announcements and introductions, McAvoy called the two gladiators together, gave them their instructions and sent them back to their corners to await the opening bell.

As Braddock's biographer Michael C De Lisa aptly put it: 'So often the first punch of a fight is like the first kiss in a love affair, and this one was no different. Braddock was committed and Baer was screwing around.' Coming out with his chin tucked beneath his left shoulder, Braddock fired some flicking left jabs before moving in fast and cracking the first solid punch of the fight, a hard right to the chin which made Baer blink. The cocky world champion went after Braddock and connected with solid right uppercuts to the body, but James J's better all-round work won him the round.

Several clinches marred the opening rounds but Braddock was boxing well while Baer, the heavier puncher, was always looking for that big punch that would make the scorecards of the referee and two judges unnecessary. Baer was starting to break through in the fourth with long rights to the head and body that made the challenger, at 29 the older man by three years, back away but he rarely followed up.

By the fifth round, the confident Baer was smiling as he connected with his punches and putting on a mock grimace whenever Braddock connected. Max was living up to his reputation as a fun-lover who would probably have been just as happy sitting in a ringside seat, or any other kind of seat in the Bowl, and looking on. In the sixth round, Baer jabbed his man before patting him on the head with his right glove. The grim challenger was not amused and replied with four successive jabs to the head.

In the seventh, the fans were calling for more action than they were getting but Braddock had his plan to keep moving and punching while avoiding too much close-range work. One solid blow on the chin from a man with Baer's power could wreck Braddock's chances so he kept moving as best he could, punching mainly from long range. Baer missed a golden chance in the seventh.

As James P Dawson wrote in the *New York Times*: 'After six rounds of idling, clowning and everything but fighting, Baer suddenly let fly with a wild right and Braddock actually walked into the blow. The Jersey man's knees sagged, his vision clouded, and he was in distress. But with the opportunity beckoning, Baer was lethargic, indifferent. Where he might have gone in, following his advantage, and at least floored his foe, he failed to grasp the chance. He never had another so bright.'

Nat Fleischer of *Ring* magazine had Baer ahead by the seventh round. 'Up to then, Max had the upper hand,' he wrote. 'He rocked Jim with several flaming rights to the head, and had the better of the exchanges whenever Braddock was forced into slugging it out. But then Baer tired, while Braddock plodded steadily, relentlessly on, landing that cutting left jab with merciless precision.'

Braddock rarely deviated from his task, to keep Baer on the move while still scoring at long range, but the world champion kept going forward seeking the finishing punch to end the fight once and for all. In the eighth, Max pretended to fall from a right swing by Braddock in an attempt to bring James J close, where he could land his big bombs. Braddock fell for the trap and Max shook him to his fingertips with a smashing right to the head and at the bell looked in command, although it was still only the halfway stage.

It was getting rough by now, but after all, this was no dinner party. It was a battle for global supremacy, with boxing's richest prize on the line. In the ninth round, Baer hurt his man with a right hook that went low and was warned by referee McAvoy. In the 11th, Braddock was reprimanded for careless use of the head. Baer resumed his clowning in the 12th by hitching up his shorts and beckoning Braddock to come and have a real fight, but James J simply moved around, jabbing and hooking with both gloves. When the bell clanged Baer was still throwing punches, prompting one of Braddock's handlers to rush over to the referee to complain. McAvoy waved him away.

Braddock clearly won the 13th with jolting lefts to the head and following through with right uppercuts that made Max blink. Baer came back with a tremendous right that caught the New Jersey fighter full in the face and made his nose bleed. Max's corner had told him the fight was slipping away and that he would have to do something really big to hang on to his title. But try as he might, he still couldn't connect solidly with his right to put his persistent challenger on the boards.

By round 14, the crowd was rooting for Braddock, as they do for the underdog. It was certainly looking like a win for the challenger. Edward J Neil, the Associated Press boxing writer, who would die in January 1938 of wounds received in the Spanish Civil War, wrote: 'In the last two rounds of the fight, you could feel the tension increasing, feel breaths shortening, until the hair stood up on the back of your neck.'

With victory ebbing away fast, Baer fired punches from all angles in those final two rounds, the last six minutes of action. Long left hooks, right uppercuts, crosses, every blow in his repertoire was tossed but Braddock only had to stay on his feet to win. A smashing right missed Braddock by inches in the 14th as James J continued to jab away and use his right effectively. A final burst of blows from a desperate Baer drove Braddock back a few paces in the 15th, but the challenger came back and appropriately got through with the final punch of the fight, an overhand right to the jaw just as the bell clanged to end a memorable night, at least for the man given so little chance beforehand.

The decision seemed a formality, and was well received by the crowd. Referee McAvoy made it 9-5 in favour of Braddock with one round even while judge Charley Lynch marked his card 11-4 for Braddock. Judge George Kelly made it 7-7-1 but awarded the verdict to Braddock on the New York points scoring system. Boxing had a new heavyweight champion. Baer immediately went over to Braddock's corner and shook the new champion's hand. 'Congratulations Jim. You fought a good fight and I hope you make a lot of money out of the title.' Braddock thanked Baer and said: 'Hard luck Max, but that's boxing.'

Interestingly, the sportswriters had thought so little of Braddock's chances that when Francis Albertini, who had been handling James J's press relations, went around before the fight offering to give them copies of Braddock's biographical history and background, they ignored him. When they didn't want them, Albertini said to hell with it and threw an armload of them under the ring. When Braddock was declared the winner, all the writers scrambled under the ring looking for the releases. Writer Damon Runyon christened James J the 'Cinderella Man' following the upset win and it was a nickname that stuck.

Nearly 40 years later at his home in North Bergen, which he had bought back in 1937, Braddock told the author and historian Pete Heller for the latter's book *In This Corner*: 'I always thought I could lick Baer. I felt I could outpoint him. Really, I thought he should have been an actor rather than a fighter. From the eighth or ninth round, I knew I'd win because he wasn't getting any better and I was. It was sheer bedlam at the end and I remember it was tougher getting back to the dressing room that night than ever before. They were pulling my hair, reaching over and shaking his hand. I had bodyguards taking me, though. It was a great night and we got a lot of nice accolades from different people around the country.'

Braddock held the title for two years before losing it to Joe Louis on a knockout in eight rounds on 22 June 1937 in Chicago. The former champion had one more fight, a close points win over the Welshman, Tommy Farr, at Madison Square Garden on 21 January 1938 before hanging up his worn gloves for the last time with a 46-23-4 record. He invested in several businesses and maintained a close interest in boxing. Braddock died in his sleep on 29 November 1974 at the age of 68. Interest in his career was revived in 2005 with the release of the successful Hollywood movie *Cinderella Man* starring Russell Crowe in the title role.

Baer continued his career after the Braddock defeat but never got another shot at the heavyweight title, particularly after being knocked out three months later by the formidable contender Joe Louis. He continued to box for another six years before stepping down with a 72-12-0 record. Max went into movies, had a successful nightclub act with former world light-heavyweight champion Maxie Rosenbloom, refereed boxing and wrestling matches and was cheerful right to the end. He died of a heart attack on 21 November 1959, aged 50.

Chapter 6

Blondes, brunettes and bruises

Jack Doyle v Buddy Baer
Madison Square Garden,
29 August 1935

BOXING has thrown up its share of colourful characters since the first world heavyweight championship bout with gloves in 1892 in New Orleans. Some couldn't fight a lick. Others could. In the latter category was Jack Doyle. The tall, handsome Irishman with the right-hand wallop to send opponents to sleep early on looked at one stage to be destined for the heavyweight title but for a series of reasons, mainly of his own making, he never quite made it. But during the years when he was part of the British and American fight picture before the Second World War, he grabbed the headlines for his antics both inside and outside the ring. A playboy in every sense of the word, he once had three chauffeurs, 25 Savile Row suits and dined on caviar washed down with the finest champagne. There was always much more than a little excitement about the big, humble man known as the 'Gorgeous Gael'.

'An easy-going extrovert with an appetite for life well beyond anything boxing had to offer, Doyle transcended the sport in the 1930s,' wrote author and boxing historian Bob Mee in his excellent book *The Heavyweights*.

When Doyle ducked between the ropes to take on the unbeaten Buddy Baer, younger brother of Max, who had lost his world heavyweight title to James J Braddock two months earlier, there were high hopes that this would be his breakthrough fight. Victory would make him a serious contender for Braddock's championship. It was all to fight for in the Battle of the Giants pitting Doyle, 6ft 5in and unbeaten in 15 bouts, against Baer, 6ft 6in and without a loss in 20 outings. It was a battle of high promise. Jack had a large following of female fans wherever he went, and many could be spotted among the big crowd.

Blowing kisses to them as he walked down the aisle, the Irishman was looking pleased that he would emerge victorious and impress his supporters, particularly the ladies. Blondes, brunettes and redheads, they all came to the charmer, who was said to have kissed the Blarney Stone, the inscribed stone at the 15th century Blarney Castle in Cork said to impart 'the gift of the gab' as well as flattery and persuasion to anyone who kissed it.

Doyle was born on 13 August 1913 in the British garrison town of Queenstown, now Cobh, in County Cork, from where the *Titanic* sailed on its ill-fated voyage the previous year. One of six children born to local sailor Michael Doyle and his wife Anastasia, Jack was a strong youngster and grew fast. He would remember listening to his father's tales of the Doyles of old, some of whom were said to have supported Brian Boru, the fabled Irish chieftain of the 11th century, who helped banish the Danes from Ireland.

At 16 and 6ft, he found employment as a bricklayer on a local building site. Like most lads, he also got into lots of street fights and it was in these skirmishes that he discovered he had a solid right-hand wallop. 'The thought occurred to me that maybe I could become a boxer someday,' Jack recalled. With this in mind, he filled in an application form to join the Irish Army with the intention of becoming part of their boxing team. However, he had a reply to say that he was too young and that he should wait until he was 18.

Undeterred, he said goodbye to his family and took the boat to Holyhead and the train on down to London for what he hoped would lead to a new life. His plan was to join the British Army if they would have him and get involved with their boxing squad. 'I knew that one of my uncles was a boxing champion in the British Navy and I remember hearing tales of his exploits in the service,'

Doyle would recall. 'I became very interested in boxing and he used to tell us about the great Jack Dempsey and his famous fights with men like Georges Carpentier and Luis Firpo and Gene Tunney. Dempsey became my idol and I wanted to be like him. He was known as "the Manassa Mauler" after the town in Colorado where he was born.'

Unlike his application to the Irish Army, Doyle was accepted into the Irish Guards, a regiment of the British Army, where he would develop his fine physique even more in their boxing team. Based originally in Caterham in Surrey for training, he was transferred to Windsor just outside London. It was there that he learned the rudiments of the noble art but he always found that when he was entered for their boxing tournaments he couldn't resist going for the knockout with his lusty right hand. On one occasion, Doyle knocked an opponent into the lap of his commanding officer at ringside. 'No problem Jack,' said the top brass, 'but when you get out of the army, you should take boxing seriously. I think you have the making of a pretty good fighter and it would be a shame to waste that talent.'

The Irishman took the advice and after being demobbed, Guardsman Jack Doyle became boxer Doyle. He made his debut as a paid heavyweight on 4 April 1932 at Crystal Palace, London and knocked out Chris Goulding in 30 seconds flat, including the count. Big Jack was on the way to what he believed would be fame and fortune. Winning his first 11 fights, all inside two rounds, he qualified for a crack at the British heavyweight championship, held by the stylish Jack Petersen. A fine technical boxer with an excellent left hand and a right that packed both speed and power, the handsome Welshman was inclined to be a bit impetuous and wasted a lot of punches by flinging wildly when more controlled hitting would have gained him quicker and more decisive results.

To the dismay of his legion of admirers, too, he did not gain sufficient weight to allow him to compete successfully among the world's best heavyweights. For all that he was the idol of British fans, who were assured of thrills and excitement whenever he climbed into the ring. So it was on 12 July 1933 at the White City Stadium, a big venue normally used for greyhound racing, that Doyle and Petersen clashed for the British heavyweight championship over 15 rounds. It was all over in two.

After a brawling first round in which Doyle wrestled his opponent around the ring after being staggered by a heavy right and forced to hang on, the Irishman was rocked by another hard right in the second round that stung him into action. Tossing punches from all angles and after landing two decidedly low blows that caused Petersen to double up in pain, referee Cecil 'Pickles' Douglas shouted: 'Go to your corner, Doyle. You're disqualified!' When he got back to his dressing room, Doyle adopted a devil-may-care attitude, typical of this punching playboy. 'I did my best, no more,' he said. 'There will be another day, mark my words. I wished it had gone another round because I had him on the run and I would have knocked him out. Before the fight, I had a telegram from Jack Dempsey and he said he wanted me to go to America. I may well do that.'

Doyle's attitude changed dramatically the next day when he was informed by the British Boxing Board of Control that a hefty £2,740 fine was being deducted from his £3,000 purse and that he was being suspended for six months. Taking the BBB of C to court, Doyle won, but they appealed and he lost, with the original fine and suspension still standing. Now completely disillusioned with the boxing set-up in Britain, he had just one more fight in the UK, a knockout over Derby's Frank Borrington in 83 seconds, before taking Dempsey's advice and going west. After all, America was the land of opportunity.

Doyle would also continue his singing career there. Possessing a fine tenor voice, he had toured halls and theatres in Britain, including shows at the London Palladium. He also cut his first record, a single with 'Mother Machree' on the A side and 'My Irish Song' on the B side. 'As well as the boxing and the singing, I hope to break into the Hollywood movie scene as well,' he told friends.

First, however, was the not inconsiderable matter of celebrating his 21st birthday on 31 August. This notable event took place in a Dublin hotel where several hundred guests got through over 100 gallons of champagne. Not surprisingly, with Doyle's large circle of friends and acquaintances, many coming from his native Cork, the party went on for several days, with more than a few lingering hangovers.

With that out of the way, Jack finalised arrangements for America and returning to Cork he packed his bags. A huge crowd gathered outside the Atlantic hotel in Cobh to say farewell, at least temporarily, to their favourite son. Doyle spoke eloquently from the balcony and proclaimed he would not return to Ireland until he was heavyweight champion of the world. He would settle down and marry 'a sweet Irish colleen', a statement that was viewed with a sense of cynicism considering his philandering reputation. Just before boarding the USS *Washington* for New York, he sang 'Mother Machree' in full throttle to tumultuous cheers. Several women were said to have fainted at the sad departure of their 'lover boy'.

On arrival in New York harbour, he was met by a horde of newspapermen who wanted to meet the man Dempsey described as 'a broth of a boy from the old country who's come to America and hopes to win the heavyweight title'. Doyle called for silence and proclaimed: 'I'm delighted to be here in your great country and I aim to fight like Dempsey and sing like Caruso.' This statement prompted Jimmy Cannon of the *New York Daily News* to turn to a colleague and remark quietly: 'From what I hear from England, this boyo fights like Caruso and sings like Dempsey!'

Doyle's personal style of showmanship and charisma made him an instant hit in the US. He worked out at a local gym and impressed boxing people with his all-round ability in sparring sessions. He also spent a lot of his time in Broadway bars, hot-spots, clubs and fancy restaurants, often three or four a night and invariably surrounded by beautiful women. Jack confessed to Geraldine Sartain of the *New York World-Telegram*: 'I have a preoccupation with the ladies. I can't get along without the beautiful creatures. I adore them. I love them. I simply must have them around me all the time. Blondes? Brunettes? Redheads? I prefer blondes and brunettes rather than redheads but then again, I wouldn't be too fussy.'

While Doyle was waiting for his American manager Walter Friedman to arrange some fights aimed at making him a genuine contender, he made a quick trip to California to see if there were any movie roles available. He already had a number of singing engagements lined up on the West Coast and those would keep him busy too. While in Hollywood, he fell in love with movie starlet Judith Allen, a divorcee. They flew down to Mexico and married in a registry office in Ague Caliento. At the time, Judith was the regular girlfriend of world heavyweight champion Max Baer but Doyle tended to ignore such trivialities.

It was a romantic occasion but sure enough the judge who performed the ceremony apparently did not think so. After getting the new bride and groom to kiss each other, he handed Jack and Judy a couple of business cards on which was printed the name of a lawyer. Underneath his name were four words – Legal Mexican Divorces Secured. Quite clearly, the judge was looking ahead. 'This one's for keeps,' said Doyle and he put his arm around his new bride and kissed her passionately.

Meanwhile, Friedman had fixed up Doyle with his first fight at a New York venue to be decided. Stanley Poreda, an experienced campaigner who had beaten future world champion Primo Carnera and taken on the rising Joe Louis, would be the selected opponent. But Doyle, an astute businessman despite his playboy image, pulled out when he discovered that his manager had not secured his purse up front. An angry Doyle sacked Friedman and linked up with two wealthy Brooklyn businessmen of Irish extraction, the McGovern brothers Tom and Andy.

They arranged for his US debut against Phil Donato at the Dyckman Oval in Manhattan on 24 June 1935. Americans saw very little of the highly publicised Irishman as he knocked out Donato in 66 seconds. Donato rushed from his corner intent on destroying the 'Gorgeous Gael' and rocked him with a heavy right to the head. Doyle, more surprised than hurt, countered with a combination of blows that dropped his man for nine. Donato climbed unsteadily to his feet but Jack, encouraged by the cheering crowd, went in fast, shook him with a powerful left hook to the head and followed with a terrific right hook to the jaw that sent him crashing on his back for the full count. Doyle and Judith celebrated in an expensive Broadway nightspot until the early hours.

Next it was to Meadowbrook Field, New Jersey, where Doyle faced Jack Redmond on 15 July. Redmond was a rugged rival who had gone the full ten rounds with former world light-heavyweight champion 'Slapside' Maxie Rosenbloom and was one of Primo Carnera's chief sparring partners. Redmond set the pace for the first two rounds by continually boring in from a crouching stance and was in the lead. By the fourth round, Doyle had solved his rival's confusing style and floored the American with a powerful right cross to the head.

When Redmond regained his feet, the Irishman tore in and a roundhouse right to the jaw knocked his opponent against the ropes. Another punch, a swinging left hook, sent Redmond hurtling through the ropes and into the laps of the ringside writers. As Redmond struggled to get back into the ring, it was all too late and he was counted out. Some thought that Doyle should have been disqualified for landing the finishing blow because, under New Jersey rules, a boxer is down if he is hanging on the ropes. Nevertheless, rousing cheers again greeted the victorious Cork boxer. One newspaper the next day called Doyle 'one of the most promising heavyweights around today' and another said that 'Doyle could well present champ Jim Braddock with some serious problems if he continues to make this kind of progress'. Back home, the *Irish Press* proudly hailed the nation's favourite son as 'the next heavyweight champion of the world'.

On went the Doyle rollercoaster. Next stop was a small open-air arena in Elizabeth, New Jersey. The opponent: Bob Norton. The date: 30 July. With the noisy, unruly crowd baying for blood, Jack's blood, Doyle went straight on the offensive and very nearly had the American out in the first round with a sustained attack from both hands. A stunning right cross in the second round sent Norton tumbling through the ropes and while he climbed back just in time, blood was streaming from a bad cut over his left eye. Doyle rushed in and applied the finisher, a smashing right to the chin, and he was counted out at 2.18.

The previously hostile crowd had changed their allegiance to the visitor but Doyle, in no mood to hang around, rushed back to the dressing room, grabbed his belongings and along with his cornermen left town immediately by taxi.

Doyle's manager Tom McGovern arranged for Jack to box the dangerous Leo 'One-Punch' Williams at Miller Field, just outside Newark, New Jersey on 9 August. Madison Square Garden promoter James J Johnston advised McGovern to pull out and accept a more prestigious bout with Buddy Baer at the outdoor Madison Square Garden Bowl. 'It'll be a major fight with all the top newspapermen in attendance, and there will be a crowd of 22,000 to see it,' said the canny Johnston with his eye on a big gate. 'There will be nobody important at Miller Field. Pull out and claim an injured shoulder or something. Victory over Baer would make Jack Doyle a major player on the world heavyweight scene.'

McGovern and Doyle agreed but there was a problem. McGovern declined to have Doyle examined by a doctor for the simple reason that there was no injury and they would be found out. The result was that the New Jersey State Athletic Commission slapped a ban on Doyle not only from boxing in New Jersey but in all the 37 other states under the jurisdiction of the National Boxing Association, later known as the World Boxing Association. Luckily, the ban did not cover New York, which was ruled by the New York State Athletic Commission. But a Doyle–Baer fight could only be a four-rounder because of a rule that Buddy was 20 and was technically a minor. Doyle and McGovern dismissed that issue, with the manager proclaiming: 'The fight won't go more than two rounds anyhow. That's all that Jack will need.'

Promoter Johnston set the date for 22 August at Madison Square Garden Bowl. It would be Doyle's fourth fight in as many weeks. Jack wanted to keep busy anyhow and get his name, and his reputation, out there for American consumption. This was what he came to the US for in the first place, to campaign for a world heavyweight championship fight and fight regularly until the big opportunity came along. Baer would be his first important fight there and victory for Buddy would go a long way towards establishing his fistic credentials.

Like his more famous older brother, former world heavyweight champion Max Baer, Buddy was a popular boxer in the 1930s and early 1940s and while he may have lacked the charisma and overall talent of Max, shrewd boxing experts believed that he could well have been world champion had Joe Louis not come on the scene. At 6ft 6in and a heavy hitter with a commanding reach, he would be ranked as the 69th greatest puncher of all time by *The Ring Record Book* in 2003. Was it any wonder that he was going to be a formidable opponent for Doyle?

Born Henry Jacob Baer on 11 June 1915 in Denver, Colorado, the family moved to Durango, Colorado shortly after his birth and settled in Livermore, California, where Jacob Baer purchased the Twin Oaks ranch. Raising cattle and hogs, the family thrived. Buddy developed his powerful physique working on the family ranch, swinging an axe and hauling the heavy carcasses of cattle and hogs.

Inspired by the ring success of Max, Buddy decided to bypass the amateurs and go straight into the professional ranks. He made his professional debut in Eureka, California on 23 September 1934 by knocking out Milton 'Tiny' Abbott in the first round.

The fight was billed as the Battle of the Giants, with the 6ft 6in Baer almost dwarfed by Abbott, who stood 6ft 8in. Known as the Redwood Giant, Abbott started fast, jabbing the oncoming Baer with his long left and moving around trying to spot an opening for his big right. Baer was watching his every move when, midway through the round, he caught Abbott with a short right uppercut to the chin. The Redwood fighter wobbled as Buddy slung across a tremendous right with all the power of his 248lbs frame. The punch landed flush on Abbott's chin and sent him down and very much out.

After winning his next 12 fights by knockout, nine in the first round, Baer suffered his first defeat when he was outpointed over four rounds by the crafty Babe Hunt, a veteran of more than 100 fights, in Boston on 10 January 1935. Encouraged by brother Max to carry on, Buddy resumed his unbeaten run and by the time he was matched with Doyle he had run up another eight knockout victories.

Baer trained at Speculator, a camp well away from the hustle and bustle of New York City and where he enjoyed the fresh mountain air. As it happened, his brother Max was training there for his upcoming fight with Joe Louis and they regularly sparred together. Doyle worked out at the equally attractive Kingston camp high up in the Catskills in Upper New York State, and by the time they left for the weigh-in in New York both boxers were reportedly 'in the best condition of their careers'.

Several weeks before the fight, Doyle's manager had confidently predicted that the contest would not last more than two rounds. It didn't, at least not in the way McGovern had forecast. After both men stepped off the scales at the offices of the New York State Athletic Commission on the afternoon of the fight, with Baer weighing 227lbs and Doyle 204lbs, Doyle declared to newspapermen: 'Y'know boys, I'm going to put over the finest knockout ever known. They can talk all they like about Maxie Baer and Jack Dempsey and John L Sullivan, all heavy punchers, but this knockout will top them all. I never felt better. I'm in the pink of condition and just want to get the thing over, taking another step towards my ultimate goal, the world heavyweight championship.'

Baer did not say much except to state that he expected an early victory. He left the talking to his manager. 'We don't intend to stay very long in the ring,' predicted Hoffman. 'We know, we all know, that Doyle is a good fighter with a fine knockout record and he has high ambitions to beat Buddy and go on to fight for the world title. It's just that he's not going to get by Buddy. I confidently predict that Buddy will put Doyle away in one round.'

Heavy rain caused a postponement of the fight for a week. Promoter Johnston also switched the location to the indoor Madison Square Garden in Manhattan. The new date was 29 August. At the rescheduled weigh-in, Baer was a pound and a half heavier and Doyle lighter by two and three quarter pounds. Buddy remained a 13/5 favourite. Little money was wagered on Doyle despite the advice of his handlers to back him and 'make a pile'. In the dressing room, he told a reporter covering the fight for the *Irish Press*: 'I feel fine. I've trained hard and expect to make good. I won't let anybody down, either here or back home.' In Baer's dressing room, Buddy chatted with his cornermen and friends who had come in to wish him good luck.

Baer entered the ring to the accompaniment of applause from the crowd, estimated at 13,000. There were more cheers when Doyle climbed through the ropes and he acknowledged the support. Among the celebrities at ringside were former champion Jack Dempsey, contender Joe Louis and the German heavyweight Walter Neusel.

Following instructions from referee Billy Cavanaugh, both men went back to their corners to await the bell. Each came out cautiously and Doyle was first to score, landing a heavy right to the jaw. The American wobbled but did not go down. Instead, he shook off the effects quickly, an indication of his superb fitness, and started moving around, looking for an opening. He found it and got home with a thudding right to the body. The punch landed on the belt-line and Doyle, clearly hurt, indicated to the referee that it was a foul blow.

Cavanaugh seemingly did not think so and waved the fight on. With the Irishman looking decidedly unsteady, Baer suddenly moved in close and connected with a smashing right to the body, in the same spot, and Doyle sank to the canvas for a count of three, ignoring shouts from his corner to take advantage of the nine count. Pride had got in the way of survival. Back on his feet, Jack attempted a long left jab to set up a follow-through right but Baer was quicker. Buddy fired a powerful right cross and an equally hard left hook, and Doyle crashed down for the second time. He was up at the count of six but was staggering around the ring, his arms hanging aimlessly by his side.

The American rushed in to finish him off, and with yells of 'stop it, stop it' from the crowd, Cavanaugh got there first and shouted: 'That's all.' He quickly moved between the two heavyweights to prevent Doyle from taking further unnecessary punishment. The time was 2:38 of round one and the official verdict was a technical knockout for Baer.

As Doyle made it to his corner to be comforted by his handlers, he seemed unable to believe that he had been beaten so decisively. Then, not too steadily, he was led to a radio announcer's microphone, where he expressed sorrow at letting down his supporters, both in America and Ireland, as Baer's beefy arms were raised as a token of victory. Buddy then came over to Doyle and both men embraced. Meanwhile, Doyle's wife Judith, who had paid a visit to Jack's dressing room before the fight to deliver a good-luck kiss and wish him well, had fainted before the finish and was escorted from the arena by officials and taken to her hotel. The sight of blood streaming from the face of her beloved husband and the utter shock of seeing him stagger drunkenly around the ring proved too much.

In Baer's dressing room, the victor, with a happy smile on his face, told an Associated Press reporter: 'The first punch that I thought hurt Doyle was a right to the body but it certainly wasn't low. Earlier, he did hurt me with a right hand and it made me jump. There's no dispute about that. But I always felt I could take him, from the moment we signed for the fight. I'm delighted I'm still in the running for a world title fight with Louis and I hope it will happen soon. I wished Jack good luck when we embraced at the end. His chance may come again.'

Doyle claimed Baer had deliberately fouled him with the first right-hand blow and said it produced a massive bruise in his groin which paralysed his legs, leaving him with very little resistance when Baer applied the pressure. 'The punch hurt terribly,' he proclaimed. 'Still, I got up from the first knockdown and gritted my teeth. I swore I would continue because if I didn't, the Americans would be saying that here was another horizontal heavyweight.

'When he sent me down again, I wasn't too hurt and I was amazed when the fight was stopped. When the referee came between us, I just thought that the round had ended and neither of us had heard the bell with all the noise in the arena. At the stoppage, I was sure I could have lasted out the remaining 22 seconds to the end of the round. Then I would have recovered in the interval, when my handlers would have worked to restore the use of my legs. I would have answered the bell and gone out and blasted Baer to defeat. In an earlier fight, I had come from behind to win after taking a bashing in the first round. More power to Baer but I hate to see a fellow get away with things like that.'

The following day, Baer's manager Ancil Hoffman announced that they had offered Doyle a return fight, but the Irishman declined. Jack was now discouraged with boxing, especially with his world championship aspirations dashed. Doyle and Judith took the train to Los Angeles the following day in the hope of continuing both his concert and movie careers. Heading straight for Hollywood, Doyle got an agent to find him work, particularly in the movie industry, where the big money lay.

It was also where glamorous women resided and before you could say 'lover boy', Jack's reputation with the ladies spread like a Californian bush fire. He was reportedly seen in the company of established actresses and starlets in nightspots around town. Whenever he was with Judith, which was not too often, Doyle was the ever-faithful husband, but it was a different story with somebody else.

At one Hollywood party, unaccompanied by his wife, he claimed he fell head over heels with one of Hollywood's major stars, Carole Lombard, and aimed to take her away from her husband Clark Gable, the acknowledged 'King of Hollywood'. Doyle told this to Gable when they met but Clark said in that familiar husky voice: 'Don't fool yourself. Carole loves one man and that man is not Jack Doyle.'

At another party, which Doyle and Lombard attended without their spouses, they got into conversation. At the end of the night, or rather the early hours of the morning, Jack escorted her to her home nearby and went in. At daylight, they were awoken by a loud hammering on the door. It was Gable, who had forgotten his key. When a furious Gable found Doyle hiding under the bed as his feet were showing, he demanded to know what was going on. 'Nothing,' said Jack. But Clark seemingly did not believe him. Soon, the two men began exchanging blows, with Doyle firing a right hand that sent the Hollywood star sprawling across the room, smashing a chair and knocking over a lamp.

When Gable regained his feet, he rubbed his jaw reflectively, smiled and offered Doyle his hand. 'You've a fine right there, me boyo,' he said, before taking out a bottle of champagne, pouring two drinks and proclaiming: 'A toast to the man who nearly knocked out Clark Gable.' Doyle promised to leave Carole alone and the three remained firm friends from then on.

With further liaisons with what used to be known as the fair sex, the patient Judith had become tired of all her husband's philandering. She served divorce papers on him, which Jack did not contest. The shaky marriage had lasted less than two years. Returning to Britain, he went back on the concert stage as well as cutting some records before going back to his first love – the boxing ring.

Out of competitive action for nearly 18 months, Doyle had two early wins before tangling with the tough American King Levinsky at Wembley on 27 April 1937. Doyle won on points. This is how Peter Wilson colourfully described the fight in his book *Ringside Seat*: 'The fight was the only one in Doyle's career that went the distance, in this case 12 rounds. It was not without incidents. Outstanding among them was the occasion when Doyle, trying to call attention to the fact that he thought the "King" was holding, allowed his arms to be pinioned and then whirled round and round with Levinsky still holding on like a strap-hanger in the rush hour.

'The referee duly intervened but the "King" had enjoyed this Terpsichorean interlude, and at the first opportunity he grabbed Doyle again. Once more, the Irishman started to circle and this time Levinsky joined in with abandon, cavorting around the ring in a kind of elephantine waltz and taking Doyle with him, to the astonishment of the cash customers, who were unused to beholding nearly a fifth of a ton of raw beef on the hoof cavorting and galumphing around the hempen square which was designed for sterner stuff. Generally speaking, a good time was had by one and all, not excluding the fighters.'

Doyle won only one of his next four fights before retiring from the ring for good after being knocked out in three rounds by Butcher Howell, a fellow Irishman, in Dublin in August 1943. The 'Gorgeous Gael', with a 17-6-0 ring record, including 16 by the quick route, died of cirrhosis of the liver in London on 13 December 1978 at the age of 65. His wild days of wine, women and song had finally caught up with him.

Baer would outlive Doyle by six years. Following his lightning win over the Irishman, Buddy built up an impressive record and by 1940 he had qualified for a world heavyweight championship fight with Joe Louis, having stopped former Louis opponent Nathan Mann in seven rounds and forced the formidable 'Two-Ton' Tony Galento to quit in the seventh round with an injured left hand. Galento, from New Jersey, had been in brutal slugfests with both Max Baer and Louis. His boast was that he put the 'Brown Bomber' on the canvas in the third round, so Buddy's good win over the rugged Galento effectively clinched the Louis fight.

They faced each other at Griffith Stadium in Washington DC on 23 May 1941 in what was Louis' sixth defence of the title in six months. Baer would be the tallest opponent the champion ever faced but Louis was confident he would be able to take care of him. A crowd of over 20,000 witnessed what turned into a torrid punching contest with a very controversial finish. In the very first round, Baer nailed Louis with a quick barrage of heavy punches, culminating in a powerful left hook that knocked Louis through the ropes, where he dangled for a few seconds, his legs brushing the ring apron and becoming entwined in the ropes. At the count of four, Louis was back in the ring, ready for action. He kept Baer at a safe distance until the bell rang, ending the first round.

Through the next four rounds Buddy, although getting the worst of the exchanges, kept Louis on his toes, anxiously awaiting openings. In the sixth round, Joe floored Baer for a count of six with a smashing right cross. As soon as Buddy was on his feet, Louis landed another hard right that put Baer down for the second time. Joe was anxious to end the fight before the bell, for time was short. Baer climbed to his feet, rather groggily, as referee Arthur Donovan was shouting 'ten'. Louis rushed across the ring and landed a last desperate right-hand punch as the bell rang, putting the challenger on the canvas for a third time.

Baer's seconds rushed into the ring shouting that Louis should have been disqualified for landing a blow after the bell sounded, thereby committing a foul, but Donovan refused to admit the claim. When Buddy refused to go out for the seventh round, Donovan disqualified him. Clearly Louis had not fouled intentionally as he was well in the lead, but it was plainly clear that it was an illegal blow and merited disqualification. It seemed remarkable that a referee could refuse to rule out one boxer and favour another. It was felt at least that he should have given Baer extra time to recover from Louis' controversial punch. Then again, Donovan was a close friend of both Louis and promoter Jacobs and in a long career would referee 12 of Louis' 25 title defences.

Baer and Louis met in a return fight eight months later at Madison Square Garden for the Navy Relief Fund, a charity for the families of servicemen killed in action. Louis donated $47,000 of his purse, with promoter Jacobs giving $37,229 and Baer handing in $4,078. The following day, Louis joined the army and Baer would put on a uniform later in the year. For this return fight, Buddy promised to settle all disputes with an undisputed victory, but not surprisingly he refused to have Donovan as referee. Frank Fullam, another leading official, got the job.

In Louis' dressing room, his old trainer Jack Blackburn was looking worried. 'What is it, Chappie?' Louis asked, trying to keep worry from his voice. 'That old arthritis got me again,' responded Blackburn. 'I reckon you'd better get into the ring without me. I'd never make it up those steps.' Louis put his hand on Blackburn's shoulder. 'Look, we've been together a long time and I wouldn't be any good without you,' he said. 'Besides, you won't have to go up the steps more than once.' Blackburn saw the determination in Louis' eyes and agreed to the request.

The 'Brown Bomber' kept his promise. Baer opened fast with leaping left hooks but the champion was quicker, with counter-punches to the head and body which rocked Baer to his bootlaces. A long right caught Buddy in the face and Baer started swinging wildly before Louis unleashed his heavy weapons, dropping the challenger for a quick count with a left-right.

When Baer got to his feet, Louis floored him for a count of nine with a powerful right. Baer tried to haul himself up by the ropes but failed to make it as Fullam reached 'ten'. The result was a knockout at 2:56 of round one. Baer never boxed again, maintaining his 51-7-0 record, with 47 either by clean knockouts or stoppages. 'Louis was a great fighter,' Buddy recalled in his retirement years as he looked back on the return fight. 'But the only way I could have beaten him that night was to hit him with a baseball bat. You know, I never liked to hurt people, and I never liked to get hurt myself.'

Like Doyle, Baer went into the entertainment business. Starting off as a nightclub singer, he went on to make 16 movies, including the blockbuster *Quo Vadis*. With the advent of TV, he was cast in nearly 100 shows, including *Gunsmoke, Rawhide, Peter Gunn* and *Have Gun, Will Travel*. Baer died on 18 July 1986 in Sacramento, California at the age of 71. He had been suffering from diabetes, hypertension and Alzheimer's disease.

Chapter 7

Gritty Welsh miner who dug in with the best

Joe Louis v Tommy Farr, Yankee Stadium, 30 August 1937

WHEN Joe Louis noticed scars and scratches on Tommy Farr's back at the weigh-in for their world heavyweight championship fight at the Yankee Stadium, he enquired of his Welsh challenger who spent much of his early years down the coalmines: 'Where did you get all those scars from, Tommy?' 'To tell you the truth, Joe,' said Farr, doing his best to keep a straight face, 'I got them wrestling with tigers in circuses back home. Those big cats can be pretty dangerous, y'know.' 'Gosh,' replied the Brown Bomber, turning to his trainer Jack 'Chappie' Blackburn. 'I guess this is gonna be a real hard fight.'

Farr entered the ring before a crowd of 36,903 as the first Welsh boxer ever to fight for the heavyweight championship of the world and the first Britisher to challenge for the title since Jewey Smith, a Londoner, 29 years earlier. 'I'm here to win the title and I don't intend to go back home without it, mark my words,' Tommy had told a large gathering of newspapermen on arrival in New York. It was a brash, confident statement which impressed the hardened American scribes, who remembered only too well the antics of

Britain's 'horizontal' heavyweight Phil Scott, whose habit of claiming foul whenever he was hit in the body became legendary, earning him the nickname 'Phainting Phil'. Lou Magnolia, the referee who was the third man in Scott's fight with Jack Sharkey in New York, remembered: 'Scott claimed so many fouls in this country that I expected him to claim foul when I was giving instructions.'

Farr was certainly one of the best heavyweights Britain ever produced and would be in most people's top five at the very least. Not a particularly hard hitter, he was a fine scientific boxer who developed a crouching, weaving style, knew how to whittle away a rival's stamina, had a strong chin and was a good finisher. He tangled with the world's best in the 1930s, including three world heavyweight champions, and never refused a challenge, no matter how big.

The son of a 17-stone Irish immigrant from Cork and one of eight children, Farr was born on 12 March 1913 in Blaen Clydach, a coalmining community overlooking the town of Tonypandy in south Wales. His father, George, worked underground at the Cambrian pit as a haulier. The need for extra money was so great that, like other men, he engaged in bare-knuckle battles, with many of his fights taking place in the hills behind Tonypandy.

'As a child, Tommy was brought up among grime and coal dust during the desperate conditions of the Welsh mining depression,' said his biographer Bob Lonkhurst. 'To make matters worse, World War One broke out the year after he was born. It meant that he lived in troubled times almost from birth.'

By 1920, the family had saved enough money to move from their little cottage to a bigger, three-bedroom house. But within three years, Tommy's mother Sarah Ann had died at her home from a bout of acute bronchitis and a heart problem, and this added to their hardships. His father was soon bedridden by paralysis and could no longer contribute to the family's budget so the children became the sole breadwinners, doing all kinds of jobs in the neighbourhood. Tommy remembered doing his bit by making deliveries from a handcart for local shopkeepers.

It was almost inevitable that the young Farr would become involved in boxing like his father, and whenever the travelling boxing booths came around to their area, the youngster would always ask for a few fights. 'The few bob always came in handy to help the family finances,' he would recall in later years. In the 1920s and 1930s, there was never a shortage of young men willing to get up into the ring after the barker would call out: 'Any challengers out there who think they can go a few rounds with my man here?'

The money coming in, however, was never enough for the family to get by. At the age of 14, Farr had no choice but to go down the mines, which was the fate of many young men in this depressed area of south Wales. Within a month he was involved in an accident, an explosion causing flying slivers of coal to scar his face and body, marks which he would carry all his life.

In between his mining duties and fights in the booths, Farr took part in official contests around the halls, so he was technically a professional boxer. In 1930, at the age of 16, he met up with Job Churchill, a former miner who had lost a leg in an accident down the pits and now ran a saddlers shop in the area. Churchill had seen Farr in action and told the young man that he had a future in the sport. Job got him back in the booths, where Farr often fought up to five times a day against all-comers.

After a few months in the booths, where he was quite successful, Farr became depressed, due to the abject poverty all around him and the death of his father after nine years as an invalid. 'I realised I was never going to get anywhere in Wales so I made up my mind to go to London,' he recalled in his autobiography. 'I had made up my mind that London was a good boxing city, with good fighters and regular tournaments. The only problem in getting to London was that I had no money except a few shillings in my pocket for lodgings until I got a job, so I walked the 200-odd miles to the city.'

Farr had always been told that the streets of London were paved with gold but he would remember that he never found any. He was beginning to be overcome by a cloak of loneliness and several times felt that he might return to Wales, as bad as things were, but he had no money as jobs were hard to find. With the help of a nightwatchman, Farr managed to get a job on a rubbish dump but the pay was poor. By counting every penny, he just about managed to pay for lodgings on the Edgware Road.

Finally, he made up his mind to return to Tonypandy. 'At Paddington station I got chatting to a man from Tonypandy and he very kindly said I could have his return ticket as he wasn't going back,' Farr would remember in later years. 'I was first in the train that headed back to Wales. I had to get off at Cardiff but the walk back to Tonypandy was a mere doddle – 14 or 15 miles. When I reached home I threw a few handfuls of pebbles at the window, and when my brother came down he threw his arms around me. It was great to be home.'

With Job Churchill's help, Farr resumed boxing with mixed success but it was not until he won the Welsh light-heavyweight championship on 22 July 1933 with a points win over Randy Jones in Tonypandy that notice was taken of him in the press, with one writer referring to him as Kid Farr. In 1934 he had 15 fights, with just five defeats. It was in 1934 that his fortunes really changed when a rising London manager named Ted Broadribb came into his life.

Broadribb, like Farr the son of a bare-knuckle fighter, began boxing as a bantamweight in 1909 under the name Young Snowball. In 1910, he became the only British boxer to beat the French idol Georges Carpentier, and inside the distance in Paris at that. In 1911, Broadribb's ring career was cut short when he developed eye trouble and he turned to promoting, matchmaking and management. Broadribb managed several outstanding British champions and in 1948 he guided Freddie Mills to the light-heavyweight championship of the world.

Broadribb was at ringside on 1 February 1934 in London to see Farr against the local light-heavyweight Eddie Phillips and while Tommy lost a close decision over 15 rounds, Broadribb was impressed and suggested to a rising promoter named Jim Wicks that he should re-match the pair in a final eliminator for the British 175lbs title. Wicks, who would later manage British legend Henry Cooper, agreed and the Farr–Phillips fight was set for Wandsworth Stadium in London on 13 June 1934. After having the best of the exchanges for two rounds, Farr cracked home a hard left to the stomach that sent Phillips to the floor in the third. With Phillips gasping for breath, Farr was disqualified for a low blow.

'Undeterred, I knew that was just a bad day and I'd have better nights,' he remembered in later years. 'I had won the Welsh heavyweight title the previous year and defended it against Charley Bundy, winning on points, in September 1934. The following February, I ran up against my old rival Eddie Phillips for the vacant British light-heavyweight championship and he beat me over 15 rounds. He was my jinx fighter, certainly. But despite my loss to Phillips, 1935 was a good one for me. I had 13 fights, with ten wins, one draw and a no-decision. I felt I was going places.'

Farr's first real test against serious international opposition was in the shape of the veteran Philadelphian stylist Tommy Loughran at the Royal Albert Hall, London on 15 January 1936. Described by the *Boxing Register*, the official Record Book of the International Boxing Hall of Fame in New York, as 'a gifted boxer with one of the greatest left hands in history', Loughran was world light-heavyweight champion in the 1920s before moving up to heavyweight, where he also compiled a solid record. Overall, he faced 14 boxers who were, or became, world champions from welterweight to heavyweight. His victims included greats such as Harry Greb, Mickey Walker, Max Baer, Georges Carpentier and James J Braddock.

For the first three rounds it was all Loughran as Farr seemed dazzled by the American's speed and dexterity. Farr did not seem to be able to cope with the clever Philadelphian. Farr managed to connect with a few glancing blows in the fourth round, often driving Loughran to the ropes, but the American never seemed unduly worried. Loughran was told by his corner before going out for the sixth round that he was well ahead on points and to just keep going and using mainly his snappy left hand to jab and hook. He was being as slippery as a wet bar of soap. Farr impressed in the ninth and tenth rounds with strong attacks but ringside reporters agreed that he did not seem to have done enough to wipe out the American's strong lead.

At the last bell, referee Wilfred Smith, officiating in his first major contest, looked at his scorecard and started to go to Loughran's corner. He stopped, made a few adjustments on his card, shook his head as if puzzled, then walked over to Farr's corner and raised the Welshman's right hand. This was the signal for a storm of booing and shouts of 'robbery, robbery' from the crowd. Loughran looked shocked, as did everybody else in the hall, but showed his sportsmanship by walking across the ring and congratulating his conqueror.

The uproar showed no sign of abating and would continue for a full 20 minutes, drowning out the announcements of the next fight, which had to be delayed. While Loughran had to have police protection as he was escorted to the dressing room by his seconds, his manager Joe Smith jumped out of the ring and rushed over to Colonel Myddleton, chairman of the British Boxing Board of Control, demanding to see if he could have a look at the referees' scorecard. 'You can't do that, Mr Smith,' said Myddleton. 'It's private. In any case, under our rules, a referee's decision is final. Any protests you may have should be in writing to the board. In any event, I see nothing wrong with the verdict.' Writing out the address to which any complaints should be made, Myddleton handed it to Smith. As it happened, nothing would come of the protest and the decision stayed.

Peter Wilson, covering his first big fight for the *Daily Mirror*, recalled in his autobiography in 1977: 'After all these years, I hope Tommy Farr will forgive me but if I were on my death bed and under oath I would still swear that Loughran won that fight. So you can imagine my round-by-round report, each round phoned in to be in time for the early editions: Loughran's round...Loughran's round...even round...Farr's round...Loughran's round...Loughran's round...Loughran's round and so on. Imagine my horror when Farr got the verdict.'

Loughran told reporters in the dressing room: 'I'm not a moaner but this is the worst decision I've ever had in my long career. I thought I won at least seven rounds. I could have knocked him out at one stage but he's a promising kid and has every chance of becoming a world champion, so I contented myself in just outpointing him.'

Farr said he felt the verdict was the correct one and that more importantly he had claimed the scalp of a former world champion. His always vocal manager Ted Broadribb did most of the talking, saying: 'Boys, Farr won every round. He skated it!' In his autobiography 53 years later, Farr said he still felt he won the fight, 'and according to my reckoning, justly so'.

Following an unimpressive points win over the Dutch champion Pater Van Goole in Swansea two months later, Broadribb matched Farr with another American, like Loughran a former light-heavyweight champion of the world, Bob Olin. They met at the Royal Albert Hall. The New Yorker was an experienced campaigner in the tough school of American rings and was coached by Ray Arcel, known as the 'Trainer of Champions'. The ten-rounder resulted in another controversial verdict in Farr's favour and was booed, though nothing on the scale of the Loughran affair. It was always going to be a close fight, with one and then the other scoring heavily. The hard-hitting American had Farr down in the fifth and ninth rounds and both men were swapping blows in the centre of the ring in the tenth when the bell rang. Referee Charlie Thomas unhesitatingly walked to Farr's corner and declared him the winner.

In the dressing room, Olin sobbed like a child who has had its favourite toy taken away. 'What do you do to get a decision in England?' he said. 'I heard Loughran was robbed here and now it's my turn. I had expected to be shown some fairness in this country, but no. I won't be boxing here again, I can assure you.'

Olin's manager Paul Damski, who also looked after the German heavyweight and world title contender Walter Neusel, said: 'This was a dreadful verdict. Olin played with Farr as a master does with his pupil.' Damsky made an official protest to the British Boxing Board of Control but as in the cases of Loughran and Olin, nothing ever came of it.

When told of Olin's complaints, Farr said: 'If that's how he feels, that's his business. I can sympathise with him but remember, I've had a lot of raw deals in my career. The verdict was correct and his claims that he should have been given the verdict are nonsense. He caught me with a big left hook in the ninth and I went down but apart from that, he never hurt me.'

Farr won the Welsh heavyweight title by knocking out Jim Wilde in seven rounds in Swansea in September 1936 and captured the British and Empire championships five months later by convincingly outpointing South Africa's Ben Foord over 15 rounds at Harringay Arena, London. Foord entered the ring as a 4/1 favourite, with an impressive 35-8-4 record but he had met his match in the gritty Welshman now billed as the 'Tonypandy Terror'. Farr now seemed to be on a roll and there were high expectations that he might get a world heavyweight title fight with James J Braddock, the New Jersey veteran.

But first he would have to get himself into the world championship picture, which would require a victory over a leading heavyweight to achieve that position. Former champion Max Baer, who had lost the title to Braddock is a stunning upset in New York two years earlier, had been at ringside for the Farr–Foord fight as there had been talk earlier of a possible fight with Farr at some stage. 'I've heard a bit about your boy,' Baer told a reporter at ringside, 'and he seems to be making progress. Who knows? We might get together some day. Mind you, I don't rate British heavyweights too highly as they don't punch with the knuckle part of the glove and they are inclined to be very upright, although Farr showed me out there that he's quite clever at the bobbing and weaving stuff.'

As it happened, British promoter Sydney Hulls had been having preliminary talks with Baer for a meeting with Farr, and after several discussions Max and his manager Ancil Hoffman agreed to the Farr fight for Harringay Arena, scheduled for 12 rounds on 15 April 1937. Baer was a ferocious puncher who was inclined not to take himself too seriously, but Hulls made sure he trained hard for Farr. 'I'm paying you good money for this fight, Max, and I don't want a half-fit heavyweight climbing into the ring,' he warned Baer at the press conference to announce the fight. 'You needn't worry, buddy,' replied Baer. 'This fight means a lot to me and I'll be giving it my best shot. I can assure you and all the folks who come will see a top-class fight.'

On the big night, a crowd of 12,000 packed Harringay and as both men climbed into the brightly lit ring they looked supremely confident, particularly the tanned Baer who, at 211lbs, outweighed Farr by ten pounds. Few gave the Welshman a chance, as the betting showed. Baer was 10/1 favourite. When referee Cecil 'Pickles' Douglas, who was also a well-known Essex cricketer, called both men to the centre of the ring for their final instructions, Baer patted the surprised Douglas on the head and cracked: 'I won't give you any trouble, ref, and I imagine the same goes for Mr Farr here. Leave it to us.' Douglas would recall later: 'I've refereed many fights in my busy career but I never got a pat on the head from one of the boxers, before or since.'

Baer began by playing to the crowd, often waving to his girlfriend at ringside, convinced he could take out Farr any time he wanted to. But the gritty Welsh ex-miner stuck to his task, moving in and out of Baer's heavy punches and scoring on the counter. The American's left eyebrow was cut from a sharp right cross in the opening round and he fired off a fast combination of hooks and swings, but Farr moved out of range as the big crowd sang the Welsh national anthem 'Land of My Fathers'.

'Undeterred by Baer's advantages in height and reach, the British champion took the attack to his opponent,' wrote Farr's biographer Bob Lonkhurst. 'Tommy was in the pink of condition and his fitness saw him through as he took punches that would have floored most other fighters. Through the 10th and 11th rounds, Baer tried all he knew but to no avail. There were occasions when it seemed that Baer's tremendous strength must wear Farr down but his left hand kept him out of trouble. The American hit back with vicious swings in the last round but Farr gave as good as he got. When the bell ended one of the most memorable heavyweight contests ever seen in Britain, Baer threw his arms around Tommy and planted a kiss on his cheek. It was a well-earned victory for Farr and the crowd cheered wildly.'

With British and American promoters now clamouring to sign the Welshman, Sydney Hulls wanted him to stay in Britain, and got Farr's signature for a clash with the German puncher Walter Neusel at Harringay Arena on 15 June 1937. Known as the 'Blonde Tiger', the burly Neusel was tipped by most of the boxing writers as the likely winner and was unbeaten in five London fights, including three victories over the classy Jack Petersen. But Farr, putting up the fight of his life, dominated the action from the first bell. As early as the second round, Neusel looked a badly beaten man as Farr kept on the attack. In the third round, the 'Tonypandy Terror' dropped his rival with a powerful left hook followed by an equally heavy right to the chin as the capacity crowd roared themselves hoarse.

Neusel, his face smeared with blood from a cut right cheek as well as a nosebleed, struggled to push himself to a sitting position at the count of four but he never looked like getting up. He was still on one knee, somewhat shakily, when the count reached ten. Down at ringside, a solemn Joachim Von Ribbentrop, the German Ambassador in Britain, accompanied by several top-ranking Nazi officials, their faces showing utter anger, quickly left their seats and headed out of the arena.

The big win pushed Farr to the forefront of contenders for James J Braddock's world title. Braddock was due to defend his championship against the new sensation and heavy favourite Joe Louis a week later in Chicago. By right, it should have been Max Schmeling meeting Braddock that night as the German had knocked out the previously unbeaten Louis in 12 rounds in a stunning upset a year earlier and became the No 1 contender. But boxing being boxing, certainly in the years between the 1930s and the 1950s, Schmeling was shamefully cheated out of his rightful opportunity.

How the Braddock–Louis–Schmeling scenario came about, and how Farr was brought into the picture, was a clear example of boxing intrigue. James J Johnson, a Liverpudian who was brought up in New York's tough Hell's Kitchen from the age of 12, promoted big fights under contract at Madison Square Garden Bowl on Long Island, or Long Island Bowl as it was known. He signed Braddock to defend his title against Schmeling at the Bowl for 26 September 1937, later bringing it forward to 3 June, even though it was public knowledge that Johnston's rival promoter Mike Jacobs had lured Braddock and his manager away with a better offer to defend the title against Louis at Comiskey Park, Chicago on 22 June.

The New York State Athletic Commission threatened to withdraw recognition of Braddock, ban him indefinitely in the state and fine the champion and his manager Joe Gould $1,000 apiece if they went through with the Chicago fight with Louis. Gould boldly announced: 'Who cares about New York? Chicago welcomes us and so would the rest of America if required.' Gould's allegiance with Jacobs was enhanced by the fact that the promoter agreed to pay Braddock, besides his purse, ten per cent of Jacobs' net profits for the next ten years.

Schmeling and his team duly turned up at the Bowl with his team in the early afternoon of 3 June 1937 for the official weigh-in, stripped off for his physical examination and stepped on the scales, which registered 196lbs. But where were Braddock and his team? The Bowl was dark that night as Braddock and his people were already in Chicago for the Louis fight. The Braddock–Schmeling incident became known as boxing's 'Phantom Fight'.

As expected Louis became champion, knocking out Braddock in the eighth round after the 'Brown Bomber' was floored in the opening session. Schmeling and his party were in attendance and when Jacobs returned to his office in New York two days later the German demanded first crack at Louis, but the promoter was unable to strike a deal with him. Max wanted 30 per cent of the gate but Jacobs insisted he take the normal challenger's share of 20 per cent, which the German rejected.

Schmeling and his team walked out of negotiations and claimed he was being victimised. 'You are all afraid I'll take your precious title out of America and never defend it here,' he told a gathering of newspapermen later. 'Nothing could be further from the truth. If I beat Louis again, and I'm certain I can, then I will come back here and put the title on the line.' Leaving America, the Schmeling party turned up in London, met promoter Sydney Hulls and suggested that the British Boxing Board of Control recognise a Schmeling–Farr fight as being for the 'real' world title, or at least an official final eliminator for the championship, with the winner named the No 1 contender for Louis. Hulls agreed and started making preparations for the fight.

Once again, the scheming Mike Jacobs was up to his manoeuvres. Immediately on hearing of Hulls' plan, he hastily dispatched his lawyer Sol Strauss to London to meet with Farr and his manager Ted Broadribb and offer them the Louis fight in New York. Strauss carried a blank chequebook, a contract and a lot of promises of future fights in the US after the Louis match. It transpired that the Jacobs guarantee for the Louis fight was $60,000 plus 25 per cent of the radio and movie rights, as well as four important fights in America. The purse was nearly double what Farr would get for the Schmeling fight.

'It is too good to turn down,' said Broadribb. 'This is what we had been wanting for a long time. Our boy deserves this shot, having trounced the former world champion Max Baer and knocked out Walter Neusel. He'll not only give Louis the fight of his life but come out the winner. Then we'll give Schmeling his chance.'

The Louis–Farr fight was set for the Yankee Stadium on 26 August 1937 in the first of what would be a record 25 defences over 11 years. One of the greatest fighting men in ring history, Joseph Louis Barrow was born in LaFayette, a little town in the Alabama cotton belt, on 13 May 1914. When young Joe was 12, his father Munroe shifted the family to Detroit, where work could be obtained at the Ford motor company. In any event, the family were being hassled by the Ku Klux Klan, the hate group advocating white supremacy and white nationalism. When young Joe left school, he joined his father in the Ford factory and later an ice company, carrying blocks of ice, some weighing up to 50 pounds.

Louis took boxing lessons at the Brewster Recreation Center, where amateur boxers gathered and trained. In 54 amateur contests he would lose only four decisions and won several important titles, including the National AAU Championships in the light-heavyweight division, while 41 of his wins were scored inside the distance. Soon after his 20th birthday, two African American businessmen, Julian Black and John Roxborough, sponsored his entry into the professional ranks. In order to get a return on their investment, they found a trainer in Jack Blackburn.

Blackburn was one of the most capable trainers in America and a former contender. He told his new charge: 'It's next to impossible for a n**** heavyweight to get anywhere so you've got to be good outside the ring as well as inside it. You must never alienate the public in the way Jack Johnson did in the past.'

Blackburn gave Louis six commandments: (1) Never have his picture taken with a white woman; (2) never go to a nightclub alone; (3) no fixed fights; (4) never gloat over a fallen opponent; (5) keep a 'dead pan' in front of cameras and (6) live and fight clean. Louis kept that promise throughout his long career. Making fast progress, he ran up an impressive 26-0 record before being knocked out by the veteran former champion Max Schmeling in a sensational upset on 19 June 1936. The 'Brown Bomber' would reverse that result almost exactly two years later by finishing off the German in 2.04 of the opening round in a fight in which he was defending the title he took from James J Braddock a year earlier.

How would Tommy Farr fare against the new champion? Few gave him a chance, with Louis installed as a 5/1 favourite, even 10/1 in some quarters. Of 200 American and British sportswriters polled, only one – John McAdam of Britain's *Sunday Despatch* – went for Farr. All the others predicted a victory for the Detroit fighter, most by a knockout or an early stoppage. 'I'm not a bit worried about the odds,' said Farr at his training quarters at Long Branch, a seaside resort on the shores of the Atlantic some 50 miles from New York. 'He's got two arms and two legs just like me. Max Schmeling proved he could be hit, hurt and knocked out and Jim Braddock had him down in the very first round, and Braddock's an old man as far as boxing is concerned. I'm fully confident I can take the title so forget those ridiculous odds. They're rubbish.'

Louis set up camp at Pompton Lakes, New Jersey, and his trainer Jack Blackburn reported that his boxer, who he called 'Chappie', was in the best condition of his career. 'We're expecting a tough fight but "Chappie" will keep his title, that's for sure,' he said. When Louis was asked for a prediction, he said: 'I believe Tommy's a good fighter and I expect a tough fight. He's beaten some good men, including Maxie Baer, but I'm ready.'

Heavy rain caused a four-day postponement so Mike Jacobs announced the new date of 30 August. A week earlier, the British Boxing Board of Control announced that they would not recognise the fight as being for the title because Max Schmeling was the No 1 contender. They would only regard the Louis–Farr match as a final eliminator.

In response to the board's decision, the National Union of Boxers back in England disagreed with the BBB of C ruling and said that it was unfair to be throwing this in Farr's face with the most important fight of his life coming up. The board also stripped Farr of his Welsh heavyweight title. When Tommy was told of the board's rulings, he said: 'Rubbish. Schmeling will get his chance at the winner, which will be me. As for taking away my Welsh title, there were just no challengers available. Let the board name a challenger and I'll take him on.'

Big fight night was hot and humid, and was not helped by the blazing arc lights above the ring. At the afternoon weigh-in, Louis had scaled 198lbs and Farr 207lbs. After the challenger and the champion ducked between the ropes and waited in their respective corners for the formal announcements, the announcer Harry Balough pulled down the over microphone. He was about to introduce the largest gathering of champions, ex-champions and almost-champions, 14 in total, ever assembled in one place.

As each celebrity climbed between the ropes one by one, Balough called out their names, from heavyweight down to bantamweight. The sight of Jack Johnson brought back vivid memories of his controversial life inside and outside the ring while heavyweight champion of the world. As he brushed past Louis' corner, he substantiated the stories that he and the 'Brown Bomber' were not getting along. Johnson had pointed out weaknesses in Louis' defence and style, once calling him 'an amateur'.

The appearances of Jack Dempsey and Gene Tunney recalled their two famous heavyweight fights of the 1920s. The cheers for another ex-heavyweight king, Max Baer, were mixed with boos as many fans never fully forgave him for sitting on the floor in the fourth round against Louis in the same ring two years earlier. Baer had his arm around Max Schmeling, who got more hisses and boos than cheers, undoubtedly because, Schmeling being a German, everything with a Rhineland connection was viewed with suspicion, with war clouds gathering over Europe. There seemed little sympathy for Max being sidetracked out of the Louis fight and Farr coming in.

Schmeling nodded to his old opponent Jack Sharkey, who shared two heavyweight title fights a few years earlier and shook hands with his former adversary Mickey Walker, the former world welterweight and middleweight champion, who was knocked out by Schmeling in 1932. Barney Ross, a great champion at lightweight and welterweight, had a few words with James J Braddock, Louis' most recent opponent. Ex-lightweight rivals Lou Ambers and Pedro Montanez chatted with each other and one-time middleweight ruler Marcel Thil exchanged pleasantries with former bantamweight champion Sixto Escobar and ex-featherweight king Johnny Dundee.

The ringside was packed with celebrities from all walks of life – politics, business, high society, sport and a large number of big names from Broadway and Hollywood, including Al Jolson, George Raft, Douglas Fairbanks Sr and several movie directors and producers anxious for a piece of the action.

It was now time for the real thing. Following Balough's formal announcements, Arthur Donovan, whose long career as a referee would subsequently span 14 heavyweight championship fights, called the two protagonists together, explained the rules, and they went back to their corners. When the bell rang, they were on their way, for 15 rounds or less.

Louis started fast, jabbing and hooking as Farr came into the attack. The Welshman connected with a strong right cross but Louis was moving away at the time and the full impact of the blow was not felt. A sharp right uppercut opened a slight cut on Farr's right cheek in the second round and the sight of blood spurred the champion on. Farr was the aggressor in the main but the American was scoring with that snapping left jab.

As the third round opened, Louis was looking slightly concerned that the visitor was proving slippery and difficult to hit solidly. But midway through the round, Louis went on the attack and a barrage of blows drove Farr back. 'I rode most of the punches but he cut both my eyes with his left jabs,' the Welshman would recall in his book *Thus Farr* over 50 years later. 'The crowd yelled for Joe to finish me and with blood streaming from my slashed eyes it must have seemed that my goose was more than three parts cooked. How I cursed my luck. For I was as strong as a bull, chock full of fight, with peepers solely damaged and threatening to close tight. Nevertheless, I fired hard hooks into the stomach of Joe and forced him to box at a distance.'

Both men were looking for openings in the fourth when Farr, making light of his facial injuries, went on the attack with hard lefts and rights. Following an exchange at close quarters, Louis got his left jab working again and when Farr closed in the champion pushed him off before the bell rang. Louis would later claim that he bruised the knuckles of his right hand in the fourth after landing a right high on Farr's head. 'I couldn't use my right hand effectively after that,' he remembered in later years. 'If I hadn't hurt the hand, I'd have knocked him out. I just kept jabbing and jabbing and cut his face with the punches. I took some good shots from him in the fourth and he really surprised me with his aggression.'

By the fifth round Louis had a points lead thanks to his better long-range work, but the challenger was making him fight all the way. A looping left hook followed by a hard right rocked Louis momentarily in the sixth and both finished the round toe-to-toe, which had the crowd roaring. Louis was not allowing his suspect right hand to worry him too much and Blackburn in the corner told him to use it sparingly but effectively.

Louis had a particularly good seventh round when, after a flurry of blows from Farr, the Detroit fighter unleashed some cracking punches from both gloves that forced Farr to duck down to avoid the worst. Louis sank a hard left into the challenger's body and followed with a fast combination of left hooks, right crosses and uppercuts that had Farr hanging on. Another smashing left hook buckled the Welshman's knees and he almost went down just as the bell rang. Louis went to his corner feeling that he had his rival under control. Farr would recall later: 'That seventh round was a particularly bad one for me, for besides my eye injuries I now had the disadvantage of badly injuring a finger in my right hand. I felt the pain every time I landed a punch but the Louis corner must never know that.'

The crowd rose to its feet in the eighth round when Farr went on the attack and drove Louis to the ropes, catching the American with a long right and a heavy left hook. Louis quickly moved to the centre of the ring, where he could jab at long range. The Welshman kept after Louis despite his injuries, with his face a red mask. It was clearly Farr's round but how long could he keep it up? Under today's rules, with more stringent referees, the bout would surely have been stopped, but not in the conditions that prevailed in the 1930s and 1940s. Even if Donovan had intervened, the Tonypandy fighter would have protested vigorously.

'Farr was taking the play away from me by always rushing from his corner and throwing all kinds of hurting punches and I had to be on my guard at all times,' Louis recalled in his retirement years. 'There was little doubt that he was the toughest opponent I ever faced in my entire career. He was always fresh, round after round. I hit him with a particularly hard left hook in the ninth, if I remember correctly, and he stopped momentarily and looked like he was about to fall but no, he charged right back. What a guy.'

Louis left his corner for the tenth round with a slight bruise over his left eye but he was now blocking Farr's long-range hooks and continuing his jabbing. By the bell, Joe's bruise had turned into a cut but good work in the corner cleaned it up. A strong left hook in the 11th shook up Farr from head to toe but the Welshman soon closed in and got back into the action. Louis was soon in command, though, with fine left jabs and hooks, as well as crosses and uppercuts with his right. In the 12th Louis' injured left eye did not look in good shape and was bleeding badly, but he was in control of the fight and dominated the fast exchanges, mainly in the centre of the ring.

Farr's facial cuts were still seeping blood in the 13th but he stuck to his task, having told his corner: 'I'm in this for the long haul. Don't throw in the towel no matter what you do.' This was a particularly good round for the Detroit fighter as he fired combinations and Farr, for the first time, was showing signs of tiredness. The Welshman stopped Louis momentarily with a looping left but the champion looked in control, moving all the time and getting home with sharp countershots. Farr's attacks were mainly wild in the 14th and again Louis replied with hard blows of his own. In a desperate effort to turn what looked like an inevitable defeat into victory, Farr threw everything into his attack in the 15th and final round but Louis was prepared. Snap, snap, snap went the American's left jabs, intermingled with hooks and uppercuts, and while Farr countered with his own shots it was Louis' round.

At the last bell, Donovan followed Farr to his corner and grabbed Tommy's right hand. Was he about to raise it? Had the Welshman won and become the new champion? There was a strange hush in the vast stadium. British hopes were raised but no result yet. The referee had come to shake Farr's hand and congratulate him on a superb performance. Donovan then added up his score before bending down to the judges to collect their scorecards and hand all three to Harry Balough, the announcer. When Balough pulled down the microphone, there was no surprise to come. Louis had retained his championship.

Judge William McParland gave Louis nine rounds and Farr six. Judge Charlie Lynch made it eight-five in favour of Louis, with two rounds even. Donovan had Louis the winner by the widest margin, giving him 13 rounds, Farr one and one even, which seemed a little harsh on the Welshman. Even Louis himself admitted in the dressing room that the referee's score did not do Farr full justice. 'I thought he may have won four or five rounds, at least,' said the sporting victor. 'But he sure is a hell of a fighter. He's easily the best heavyweight to come out of Britain, and I'm certain about that. I'd love to fight him again but that would be up to my promoter Mike Jacobs. Mike's talking about the return fight with Max Schmeling for next summer. That's an important one for me.'

Farr said in his dressing room that he had no complaints about the decision, which was greeted by a mixture of cheers and boos. 'My eyes were so bad at the halfway stage that I was hitting him from memory,' he said. 'Louis is a great fighter and I wish him luck for the future. I'm certain he'll beat Schmeling when they meet, as they surely will do.' Only 'Doc' Almy of the *Boston Post* had predicted that Farr would still be on his feet at the finish, but in the loser's corner.

In 1986, shortly after Farr's death, his mother found scribbled notes by Tommy at her home which were published in a book by Farr's son Gary three years later. Describing the scene at the last bell, he wrote: 'The battle was over. To my corner I groped. I could scarcely see. My mouth was dry and clotted with blood. Yet I was supremely happy. I had gone every inch of the hard, jagged road. I had confounded the critics. I was no pugilistic turtle, no horizontalist.'

If Louis left the ring with his title intact, he took a real hammering from the American press. Jimmy Powers wrote in the *New York Daily News*: 'Louis lost everything but his heavyweight title last night at the Yankee Stadium. His footwork is atrocious, his headwork nil.' Dan Parker in the *New York Mirror* said: 'With a punch that would hardly knock over a pillar of salt, Farr made Louis look dumb, timid and futile. Never a mental giant, Joe was the personification of stupidity in this fight. He couldn't think his way out of a subway turnstile. Schmeling would have slaughtered him.'

Harry Grayson in the *New York World-Telegram* said: 'The Alabama-born fighter was rushed to the front at a time when the field was unbelievably bad. Through the medium of a string of stumblebums, he was built up as a dark destroyer.' Wilbur Wood in the *New York Sun* wrote: 'Farr presented final proof that Louis is not a great fighter by going the Derby distance with him without a right-hand punch and with only cleverness, courage and a fair sort of straight left.' Nat Fleischer, editor and publisher of *Ring* magazine, was critical of the fans: 'If Louis knocks his man out in a jiffy, they call his opponent a set-up. If he fails to score a knockdown he is a phony and when the fans find his opponent on his feet at the end of the bout, then "bum" is the title they give him.'

All that would change dramatically ten months later when Louis destroyed Max Schmeling in 204 seconds of the first round. The same writers who savagely criticised Louis for what they termed a very disappointing performance against Farr were now calling him a superman of the ring, one of the greatest fighters of all time and way above anybody of his era.

Farr did not fight again in 1937 except to box exhibitions. He returned to competitive action on 21 January 1938, when he faced the former world heavyweight champion James J Braddock, Louis' predecessor, in a scheduled ten-rounder at Madison Square Garden. Promoter Jacobs told Farr: 'Beat Braddock and a return fight with Louis is yours.'

On fight night it was bitterly cold and a heavy carpet of snow covered Manhattan as a near-capacity crowd of 17,369 fans passed through the turnstiles. Braddock, from New Jersey, had made a remarkable comeback when he upset Max Baer over 15 rounds to win the championship in June 1935. Out of the ring since losing the title to Louis seven months earlier, he was a 2/1 underdog going in against Farr. Asked about his chances at the weigh-in, he replied: 'I'm not too worried really about Farr. He is not a heavy hitter, unlike Louis, and I think I can handle him.' Farr said: 'With all due respect to Braddock, he's an old man on the comeback trail. I'm sure I can defeat him and get that return with Louis.' Braddock tipped the scales at 199lbs as against Farr's 207lbs.

After final instructions from referee Johnny McAvoy, the big fight was on. The Welshman started off on the attack, hooking and swinging, but Braddock was able to tie him up and push him off. Farr, as he had done against Louis, boxed out of a semi-crouch. After hurting the American with two left hooks to the body, McAvoy ruled both punches were low and deducted a point, meaning he lost the round. Not a good start but Farr increased his output in the second and third rounds with consistent body attacks. The Associated Press news agency had Farr ahead by the seventh and the 31-year-old Braddock was beginning to show his age and slow down.

Most of the newspapermen had Farr well ahead after eight rounds, and Braddock's trainer Whitey Bimstein told the ex-champion before going out for the ninth round: 'You're losing this one, Jim. You gotta start moving, and fast.' Braddock seemed to find new energy after that pep talk. 'When Farr came in with his head down like a wet mop, I hit him with a right uppercut followed by left and right hooks,' he recalled later. 'I'm sure Farr wondered where I was getting the energy from, as I guess he figured I was finished.'

The crowd were on their feet, cheering Braddock with every punch he threw. Farr was surprised by Braddock's new lease of boxing life. 'This was a completely different Braddock than the one in the earlier rounds and he started punching with both hands,' remembered Farr. 'But I had enough in reserve to weather the storm. He won't be able to keep it up.' The Welshman was wrong on that count. Braddock dominated the ninth with hooks and uppercuts, bouncing on tired legs. Farr tried to hold off Braddock in the tenth and final round, but the former world champion drove Farr to the ropes and at the last bell referee McAvoy had to pull them apart.

Ring announcer Sam Taub called for silence. Judge George Le Cron had it 6-4 in Braddock's favour while judge Charlie Lynch scored it 6-4 for Farr. It was now up to referee McAvoy, who made it 5-5, which normally would have made it a draw. But New York rules at the time allowed for a tiebreaker based on supplementary points. McAvoy awarded Braddock extra points for his inspirational showing in the last two rounds. In his final professional fight, Braddock won a split decision. The Associated Press reported that going into the ninth round, practically every scorecard at ringside had Farr well ahead.

With a mixture of boos and cheers coming from the crowd, Farr buried his head in his hands and exclaimed: 'I can't believe it, I can't believe it.' When Braddock went to the Welshman's corner, hand outstretched, and said 'Hard luck, Tommy', Farr refused to take his hand. Instead, he turned his back and stormed out of the ring, kicking his water bucket on to ringsiders and pressmen, and hurrying to his dressing room. 'I was bloody robbed,' he said. Looking back in later years, he recalled: 'I thought I got the worst of a raw decision and still think so. That fight meant about $200,000 to me in contracts which I had signed with Mike Jacobs, and now I was out.' Braddock said in his dressing room: 'I thought I held my own and maybe a draw might have been a fairer result. But I'm glad I'm going out as a winner. It's been a tough road but it's over now.'

Farr's final three fights in the US ended in points defeats, against former champion Max Baer, who he had previously beaten in London, Lou Nova and Red Burman, who he would outpoint in a return bout in London. The Welshman retired in November 1939 after knocking out Scotland's Manuel Abrew in three rounds in Dublin. Nearly ten years later, he made a comeback and won 11 of his 15 fights before finally hanging up his gloves for good after being stopped in seven rounds by Don Cockell, a former London blacksmith, in a final eliminator for the British heavyweight title in 1953. His record read 95-43-22 with 19 no-decisions. Farr died of cancer, aged 72, on 1 March 1986.

After the Farr fight, Louis would go on to defend his world title 24 more times before retiring following his knockout of Jersey Joe Walcott in 11 rounds on 23 June 1948. But heavy tax demands from the revenue commissioners forced him back into action against the new champion Ezzard Charles on 27 September 1950. Louis was decisively beaten on points but he continued his comeback until the younger, stronger Rocky Marciano pounded him to defeat in eight rounds at Madison Square Garden on 26

October 1951. Finally retiring for good, with a 68-3-0 record, he retained his interest in boxing until his death from a heart attack on 12 April 1981. The drama on that famous warm night under New York skies against Tommy Farr in August 1937 was by now just a distant memory.

Chapter 8

Drama at the Graveyard

Henry Armstrong v Barney Ross, Long Island Bowl, 31 May 1938

IT WAS raining heavily on the evening of Thursday, 26 May 1938, causing a 24-hour postponement of the world welterweight title fight between the champion Barney Ross and his challenger Henry Armstrong, who held the featherweight title, at Madison Square Garden's outdoor venue, Long Island Bowl. It rained again the following evening, even more heavily, causing a further postponement and providing another major headache for promoter Mike Jacobs of the 20th Century Sporting Club, who could not have been blamed had he pulled out what was left of his hair and swallowed his ill-fitting false teeth.

Many out-of-towners who could not stay on called the box office and cancelled their tickets. Jacobs was reluctant to hold the fight on the Saturday, when the weather forecast was good, because Saturday was not a traditional day for big fights in New York, so he rescheduled it for the third time.

It finally went ahead on Tuesday, 31 May and the crowd, just over 50,000, expected some real action from these two big names. Ross was not too worried about the Bowl's reputation as an unlucky venue. Known as the 'Graveyard of Champions' and the 'Jinxed Stadium', many champions had lost their titles there, including Max Schmeling, Max Baer, Jack Sharkey and Jimmy McLarnin.

He felt he could handle the lighter challenger and leave the ring still welterweight champion of the world. 'Henry is a good fighter with a big reputation but I'll take him,' he told a packed press conference. Armstrong said: 'The heavier weight division means nothing to me. Ross is there to be taken and I'm the man to do it.'

Armstrong was certainly a formidable fighting machine. Earlier in the year, he had sent out a challenge to the world lightweight champion Lou Ambers for a title fight but Ambers' canny manager Al Weill, who in later years would guide Rocky Marciano to the world heavyweight title, was having none of it. Weill wanted big money for a title defence but Armstrong's manager Eddie Mead considered Weill's demands exorbitant and that it was purely an excuse by Weill to avoid his boxer's most dangerous challenger. Mead reasoned that the next best thing for Armstrong was to skip the lightweight division, at least for the present, and challenge Ross for the welterweight title.

Sportswriters would put several nicknames on Armstrong such as 'Homicide Hank', 'Hammerin' Henry' and 'Mr Perpetual Motion' and each one stuck like glue. His all-action style endeared him to scribes and fight fans, not to mention promoters, because action was guaranteed whenever he climbed into the ring, which was often. In 1936 he had 14 fights, with 11 wins. In 1937 it was 27 fights, all wins. So far in 1938 he had ten fights, all wins. The big question now was: Could he move up two divisions and win a second world title?

Ross was a classy operator, an all-rounder, once the bell rang. Armstrong, on the other hand, was essentially untried in the heavier division. But his supporters put their belief in Henry's relentless aggression and powerful punching. Would it all be enough?

Armstrong feared nobody. With an abnormally slow heartbeat, throughout his career he would warm up with often ten rounds of fast shadowboxing in the dressing room before climbing into the ring to fight a 15-rounder. He stood only 5ft 5in but had the upper body of a much bigger man, with a reach, outstretched from fingertip to fingertip, of 67 inches. This was longer by an inch than Roberto Duran, considered the greatest of all modern lightweights.

Armstrong threw punches relentlessly and never let up, the blows coming from all angles. He fought so furiously that it was impossible to count the punches, though it should be said that in his haste and fury, he was often guilty of using wrists, forearms, elbows and even his head in addition to his fists. Many well-intentioned blows invariably strayed below the belt-line.

Frank Butler of the *News of the World* had access to Armstrong's dressing room shortly before Henry went out to fight and defeat Liverpool's Ernie Roderick over what turned out to be 15 hard rounds at Harringay Arena, London in 1935. Butler told a story that explained Armstrong's incredible workrate. 'His huge manager Eddie Mead warned me that Henry would shadowbox for at least six minutes before leaving for the ring,' said Butler. 'It duly happened and Henry pranced around the room at a terrific pace for two rounds. I've never seen a boxer so active in the dressing room. It was amazing.

'When the bell sounded for the first round, Armstrong didn't seem to be warmed up despite his actions in the dressing room. He came out slowly and Roderick, boxing superbly, jabbed the champion with left jabs and let go with his right several times. But Armstrong came out faster for the second round, faster still in the third and from then on threw so many punches that Ernie could never settle down and get his left working again. He was too busy defending himself.'

Boxing News said of the fight: 'He came, he saw, he conquered and left behind an impression of impregnable greatness. Armstrong can be placed in a class in which he stands completely isolated.' Some 80 years later, in a list of the 100 greatest boxers of all time in the magazine, Armstrong was placed at No 3, directly behind Sugar Ray Robinson at No 1, followed by Muhammad Ali.

Born Henry Melody Jackson on 12 December 1912 in Columbus, Mississippi, in an area close to the fields of cotton around which his early life would revolve, Henry was one of 15 children. His mother was part Cherokee Indian. When he was four, the family moved to St Louis, Missouri, to find work. His mother died a year later and the family took her remains back to Columbus, which had been her wish.

From that day on, Henry was raised by his grandmother, who was born into slavery. When his father grew seriously ill and died, Henry became the major breadwinner among those still left at home. His first jobs were resetting pins in a bowling alley, selling newspapers and shining shoes. He later worked on a local railroad by drilling pikes into the sleepers beneath the tracks.

'One day while working on the railroad a newspaper blew into my face, by chance or by some miracle, I don't know which,' he remembered in later years. 'And there, in front of me, was a headline that said the Cuban boxer Kid Chocolate had earned big money for beating Al Singer for half an hour's work. I can't remember the exact amount but it was a big purse. The article said that he had been discovered in the streets of Cuba and now he was a big star. I'd had dreams of saving money to allow me to go to college and becoming a doctor but that newspaper story changed everything.

'When I got home I showed my grandmother the story. If he can do it, then I can, I said. I told her I was going to be a boxer and that I was quitting my job the next day. She said I must be mad, crazy to even think such a thing. She said I knew nothing about boxing. 'You ain't no Jack Johnson,' she said. I told her that was true but I would learn all about the game and become good and someday be a champion. I said I was going to buy a pair of boxing gloves the next day. She kept repeating I was crazy but my mind was made up and nothing or nobody, not even my grandmother, could change it.'

Henry went down to the local YMCA gym in Pine Street to make enquiries. The coach turned out to be a former professional boxer named Harry Armstrong. After watching Henry going through his paces, Harry agreed to take him on – on one condition. Young Henry had to change his name from Henry Melody Jackson to Henry Armstrong so that the trainer could tell people the young boxer was his brother. Being the brother of Harry Armstrong would help the kid's progress.

Under his new name, Henry Armstrong had a few amateur bouts and won the featherweight championship of St Louis before Harry felt he was ready for the professional ranks. It was now August 1932. Harry took his protégé to Pittsburgh because professional fights between whites and blacks were banned in St Louis, indeed all over Missouri.

Henry had two fights, a win and a loss, before locating to Los Angeles, where he started badly with two defeats. But the pay was good, $35 a fight, twice as much as a week's wages on the railroad. Also, his style was so exciting that promoters wanted him back, but Armstrong had a plan. He would go back to the amateurs under his real name, Melody Jackson, to learn the rudiments of the sport but mainly to avoid any complications with the boxing authorities, who might well ask too many questions as to why he was leaving the paid ranks.

The truth was that the 1932 Olympics were being held in Los Angeles and he felt that if he could win a medal, preferably gold, it would enhance his standing. As it happened, he failed to make the US trials to select the team and decided to return to the punch-for-pay ranks anyhow. After all, he had won 58 of his 62 amateur contests and that record would stand to his credit.

With Harry Armstrong in tow, Henry relaunched himself as a professional and won 12 fights in a row on the West Coast. By now, however, Harry wanted to return to his old post at the YMCA gym in St Louis, where he had lots of friends. They parted on amicable terms. 'In any event Henry, you'll need a top man behind you to make progress in the paid ranks and I don't think I'm that man,' Harry told his promising young protégé. 'But good luck, and I'll be following your progress in the papers and in *Ring* magazine.'

Armstrong linked up with Wirt Ross, an influential manager who promised he would get Henry the fights that mattered, and if he did lose the occasional one, it would be put down to experience, or rather the lack of it. He lived up to his word, but he knew that the tough, cagey Alberto 'Baby' Arizmendi would be a tough one. They fought in Mexico City on 3 November 1934.

Arizmendi was Mexico's first major boxing star and led the way for future generations of warriors from the Aztec nation. A bull-necked fighter with a chin seemingly made of granite, he was born in Tamaulipas, near Vera Cruz, and began boxing as a professional at 13 to put food on the family table. Later on he lived in San Antonio, Texas, before pulling up roots and making his home in Mexico City. By the time he was 17, he was Mexican bantamweight champion and moved to Los Angeles at 18 to campaign, successfully as it turned out, among the top boxers of his day.

Armstrong felt he might be the victim of a hometown decision in Arizmendi's territory if the fight went to the full ten rounds, but Ross brushed aside any fears. 'He won't stand up to your aggression,' said the manager. 'Keep the pressure on him.' Armstrong lost the decision, though it was soundly booed even by the partisan fans. In a return two months later, again in Mexico City, Armstrong lost another unpopular verdict, amid more boos.

The last straw came after the second fight when Ross was delaying paying Armstrong his purse. When he asked Ross what was happening, the manager said: 'The promoter lost heavily on the card and can't pay any of the boxers, I'm afraid.' When Henry tried to contact the promoter, he was told he had left town. Exit Wirt Ross.

At this stage, three important people entered the picture – Eddie Mead, Al Jolson and George Raft. Mead was a well-established boxing manager with many connections while Jolson was one of the major stars of the entertainment business and Raft was a leading Hollywood star. Mead agreed to manage Armstrong but could not afford the $10,000 that Henry's former manager was demanding. Mead had once befriended Jolson's wife, the dancer Ruby Keeler, so he went to Jolson and asked him for a loan. Jolson agreed to put up $5,000 if his friend George Raft came up with the rest. The actor agreed and a new partnership was born.

'Jolson, Raft and Mead had big plans to get me more known and they seemed the right people to look after me,' Armstrong recalled. 'Jolson seemed to be the main man behind the whole project, even if Mead was my manager. Jolson had the clout and, of course, the money. Joe Louis, who was a prominent heavyweight contender at the time, was getting big gates, and Mead, Jolson and Raft figured I could draw big money too. I remember Jolson said to me once: 'Win a world title, even two, and you'll be as famous and as rich as Louis.' I said: 'A couple of world titles, Mr Jolson? You're not asking too much, are you?' 'No,' said Jolson, 'but you can do it.'

Armstrong made fast progress as a featherweight and he was keeping busy, with many of his fights just days apart. In 1934, *Ring* magazine had him at number six at his weight in their annual world ratings. On 4 August 1936, Armstrong won a ten-round decision over his old nemesis Alberto 'Baby' Arizmendi in Los Angeles for the Californian and Mexican featherweight titles.

Things were now looking extremely bright for the man born Henry Melody Jackson 23 years earlier, with Mead handling his managerial affairs. Two months after defeating Arizmendi, Armstrong outpointed Mike Belloise in Los Angeles. Belloise was recognised as world featherweight champion in his home state of New York but his title was not on the line. Petey Sarron, from Birmingham, Alabama, was the National Boxing Association (NBA) claimant. When Belloise was forced to retire through injury in August 1937, the NBA and the New York State Athletic Commission got together and gave official recognition to Sarron as champion. Petey was now Armstrong's target.

Armstrong got his chance sooner than expected, thanks to Mead's negotiating skills. The title fight was set for Madison Square Garden over 15 rounds for 29 October 1937. Armstrong had been campaigning as a lightweight for some time now but he could not allow this golden chance to slip by. At the end of a strenuous training campaign, he struggled to make the 126lbs limit and just about managed to balance the scales under the watchful eyes of commission officials.

Sarron, a month short of his 31st birthday, was six years older than the challenger but felt that his fast, shifty style would frustrate Armstrong. A member of the US team for the Paris Olympics in 1924, Sarron was part of the great influx of Lebanese people who moved to Alabama in the early 1930s and settled in Birmingham. From the opening bell, he stood up well under Armstrong's heavy punches and for the first three rounds there was little between them. In the fourth round, however, the challenger began to get on top with his constant aggression.

By the sixth, Sarron was well behind and practically defenceless. In this round, Armstrong found the opening he had been looking for, hitting Sarron on the chin with a powerful right that sent the champion to his knees as referee Arthur Donovan counted him out. The timekeeper's clock showed two minutes 36 seconds of the round had elapsed. Boxing had a new world featherweight champion. One ringside writer had a record book beside him and found that Armstrong had just recorded his 23rd fight of the year, all wins, 22 by knockout or stoppage. Compare that to many of today's champions and challengers and you will find that on average they have two fights a year, sometimes three, and that's it.

Mead now started negotiations for a match with world lightweight champion Lou Ambers but the purse demands by Ambers' manager Al Weill ruled that out. Angered by Weill's refusal to even discuss a defence against Armstrong, Mead told his charge that they would skip the lightweight division altogether and go after the welterweight champion Barney Ross. 'I can beat Ross,' said a confident Armstrong. 'Wait and see.' Boxing people thought it was a crazy idea – a featherweight against a welterweight. There was a difference of 20lbs between the two weight classes and while Ross was a little past his peak, he was still fully capable of beating the best around.

A native New Yorker, Ross was born David Rasofsky in Manhattan's Lower East Side on 23 December 1909. His Jewish parents, Isidore and Sarah, had migrated from Russia around the turn of the century and, after a spell in New York, relocated to Chicago, where he was raised alongside his five brothers and sisters. Isidore and Sarah worked hard in a grocery store owned by her uncle and which they kept open for 19 hours a day, six days a week. David's destiny was mapped out for him while he was still a boy, his father deciding that he should become a Hebrew teacher.

Although he was brought up to disdain any form of violence, the young Rasosky learned how to handle himself in the tough world of mob-ruled Chicago. Gangs of Irish, Italians and Poles opposed the Jews, and David and his friends had to fight simply to get into the local swimming pool. In spite of his small stature, he soon discovered he was pretty useful with his fists. 'I found that I was so fast on my feet that I was able to dance and weave so much that the other kid would almost knock himself out trying to hold on to me,' he recalled in later years. 'I certainly won more street battles than I lost.'

A dramatic change in his life would follow. Just before Christmas 1923, a little over a week before David's 14th birthday, his father was brutally shot to death while attempting to resist a robbery at the store. Inconsolable with grief, Sarah had a nervous breakdown. The store was sold and the family split up. The three youngest children, brothers Georgie and Sammy and sister Ida, were placed in an orphanage while David went out to get a job. With no work available, he turned to juvenile gambling rackets. One of his pals was Jack Ruby, who would later become a nightclub owner and gain infamy in 1963 as the man who shot and killed President Kennedy's assassin Lee Harvey Oswald. David would testify at Ruby's trial.

David used to read about the great Jewish boxers of the past such as Abe Attell, Joe Choyinski, Jack 'Kid' Berg, Benny Leonard, Lew Tendler and even the great bare-knuckle battler Daniel Mendoza. He decided he wanted to be a boxer. Illinois state law at the time decreed that amateur boxers must be 16 years of age, so when the 15-year-old David made up his mind to get into the sport he had to lie about his age. He also had to deceive his mother about his new interest as she disliked boxing. So to keep his activities from her, he became Barney Ross, a name he simply picked out of the air as it sounded good.

The teen now known as Barney Ross went along to Kid Howard's downtown gym, where all the big names trained, and picked up valuable tips. He made fast progress. Fast and agile with a big heart, Ross enjoyed a successful amateur career as a bantamweight, the highlight coming in 1929 when he won a Chicago Golden Gloves title in what was then a relatively new tournament created by the sportswriter Arch Ward. He also boxed in Madison Square Garden in intercity championships.

Overall, Ross had nearly 200 amateur contests, winning most of them. He became known for his speed, cleverness and stamina rather than as a knockout specialist. He also possessed a sturdy chin. In his entire amateur and professional careers nobody ever knocked Ross out, and he shared rings with many heavy hitters, particularly in the paid ranks. As an amateur, Ross found that money could be made in the sport by selling cups and medals.

There is a myth that the gangster Al 'Scarface' Capone befriended Ross by giving him dollar bills 'to tide you over, kid', and that he worked for Capone as a messenger boy. Extensive research shows that this was not the case. In truth, while Capone knew Ross and the family, the mobster recognised the inherent goodness in the boy and merely told him 'to stay in school as long as you can, then get a job but keep out of trouble'.

What is factual, though, is that the crime element in Chicago was pretty high and that the city was a hotbed of gangsterism. In later years, Ross would admit that he knew all seven of the mobsters murdered in the infamous St Valentine's Day Massacre of 14 February 1929. In a garage in town, Capone's men, equipped with machine guns, opened fire on the gang led by his hated rival George 'Bugs' Moran.

Capone would come into Ross's life in later years when he tried to fix some of his fights in the professional ranks, but Ross and his handlers weren't having any shady dealings with the mobster. As a result, Capone respected Ross' integrity and honesty. 'No hard feelings, kid,' he would say, the familiar fat cigar clenched between his teeth. 'Remember what I told you years ago. Keep out of trouble.'

When Ross was 19, with a successful spell in the amateurs behind him, he was giving a lot of thought to turning professional. Whatever was said about picking up money by selling amateur cups and medals, the real financial rewards were with the pros, especially if you happened to be good. Barney took the big step on 31 August 1929. 'I reckoned I would keep going until I could put enough money away to take my two brothers and my sister out of the orphanage, and support them until they could look after themselves,' he remembered in later years.

From his early days, Ross worked as a sparring partner for world welterweight champion Jackie Fields. When Fields had a fight lined up at the Main Street Athletic Club in Los Angeles, Barney was given a preliminary spot on the card. He made a successful debut by narrowly outpointing Raymond Lugo of Mexico over six rounds. He purse came to $75. A week later, he was back in the same ring and defeated Joe Barola, again over six rounds, and this time collected $100.

Following the win, Chicago gang leader and boxing referee Davey Miller introduced Ross to a pair of experienced fight men, manager Sam Pian and his cornerman Art Winch. They would become his co-managers and would stay with him throughout his career, which would last almost nine years. It was one of boxing's most successful partnerships. For the next three years Ross campaigned around the Midwest, moving successfully through the featherweight and lightweight divisions and running up an impressive record.

At this stage, Barney was getting a little over-confident and started to neglect his training, staying out late at night and having a good time. Al Capone had warned him that the only way to get to the top was to work hard in the gym and on the road, and now he was neglecting that advice. After one loss, against Roger Bernard, which his handlers Pian and Winch put down to their charge not being fully fit, they threw him out of the gym and told him never to come back. It took a visit by Ross to the orphanage to see his siblings to realise what he was throwing away.

Ross crept back to the gym one evening and pleaded with Pian and Winch to take him back. 'One more chance,' warned Pian as he threw Barney a pair of mitts and told him to get working on the heavy bag. Ross promised he would never stray again and he kept to his word. He was always 100 per cent in shape, especially when his mother told him she would be at ringside for his fights, despite her earlier misgivings about boxing. Sarah now fully supported him. When he boxed on a Friday, a day when orthodox Jews were forbidden to travel by car or bus, she would walk miles to see Barney in action.

On 22 March 1933, Ross beat the leading lightweight contender Billy Petrolle, the 'Fargo Express', over ten rounds in New York, prompting the *Chicago Tribune* to note: 'It looks like Barney Ross can't escape the 135lb championship.' Tony Canzoneri, an Italian-American from Brooklyn, was the champion and they were matched in a title fight at the Chicago Stadium on 23 June 1933, with Canzoneri's world junior welterweight title also on the line.

Canzoneri was a 6/5 favourite because of his heavy punching, and while Ross was behind for the first seven rounds, he rallied magnificently and won the decision after 15 fast rounds. With his surprise victory, Ross became the first boxer in history to win two world titles in the one night. Barney declined to attend the post-fight party, preferring to walk his mother the five miles home. For Barney, the victory was particularly sweet. The $10,000 purse enabled him to install his mother in a larger and more comfortable apartment, as well as being able to take his siblings out of the orphanage and set them up at home for the first time in years.

Canzoneri and his manager Sammy Goldman complained about the decision and lodged an official complaint with the Illinois State Athletic Commission, demanding a return. They were re-matched in New York three months later and Ross again won the decision, this time on a majority vote. Barney collected his biggest purse, $35,000, and relinquished the lighter title, hanging on to the junior welterweight crown. By now, he was becoming addicted to gambling and big spending. After one non-title fight in 1934, he went out on the town with friends and spent his entire purse. The world champion was regularly seen at racetracks and perpetually owed money to bookies, loan sharks and mobsters.

'Ross was a fool with his money,' wrote a contemporary boxing reporter. 'He drank, caroused, picked up tabs and lavished gifts on girlfriends and hanger-ons with the fervency of a college student stumbling on to an open bar reception. When his co-managers warned him to curb his spending, he would brush off their fears by saying: "There's more where that came from." That's how it was with Barney, the big spender.'

While he may have thrown his money around, Ross did not neglect his training. His success was hard won and he knew only too well there were lots of hungry fighters out there just waiting to topple him. Relinquishing his junior welterweight title, he moved up to welterweight, where he would have some of his most famous fights. On 28 May 1934, Ross challenged Jimmy 'Baby Face' McLarnin for the world welterweight championship and outpointed the Irishman over 15 rounds on a split decision. Four months later, McLarnin reversed the points verdict, again on a split vote. In their third meeting, on 28 May 1935, exactly a year to the day after their first clash, Ross won on points, with the three officials voting for him this time. All three fights took place in New York.

Ross put his title on the line twice more, winning decisions over Alabama's Izzy Jannazzo on 27 November 1936 and Ceferino Garcia, the Filipino who first popularised the bolo punch, ten months later, both in New York. There were reports in the newspapers that the world featherweight champion Henry Armstrong was anxious to take on Ross after talks failed for an Armstrong challenge to world lightweight champion Lou Ambers.

Ross and his co-managers were keen on an Armstrong fight. So was Henry. There would be big money for all concerned. Boxing writers were unsure if Armstrong could bridge the weight gap. After all, Henry was merely a featherweight, with his best weight inside 126lbs. The welterweight limit was 147lbs, so how could anybody even think of moving up to concede considerable weight and still be strong, even if Armstrong often ventured into the lightweight division, with its 135lbs limit? Unlikely, said some. Impossible, chorused others. In any event, Ross felt he could do with the big purse such a defence would bring in to feed his gambling habit.

The two champions ducked between the ropes at Long Island Bowl on 31 May 1938. At the weigh-in on the morning of the fight Ross had tipped the scales at 142lbs, with Armstrong surprisingly heavy at 133lbs, though still two pounds under the lightweight limit. It meant that Ross would still have an advantage of eight pounds, which could be decisive over the scheduled 15 rounds, particularly after nine or ten rounds if it lasted that long. After both boxers left the weigh-in room to get dressed, an official tipped off Major General John J Phelan, chairman of the New York State Athletic Commission, that Armstrong had cheated by using lead plates fastened to the soles of his feet to make him heavier.

Phelan sought out Armstrong straight away and questioned him about the allegation. Henry laughed at the mere suggestion of any illegalities. Phelan demanded: 'Empty the contents of your bag.' Henry duly did so. Nothing found. 'Take off your shoes and socks and let's have a look at your feet,' demanded Phelan. Again Armstrong obliged. Phelan bent down and ran his fingers along the bottom of the boxer's bare feet. 'That's enough, Commissioner,' said Armstrong. 'Besides, you're tickling me.' Phelan straightened up, said nothing and left, with Armstrong still smiling.

The ringside was full of famous celebrities from all walks of life and several former champions were introduced from the ring. After the master of ceremonies, Harry Balough, complete in evening suit and bow tie, made the formal announcements, referee Arthur Donovan called the two participants together to the centre of the ring for final instructions. The big fight was a reality. It was the first time in ring history that a featherweight champion was taking on a welterweight king. Ross was favoured at 3/1.

Ross, taller by one and a half inches and three years older than the 25-year-old challenger, won the opening round with his sharper boxing as Armstrong bored in with hooks and uppercuts. Barney also brought an effective right uppercut into play, a punch he and his handlers had worked on in training to get through to the lighter man's carefully protected chin.

Armstrong was beginning to connect with those damaging hooks and uppercuts in the second round and Ross seemed to smart from one particular left hook towards the end of the session. But the welterweight champion was still moving smartly and using that snapping left hand. By the fifth, Ross was marginally behind as Armstrong constantly forged forward with his incessant, relentless attacks, and the heavier champion appeared to be tiring.

'Armstrong's swarming style, his merciless rain of punches at an almost superhuman rate and his inexhaustible stamina was simply too much for Ross,' recalled author, broadcaster and former *Ring* magazine editor Bert Sugar. 'Ross's right eye was damaged early, and closed by the seventh. His mouth, too, was badly cut and he was bleeding from the nose. In short, he was a mess but he still fought on.

'In the second half of the 15-rounds fight, it was no longer a question of who would win but whether Ross would go down. Gasping, he tottered to his corner at the concluding bell for each round. Referee Donovan, the best of his time, would come over and examine the damage between every round. Several times he asked Ross whether he wanted to continue but a proud Ross nodded assent.'

By the ninth, Ross was well behind on points and with little if any chance of victory. Donovan was still keeping a close watch on proceedings. Barney got his left hand working again but Armstrong would not be denied, and continued to press forward, banging in left jabs, left and right uppercuts, hooks and swings in an effort to bring Ross down. But the welterweight champion had a solid chin. Hadn't he been knocked down just once before in his entire career, against Jimmy McLarnin in 1934?

Donovan went over to Ross' corner in the tenth round and said to Pian, Winch and trainer Ray Arcel: 'I'm not going to stop this fight just yet but it's up to you guys. You're going to be responsible for anything that happens, so use your own judgement.' Ross looked up at his cornermen and said through cut and bruised lips: 'If you guys stop this fight, I'll never talk to you again for the rest of my life and I mean that.'

Several times in the 12th and 13th rounds, his team suggested he call it quits but Ross would always shake his head. 'Remember what I said,' he replied. Barney knew deep down, and so did everybody else in the arena, that he would unquestionably lose his title barring a miracle but he would go out on points, battered and bleeding but still standing. That's the way he wanted it. At the final bell, Donovan gave Armstrong 12 rounds, Ross two, with one even. Judge George Lecron had it 11-2 for Armstrong with two even and judge Billy Cavanaugh, who was also a prominent referee, made it 10-4-1. Long Island Bowl once again lived up to its reputation as 'the Graveyard of Champions'.

When Ross came down from the ring, Grantland Rice of the *New York Herald Tribune* said to him: 'Why didn't you quit, Barney? Did you want to get killed?' Ross replied: 'It's a champ's privilege. A champ's got the right to choose the way he goes out.'

In his retirement years, Ross recalled: 'Armstrong was a great fighter, really great, and I mean that. I could never get to grips with him after four or five rounds. He just kept coming forward like a tank. After the fight, I went over to his corner and shook his hand. "Hang on to the title, Henry, you deserve all your success." He was a really nice guy too.'

Armstrong remembered the Ross fight: 'After the 11th round, I told my manager Eddie Mead in the corner that I was going to make a determined effort to knock him out, or at least stop him, even if his chin was so damn strong. Just before the bell to start the 12th round, Eddie got a message in the corner to say that Al Capone was down at ringside and he wanted me to carry Ross for the final four rounds for his own purposes. Well, you don't go against Al Capone so I went easy on Ross for the last four, though I still made it look as if I wanted to get it all over with. I was pulling my punches and nobody suspected anything.'

In 1991, Ross' coach Ray Arcel recalled for Dave Anderson of the *New York Times*: 'Armstrong was then at the top of his game. He gave Ross a bad licking. He had lumps on his head. His eyes were swollen. His ears were swollen. When we got back to the hotel, I put hot towels on his face. That night, I slept beside him because I didn't want to leave him alone. He had just been married but he was so busted we didn't let his wife in there to see him.

'She was yelling and screaming blue murder but Sam Pian, Ross' co-manager, said to Barney: "Look at yourself in the mirror. You don't want your wife to see you like that. Let's wait a day or so and you'll look a lot better." He agreed. I stayed with him for four days, and still put the hot towels on his face and he looked much better. He was a wonderful, wonderful man, a tremendous person.'

When Ross announced to the assembled press in the dressing room that the Armstrong fight was his last, he meant it. Leaving behind an impressive record of 72 wins, four losses, three draws and two no-decisions, he enlisted in the US Marines when the Japanese attacked Pearl Harbor on 8 December 1941. He was two weeks short of his 32nd birthday. Although assigned to work as a boxing instructor, Ross requested that he be sent into combat and was consigned to Guadacanal in the Japanese-held Solomon Islands, where some of the fiercest fighting of the Second World War took place from 1942 to 1943.

On the night of 19 November 1942, Ross and three comrades were out on patrol duty and found themselves under attack by enemy troops. His three comrades were wounded and Ross shepherded them into a crater hole for protection. During the bloody night, he fired off over 200 rounds and when the bullets ran out he hurled 22 grenades at enemy machine gun positions. Ross was credited with killing roughly 20 Japanese in this overnight period. By the morning, two of his colleagues had died and he was able to carry the third to safety. For these heroic exploits, Ross would receive the Silver Star, Purple Heart and a Presidential Citation. A true hero.

Within a matter of weeks on the frontline, his hair turned a mixture of silvery grey and pure white. Moved to a military hospital in New Zealand to recover from wounds he had received, as well as contracting a severe case of malaria, Ross was treated with morphine, to which he quickly became addicted. Happily, back home he would eventually beat the addiction and become an anti-drugs spokesman, lecturing throughout colleges and high schools on the dangers of drugs, and testified at a UN Senate hearing about his experiences. Ross would subsequently describe his war wounds and battle with malaria as 'child's play compared to the drug addiction'.

Ross' life and personal battles were depicted in the movie *Monkey On My Back*, with Cameron Mitchell playing Barney. Opening in the US in May 1957, Ross had acted as technical adviser, appearing every day on the set and gaining a rapport with Mitchell. The film was a success, artistically and financially. 'Mitchell handles the part with commendable flexibility and plays the boxer with uniform conviction,' said *Variety*. Leonard Maltin's *Movie Guide* described it as 'a well-meant, engrossing little film', with Mitchell 'turning in a sincere performance'.

While Ross was happy with the finished film, he was far from pleased with the end packaging. Later in 1957, the ever-combatant ex-champion and addiction conqueror announced he was planning to file a $5m lawsuit against United Artists film company. He alleged that the advertisements relating to the movie were misleading, conveying the notion that he was still addicted to drugs, despite the fact that he had kicked the habit several years earlier. There is no evidence, though, that he went ahead with the lawsuit.

Ross also had a small part in the 1962 movie *Requiem For A Heavyweight*, starring Anthony Quinn in the main role, and was often introduced at big fights. Barney also worked tirelessly on the political scene, lobbying for the emerging state of Israel, even seeking donations from his underworld connections to buy and smuggle weapons into that country. He also tried to create a corporation of American Jewish war veterans to send to Palestine but was blocked by the State Department. Ross had long squandered most of his ring earnings when learning that he had cancer and died in his hometown of Chicago on 17 January 1967, a month after his 57th birthday.

Meanwhile, Armstrong won the world lightweight title less than three months after the Ross fight by defeating Lou Ambers on a unanimous decision in New York to become the first and only boxer to hold three titles simultaneously, something that can no longer happen under today's regulations.

Armstrong would soon relinquish the featherweight title and lose the lightweight belt back to Ambers in 1939. In March 1940, he lost the welterweight belt to Fritzie Zivic, but not before he stepped up to middleweight and forced a draw with the Filipino world champion Ceferino Garcia in 1940. Victory would have created another record, with Armstrong becoming the first boxer to win four world titles, but it was not to be, even if several writers felt that Armstrong was robbed and should have been given the decision.

Armstrong continued boxing during the years of the Second World War, though his glory days were in the dim and distant past. He finally hung up his gloves in February 1945. Having enlisted in the US military, he helped boost morale for the troops by boxing exhibitions in India, Burma, China and Egypt. 'In Egypt, where Moses was, I had a very good feeling of Christianity,' he recalled. 'I saw the place where Ramses the Second defied God. I made a decision that when I got back to the US I was going into the ministry.'

In 1952, Armstrong was ordained a Baptist minister and was regularly pictured with a Bible in his hands. The next 37 years were spent travelling from his home in St Louis as assistant pastor of the First Baptist Church to spread the word. Distancing himself from the boxing scene, he felt that the sport had lost a lot of its glamour and excitement. On the rare occasions he attended big fights, he was given a tremendous reception and besieged for autographs. Having successfully battled alcoholism, Armstrong died in Los Angeles on 23 October 1988, aged 75.

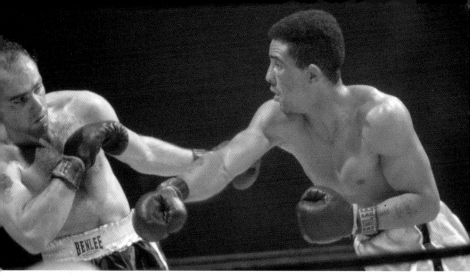

Carl Bobo Olson sways back from a Randolph Turpin right

Down goes Rocky Graziano against arch rival Tony Zale

Floyd Patterson, right, and Ingemar Johansson in action

Henry Armstrong rocks Barney Ross with a right cross

Henry Armstrong, centre, and Barney Ross have their medical examination

Jack Doyle and the author talk boxing

Jack Sharkey, left, and Primo Carnera square off at the weigh-in

James J Braddock, left, mixes it with Max Baer

Lennox Lewis, one of Britain's most popular ex-champions

Mickey Walker, left, and Harry Greb at the signing-in ceremony

Pancho Villa, left, and Jimmy Wilde minutes before their big fight

Riddick Bowe blocks a left hook from Andrew Golota

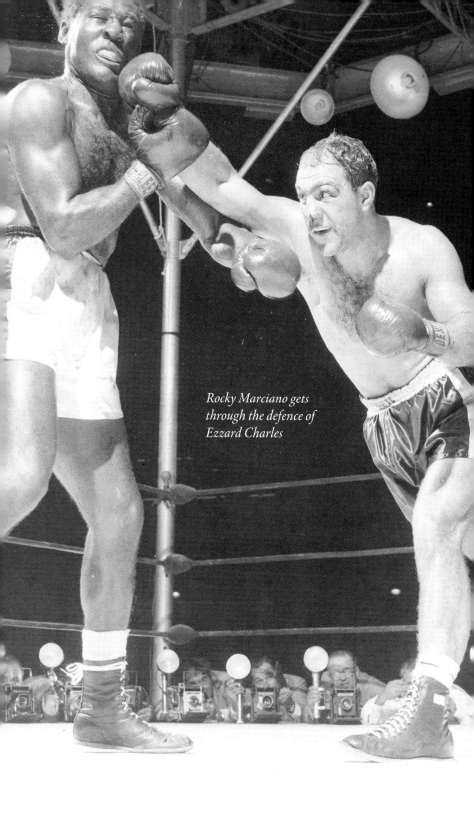

Rocky Marciano gets through the defence of Ezzard Charles

The author takes it on the chin from Ken Buchanan

Tom Sharkey, back to camera, awaits James J Jeffries' next move

Tommy Farr shoots a long left against Joe Louis

Tommy Farr, left, and Joe Louis pose for the press

Chapter 9

Somebody up there liked Rocky

**Tony Zale v Rocky Graziano,
Yankee Stadium, 27 September 1946**

BELLS rang and the streets resounded with singing and cheering as crowds packed Trafalgar Square in London and Times Square in New York City, where ticker tape fluttered down like snowflakes. The date was 8 May 1945, and the long-awaited victory in Europe, VE Day. Four months later, Japan surrendered and the Second World War was finally over after six terrible years.

With most of the world titles 'frozen' for the duration, boxing activities had gradually got back to normal by 1946, with Joe Louis defending his world heavyweight title against Billy Conn in June and Tony Zale putting his world middleweight championship on the line against Rocky Graziano in September.

The Zale and Graziano rivalry covered three fights, and each one was a war. Gilbert Odd, the esteemed British boxing writer and author, considered the trio of bruising battles 'the hardest-hitting, free-punching slugfests ever seen in the middleweight division'. The fights, which lasted a combined 15 rounds, took place within a period of 21 months. In each, both men fought until the other had been flattened, and the punishment they absorbed and what it took out of them in meting it out, effectively finished both as fighters. Graziano was never the same again, despite several exciting performances. In Zale's case, he boxed only once more after their third meeting.

In all, there were seven knockdowns and no shortage of blood. Two of the bouts were named Fight of the Year by *Ring* magazine. While the trilogy defined both of their careers, the series was a microcosm of the 11 gutsy years Graziano spent in the ring. Rocky is considered today one of the greatest knockout artists in ring history, often displaying the capacity to take out an opponent with a single punch. He was one of the few men to put Sugar Ray Robinson on the canvas. A rough brawler with a particularly potent right and a devil-may-care attitude, it was said he hated all his opponents.

Chewing his nails in the dressing room, throwing quick, practising rights and reading comics did not take the edge off his anger. He often admitted that he did not care how he won, so long as he won. He used the illegal rabbit punch, hit out in the clinches, punched fighters when they were on their way down and, as they tried to get to their feet, clambered over the referee to get at groggy opponents and hit them after the bell. In all his years in boxing – and he was a professional for ten years – Rocky struck a single pattern. He charged across the ring with both gloves swinging, never paused or moved back, and was not happy until his rival crumpled under his attack.

'Rocky's trainers found that instructing him in technique was the most dangerous thing they could do,' wrote Rex Lardner in *Sport* magazine. 'It was as though it had been impressed upon him from the age of about five that they were there for punching. It was as though his hair-trigger temper and rages were beneficial instincts for survival. It was as though they were things he felt he owed his fans. Certainly the fans appreciated Rocky's efforts to please. He was one of the biggest middleweight attractions the world had seen, and for at least two years of his career, he made more money than any other man in the ring. Stocky, confident, heavily-muscled, with powerful legs and lungs, a powerful back and tough hands, Rocky had, on his best nights, the ability to concentrate utterly on cutting his opponent down, a concentration shaped by his blind, animal fury.'

It was boxing that prevented Graziano from becoming a confirmed criminal. Of Italian heritage, he was born Thomas

Rocco Barbella on New Year's Day 1922 in a cold-water tenement flat in Manhattan's gritty Lower East Side, where robbery and thuggery was a way of life. The family later moved to Coney Island in Brooklyn 'where the air was a bit fresher', as his mother said, but it didn't change young Rocco's way of life. He grew up as a street fighter and learned to look after himself before he could read or write. He spent years in and out of jail and reform schools. His father Nick, who got occasional work on the docks, was a former professional welterweight boxer and kept boxing gloves around the house, encouraging Rocky and his brothers to fight one another.

'We never had a doctor in our house,' Rocky would recall in later years. 'No matter what happened to us, no doctor. My mother believed, like her own mother, and all the old Italians, that you didn't need doctors if you knew how to make your own cures. I won't go into what she did but none of us ever got any infection or anything like that, so her cures obviously worked. I loved my mam, and my dad too. When I was about six, I was wild. When my dad was not out looking for work, he was looking for me. My mam moved me from this school and that school as the teachers used to say I was too hard to handle. I ended up in reform schools.'

As it happened, reform schools did not change Rocky. In between spells in these schools, he constantly got into trouble with the police for robberies. 'I wandered all over the city, stealing what I could find to eat, sleeping when I got tired, wherever I was,' he remembered. 'But I only stole things that began with A, like a car, a truck, a bike, a watch, a camera, a slot machine, that sort of thing. But I paid for my crimes. Let's not forget that. I tell kids now to keep out of trouble and you'll keep out of reform schools.'

Rocky told Peter Heller for his book *In This Corner*: 'I grew up on the East Side. Like everybody else I had a rough time at the beginning, like these kids that are on drugs or whatever. Eventually, they get out of that drug programme. They find out they're a man or a woman and that's what happened to me. I found later on that this crap was not for me and I got out of it. I went to a couple of reform schools but then I got out of that and I said to myself, "Rocky, this is not the way to go." Then I went into boxing and found something in my life that I was interested in and liked it. I earned an honest living and I was happy being honest.'

Encouraged by Graziano Sr, Rocky began boxing as an amateur in his mid-teens and won several boys' club championships, but it was not until around his 18th birthday that he took the sport seriously. Two cousins told him the organisers of the upcoming Metropolitan Amateur Athletic League Championships, due to be held at the Broadway Arena in Brooklyn, were looking for a replacement for one of their boxers, who had had to pull out of a preliminary bout.

Rocky agreed to help out, even though he had never pulled on a boxing glove in his life. He went down to the Boys' Club and looked up the trainer, who happened to be Cus D'Amato, later to become famous as the man who guided Floyd Patterson and Jose Torres to world titles. In later years, D'Amato would become involved with Mike Tyson.

With just a few weeks to go before the start of the tournament, D'Amato worked on getting Rocky to improve his jab, how to get the best out of his hooks and uppercuts, and how to move around and protect himself. Hitting the heavy bag was easy but the speedball proved more difficult, although he eventually got the hang of it. Come the Friday night of the fight, and with all his pals cheering him on, Rocky won his fight and the title with a first-round knockout.

Rocky would soon sell his gold medal for $6, which he gave to his mother. 'Rocco, you didn't steal this for momma, did you?' she said, but he replied: 'Don't worry. The way I got this was easier than robbing.' He did not tell her he got it through boxing as she never liked Rocky's dad's participation in the sport and he was sure she would feel the same about her son's involvement. Eventually, though, she found out and gave her full approval.

'From that day on, I couldn't walk down Fifth Avenue or 10th Street without people stopping me and shaking my hand,' he recalled later. 'They were either at the fights or had seen my name in the papers. I felt it was upwards from there on.'

Or so he thought. Encouraged by his old pals who regarded stealing as an exciting adventure, he went back to muggings and robberies and spent time in the notorious Tombs prison, where persons accused of crimes were confined while awaiting trial or sentence, if any. Rocky was put on parole and though he hated authority of all kinds, particularly the police, he vowed to go on the straight and narrow – and boxing came back into his thoughts.

Rocky realised he could make good money in boxing and with that thought in mind he looked around for a manager, eventually signing up with Eddie Coco, who had a lot of connections in the New York boxing scene. Under Coco's guidance, Rocky turned professional as a welterweight on 31 March 1942 with a knockout win in two rounds over Curtis Hightower in Brooklyn. He followed it up with four more fights in April and three in May to run his record 5-1-2 before he was drafted into the US Army. But if anybody seriously thought that Private Rocco Barbella would settle down to army discipline and regulations, they were hopelessly wrong. Despatched to Fort Dix, New Jersey for basic training, he was in trouble on the very first morning when he threw punches at the corporal who was shouting at him. Brought up before the captain, he slugged him as well and went on the run.

Caught by the army authorities back in Brooklyn, Rocky was court-martialled, given a dishonourable discharge and sentenced to 12 months at Leavenworth maximum security prison in Kansas. Freed in the spring of 1943, and still only 21, he asked around about managers and found several. But once they discovered Rocky was inclined to go off the rails from time to time and detested training, they lost interest.

One day in the company of some friends, and still looking for a good manager, somebody brought up the name of Irving Cohen. Born in Russia in 1904, Cohen left his homeland in his early years and headed for America, 'the land of opportunity'. Though he boxed as an amateur, he didn't find a career in the sport immediately and worked as a lingerie salesman before becoming a boxing manager in 1935.

Rocky looked up Cohen's address in *Ring* magazine, made contact with him, liked what he heard and signed a contract there and then. Calm, quiet and distinguished, the 5ft 6in Cohen did not fit the stereotype of the loud, insensitive, cigar-chomping fight manager. It was estimated that he managed over 500 boxers in a career spanning over 30 years, notably top welterweight contender Billy Graham, a New Yorker, but he would always be associated with Graziano.

Cohen would skilfully and carefully guide Rocky throughout his 83-fight career, which was not an easy task considering the fighter's lack of interest in training and discipline. For a while, he let Rocky live with his own family. It was Cohen who changed Rocco Barbella into Rocky Graziano when they signed up.

Under Cohen's guidance, Rocky made steady progress, spending many hours a week in Stillman's famous gym on 54th Street and Eighth Avenue, where all the greats had trained over the years. Cohen tried in his subtle way to get Rocky overmatched, have him defeated and thereby show him the value of conditioning. Cohen even tried to get him a match with the great Sugar Ray Robinson, who would give Rocky a lesson and knock some of the cockiness out of him, but no success there. Graziano carried on and his big punching was always in evidence. In 1943, he had 18 fights, winning 16. In 1944, he had 20 fights, scoring ten knockouts and losing two decisions to Harold Green.

'I fought Green in the main event at Madison Square Garden, which was a big thrill for me, but the guy just got on his bicycle every time I charged him,' Rocky remembered. 'When he didn't get on his bicycle, he grabbed and held and I could never get a clean shot at him. We met again three weeks later, again at the Garden, and this time he ran, ran, ran. But with ten seconds of time left, and the crowd on their feet yelling, I caught him with a good roundhouse right and he went down, most likely for the full count. But the referee only got to six when the bell rang. It took the referee and both Green's handlers to lift him off the canvas and hold up his right hand as the winner. He was a lucky guy that night.'

By now, Cohen had brought Morris 'Whitey' Bimstein on to the team as Rocky's trainer and cut man. Like Rocky, he was born on Manhattan's Lower East Side. There were few, if any, better coaches and cornermen than Whitey, and over the years he worked with the likes of Gene Tunney, Harry Greb, Georges Carpentier, Benny Leonard, James J Braddock, Barney Ross, Ingemar Johansson and many others.

Bimstein was known as a 'magician with the swabs', which could be seen protruding from his mouth while working in the corner, complete with various ointments and chemical substances he used on his boxers. Countless times, he was able to keep a fight from being stopped due to excessive bleeding on a closed eye. Whitey was doing his job and doing it superbly well.

Rocky would remember 1945 as his best year to date. Billy Arnold, a highly talented welterweight contender from West Virginia, was being touted as a future world champion by newspapers and *Ring* magazine, and they were calling him 'the new Sugar Ray Robinson' and 'the new Joe Louis'. Aged 19, he had lost just once and scored 28 knockouts. A brilliant all-rounder who could box and punch, he was a 6/1 favourite to beat Graziano in Rocky's opening fight of the year, at Madison Square Garden on 9 March. For two rounds before a crowd of 14,037, Arnold handed out a battering to Rocky, hitting him with every punch in the book: jabs, hooks, crosses, uppercuts, the lot.

That all changed in the third round of the scheduled eight-rounder when Rocky lashed out with a looping right to the chin and Arnold went sprawling through the ropes. He staggered to his feet just before the ten count as Rocky jumped in again and dropped him for the second time with another looping right and he slid down in the neutral corner. Somehow he managed to get up and was met by an enraged Rocky, who put him down for the third and last time as referee Frank Fullam called it off. It was all over and Rocky had won his most important fight to date.

In his autobiography *Somebody Up There Likes Me*, Rocky would say: 'I heard later that Damon Runyon, the famous boxing writer, passed a note to a colleague, which said: "There's your new Stanley Ketchel." That was some praise as old-timers used to say that Ketchel was the toughest who ever fought in the ring. A killing puncher, he was called the "Michigan Assassin" and he once put the heavyweight champion Jack Johnson on the canvas.'

Rocky was now attracting a large following as an exciting, destructive puncher always on the attack. On 25 May, at the Garden, he faced Al 'Bummy' Davis, a tough contender from the Brownsville district of Brooklyn. Al Buck of the *New York Post* reported: 'Rocky Graziano knocked out Al "Bummy" Davis with a right to the jaw that landed seconds after the bell had sounded ending the third round. Officially, the end came in 44 seconds of the fourth but the blow that did the damage came at a time when the ring was full of handlers of both fighters.

'It was clearly an illegal punch but Young Otto, the referee, ignored the protests of Lew Burston, Davis' manager. "I asked Otto to stop the fight and disqualify Graziano but he refused," Burston explained. "Instead, he ordered the fight to continue." Davis, hurt and bleeding, was knocked down and took a count of nine. When he got up, Rocky smashed right after right to Bummy's chin. Al was on his feet when Otto stopped it.'

Within six months, Bummy was dead. On 21 November, he was drinking with some friends in a bar in Brownsville when four armed robbers walked in. Davis attacked the gunmen and knocked one of them down, but was shot three times. Bleeding badly, he managed to chase the other three but they turned around, opened fire and shot him dead.

The reigning world welterweight champion Freddie 'Red' Cochrane fancied his chances against Rocky and they were matched in a ten-rounder at the Garden on 29 June 1945. Now a fully fledged middleweight, Rocky wanted to get down to the 147lbs welterweight limit but his trainer Whitey Bimstein would not allow him to lose weight which would weaken him. Instead, the fight was a non-title affair.

Cochrane, from Elizabeth, New Jersey, was a slippery opponent with a big pull in experience. Moving smartly, he was well ahead on points after eight rounds before Rocky caught him with a looping right to the chin in the ninth. He went down but was saved by the bell. Rocky came out fast in the tenth and landed another big right on the champion's jaw, dropping him as though he had been shot. The ten count by referee Benny Leonard, the former great world lightweight champion, was a mere formality. They met again two months later and it was practically a replica of the first fight. Once again a non-title bout, Rocky was well behind on points before catching up with the welterweight champion in the tenth round and finishing him off.

Before the year was out, Graziano avenged his earlier two defeats by Harold Green by knocking out his fellow Brooklynite in three rounds. 'I got great satisfaction out of that win,' Rocky said in his retirement years. 'Green was the only guy who ever licked me in the Garden and now I'd evened the score.'

Seconds after Green was counted out, he sprang up and charged at Rocky, throwing punches in all directions. Green's cornerman Charles Duke joined in the attack before officials intervened and helped restore order. Green was subsequently suspended and fined $1,000 for inciting a riot and Duke had his licence suspended. In his book *Men of Steel*, author Peter Walsh quoted an article in *Ring* magazine 45 years later in which Green claimed the fight was fixed and that by going down he was promised a title fight later. It never materialised.

Graziano was now the biggest attraction in boxing, excluding heavyweight champion Joe Louis. He was an exciting fighter with the ability to end a fight at any time. On 29 March 1946 he faced

Marty Servo, who had taken the welterweight title from Cochrane four weeks earlier. Servo's title was not at stake as Graziano was now an official middleweight. It was all over in two rounds after Servo was down for counts of two, eight and seven before referee Arthur Donovan intervened. Servo would announce his retirement from the ring some months later when his nose, badly injured by one of Graziano's heavy rights, failed to respond to treatment. He would be succeeded by Sugar Ray Robinson, who had been the uncrowned champion for several years.

By this time, Rocky was officially the No 1 contender for Tony Zale's world middleweight championship, which Zale had won on 19 July 1940 by stopping Al Hostak in 13 rounds at the Chicago Stadium. He made three successful defences in 1941 before being called up for service in the US Navy, with America now at war. Consequently the title, as in other divisions, was frozen until the end of hostilities. Joe Louis' heavyweight title was put in mothballs, as was Gus Lesnevich's light-heavyweight championship, and so on down the line.

With the end of the war in Europe and Asia in 1945 and the promised millennium of world peace still unfulfilled, disenchanted Americans turned from the rigours of problem-solving to the rituals of pleasure-seeking activities. The major form of escapism was the movies. Big films in 1945 included *The Lost Weekend*, *The Bells of St Marys*, *Spellbound*, *A Tree Grows in Brooklyn* and *Mildred Pierce*. In 1946, it was *Duel In The Sun*, *The Razor's Edge*, *Gilda*, *My Darling Clementine* and *It's A Wonderful Life*.

On stage, a big, brash musical *Annie Get Your Gun* opened on Broadway, and from the hit parade could be heard the voices of the most popular singers of the day, such as Bing Crosby, Frank Sinatra, Judy Garland, Nat King Cole, Perry Como and a very promising newcomer named Ella Fitzgerald. The big bands still held sway, such as Benny Goodman, Count Basie and Les Brown, along with a new form of jazz known as be-bop, or bop for short. Some were saying this was the beginning of modern jazz as distinct from traditional, with one of the leading exponents being the brilliant trumpet player Dizzy Gillespie.

In boxing, fans looked to the return match between Joe Louis and Billy Conn for excitement. They had met five years earlier and in a thrilling finish Louis came from behind to knock out the Irish-American in 13 rounds. Unfortunately, the second bout lacked the same kind of excitement and Louis won on a knockout in the eight round of a very dull, dismal match.

The Zale–Graziano match promised real excitement, a clash between two heavy punchers, and there was no way that anybody would be disappointed. As it happened, they weren't. Graziano was hungry for the title and Zale was determined to proved he was a genuine champion. A crafty boxer and strong body puncher, Tony punished his opponents and steadily wore them down before knocking them out. He also had the reputation of being able to absorb heavy punishment and still rally to win.

Zale was born Anthony Florian Zaleski on 29 May 1913 in Gary, Indiana, a steel town that would give him his nickname 'Man of Steel'. It is still said in Gary that 'some of the steel from the mills must have poured into Tony's veins'. His parents were Polish immigrants who first moved to Chicago but, struggling to pay the rent in their tenement flat, they moved to Gary, where rents were cheaper. When Tony was two years of age, his father Josef was killed in a car accident and it was left to the mother, Catherine, to raise the young family.

Tony and his two elder brothers found work in the oven-like steel pits, where they toiled long hours. The boys were interested in boxing, having read about the exploits of famous fighters, so after work they set up a makeshift ring at the back of the house. Here, they would invite neighbourhood kids in to have boxing sessions. Tony, the youngest of the siblings, used to watch these impromptu matches but declined to take part. It was not until he was assailed by a local gang and beaten up that he made up his mind to take up boxing and be able to defend himself against all-comers. 'The whipping I got was the best lesson I ever received,' he would recall in later years. 'It turned me into a man.'

After some enquiries the following day, Tony discovered that Gary had a boxing club and decided to join. He enjoyed the sparring sessions and workouts, hitting the heavy bag and doing the various exercises on the floor. The one good thing that came out of toiling long hours in the steel mill was that it developed his strength and fine physique, which would later be beneficial in his boxing career.

In between stints in the mills, Tony entered local boxing tournaments and started to win amateur titles at welterweight and middleweight. Eventually, he would win 87 of his 95 bouts and made up his mind to quit the mill and become a professional boxer. Making his paid debut on 11 June 1934, a fortnight after his 21st birthday, at the Marigold Gardens, Chicago, he scored a points win over Eddie Allen. In that first year, he racked up 15 wins, dropping six decisions. In 1935, he won only two of his five fights, with two of his three losses inside the distance, a stoppage in nine rounds by Roughhouse Glover, who lived up to his name, and the other by a knockout in six rounds by another toughie, Johnny Phagan.

'I realised then that I wasn't getting anywhere in boxing,' he recalled. 'I had the wrong type of managers, who were only looking after themselves. I seriously considered quitting the game and looking for a steady job. As it was, I only had one fight in 1936 and could only manage a draw. It was when I met a genuine guy named Benny Ray, a fatherly type, that things changed. Benny made good matches without the risk of me getting killed.

'When the summer season opened at the famous Marigold Gardens in Chicago in 1937, I boxed on that card and won. Benny would have been with me longer but he had a bright prospect named Milt Aron, who was requiring more and more of his time. After all, I was just a beginner more or less. Benny was also the matchmaker at the Marigold and the authorities were none too happy about the double jobbing. But he did put me in touch with two influential managers, Sam Pian and Art Winch, who had a small team a boxers on their books. "These are good guys, Tony, take my word for it," said Benny. "They'll be your new managers. I know them well and they'll take you a long way, hopefully to a world title." How right he was.'

Winch would remember in later years: 'We knew that Zale was a good fighter but we wanted to find out how good. I knew of a good young middleweight down in Youngstown, Ohio named Al Wardlow and I told Sam to try and make the match. He did, so we took Tony all the way to Youngstown to see what he was really made of. What happens? Tony belts him out in three rounds and the fans cheer him all the way to the dressing room. We had a great prospect, sure enough. He had passed the test.'

It was Zale's points win over world middleweight champion Al Hostak in a non-title fight in Chicago on 29 January 1940 that turned him into a genuine contender. Hostak, of Czech parentage and known as the 'Savage Slav', was not too keen to put his title on the line against his conqueror but a big purse made him change his mind. The title fight was set for the Civic Stadium Field in Hostak's home ground of Seattle, Washington on 19 July 1940.

Hostak won the early rounds on his sharper boxing and superior hitting but by the sixth round Zale was gradually coming into the fight, landing solid punches to head and body. In the eighth, Zale opened a cut over the champion's left eye and with the right eye closed tight, Hostak looked set for defeat. Zale had him down in the 12th with a strong left hook and again in the 13th with a damaging right to the heart. The game Seattle man climbed to his feet only to be met with a powerful body blow that dropped him for the third time. As he wobbled to his feet, referee Benny Leonard said: 'That's enough.' The time of the finish was 1:23 of the 13th round. Tony Zale was the new middleweight champion of the world, the first king of the ring from the Steel City of Gary, Indiana.

Tony had three more fights in 1941, all wins, before America entered the Second World War following the attack on Pearl Harbor on 8 December 1941. On 13 February, he boxed the former world light-heavyweight champion Billy Conn at Madison Square Garden. Conn, who had almost toppled heavyweight king Joe Louis eight months earlier, had a 14lbs weight advantage over Zale and proved too smart for the middleweight champion, winning a decision after 12 rounds. Billy's long left jabs and fast combinations proved too much. There were some boos at the finish, with some saying that Conn should have put him away, but Zale was too tough for that. The Associated Press gave Conn ten of the 12 rounds.

Shortly after, Zale receved his call-up papers and joined the US Coastguard based in Puerto Rico, but his world title was safe. It was frozen until the end of hostilities.

When the war ended, Zale resumed his ring activities in 1946 with six wins before taking on the most formidable challenge of his career, against his No 1 contender Rocky Graziano, the cocky New Yorker with bombs in his gloves. The fight was set for 27 September 1946 at the Yankee Stadium. Nine years younger than the champion, Graziano was tipped to win and leave the big ballpark with the championship in his possession. Rocky was a 13/5 favourite at the opening odds and though late money came in for Zale the betting closed, making the 24-year-old challenger the favourite at 7/5. One thing everybody was in agreement over was that that Zale v Graziano had the makings of a classic and that it would surely end in a knockout, considering the power of the two participants. Rocky's impressive record read 43-6-5, with 32 of his wins by straight knockout or stoppage. Zale's record, too, looked good – 60-12-1, including 36 wins by the short route. Who would be the first to fall?

While most of the New York writers tipped the younger Rocky to come out on top, Gene Kessler of the *Chicago Daily Times* went for a Zale victory. 'Firstly, I'm convinced Zale has regained most of his old form and is very close to the durable puncher who overpowered Al Hostak five years ago,' he said. 'Secondly, I think Graziano is over-confident and, thirdly, I feel that Zale is bigger and stronger. A good big man will always beat a good little man.'

Zale had set up his training camp at Pompton Lakes, New Jersey and was reported to be in prime condition. 'I've never seen Rocky fight but I know he's a big puncher, but I'll be ready for whatever he throws at me,' he told reporters. 'I don't think he'll be able to stand up to my body shots.' Graziano also worked out in New Jersey, at Greenwood Lake. 'I'll take Zale, that's for sure,' said Rocky. 'His time is up. I reckon I'll knock him out and take the title back where it belongs, in New York. Before that happens, I will promise you all, and the fans, a good fight.' When one reporter told Rocky that Zale's people had backed $5,000 on their man winning, he smiled: 'You go back and tell them they're going to lose their money.'

As fight night drew near, with excitement building, the ABC and NBC television networks announced plans to show the fight. At the weigh-in, Zale's legal representative Sol Gold said to New York officials that he was very concerned at Graziano's illegal tactics, such as holding opponents by the throat and clubbing them in the ribs, kidneys and back.

'I think the referee should sit outside the ring, like it used to be in the old bare-knuckle days in England, and let them get on with it,' he said. 'Then, if Rocky wants to play dirty, Zale can show him just what rough and dirty fighting really is.'

Gold went on to cite three incidents in which he claimed that Rocky had taken the name of the Marquess of Queensberry, who had drawn up the first set of rules in 1867, in vain. 'Firstly,' said Gold, 'Rocky grabbed Freddie "Red" Cochrane, who was world welterweight champion at the time, by the throat and was choking him with the left hand while hitting him with his right. Secondly, after knocking down Al "Bummy" Davis with a punch well below the belt, he then hit Davis while he was on the floor. Thirdly, after knocking down Marty Servo, he stood over him the way Jack Dempsey used to hover over opponents and hit the welterweight champion as soon as his gloves left the canvas.

'There has not been a fight in which Graziano has not broken one or more of the rules,' he said. 'I don't think it is good enough in this age of modern boxing to allow such fouls to go unheeded and I expect something to be done about it.'

Alas, Gold's views, as well founded as they were, fell on deaf ears. The fans wanted action, and it did not matter how they got it, or in what form. A crowd of 39,827 filed past the turnstiles and produced the largest gate in history up to then for a world middleweight championship fight, a total of $342,497. It was also the second largest amount ever taken in for a non-heavyweight battle, exceeded only by Benny Leonard's successful defence of his world lightweight title against Lew Tendler at the Yankee Stadium in the summer of 1923. That one took in over $450,000 in receipts. Was it any wonder that the Zale–Graziano promoter Mike Jacobs was in happy mood?

The day before the fight, Zale's co-manager Art Winch told reporters that his boxer would have no trouble knocking out Graziano. 'Tony loves boxers who move in on him,' Winch said. 'Graziano's style is made for Zale. First, he'll wear him down with body punches, then he'll finish him off to the head.'

Winch's prediction almost came true shortly after referee Ruby Goldstein had called the two men together for the usual pre-fight instructions just before the bell. Less than a minute into the fight, Zale connected with one of his pet punches, a left hook. The blow caught Rocky on the chin and he went down. Bert Sugar recalled the dramatic moment in his book *The Great Fights*: 'The punch had Rocky rolling around on the floor, groping on the ropes, desperately trying to pull himself upright. The crowd was frantic. The short-end bettors jumped up and down on their chairs and threw their hats into the air. But Graziano was up at the count of four, menacing Zale with his vaunted right. At the bell, it was Rocky on the attack as Zale tasted some of the firepower he would expect in round two.'

The action was just as furious in the second round, with both men connecting with their heaviest blows. Graziano was piling on the pressure now, charging in and firing lefts and rights. Some missed the target but those that did connect were solid. There was a smear of blood coming from Zale's lip cut. Zale was fighting back but there was no stopping this human battering ram.

Rocky connected with several strong rights to the head and Zale responded with a jarring left hook to the body. It was stirring stuff. Rocky landed four successive rights and Zale went down. Rocky said later that he did not think Tony would get up and that he was just seconds away from the title. Goldstein reached a count of three as the bell rang and Zale's seconds rushed over to their man and, in the words of boxing historian and author Bert Sugar, 'literally dragged him to the corner'. The interval was now vital. They had just 60 seconds to prepare Zale for round three.

There was an additional problem, too. Tony complained of a throbbing sensation in his right hand. 'I must have busted something,' he muttered to Winch. To try and ease the pain, Winch put pressure on various parts of the hand, and when he dug his finger into the base of his man's right hand, Tony winced with pain. 'The thumb is broken, so you'll have to use your left as much as possible,' said Winch. Zale nodded.

Over in Graziano's corner, his trainer Whitey Bimstein urged his man to go for Zale's head. 'If you keep going for the head, you'll finish him. But watch out for that left hook. It's a dangerous weapon, his best punch.'

It was all Graziano in the third, and ringside reporters were agreeing that it was not looking good for Zale. His prized title seemed to be slipping away unless he could come up with something special, something out of the past, like a smashing left hook, to send this cocky Brooklyn slugger into dreamland. But so far, no luck. Graziano was belting the champion with long left hooks and looping uppercuts. Left, right, left, right from the challenger, and Zale was now bleeding badly from the mouth.

Rocky had an unassailable lead going into round four, but it was in this round that Tony seemed to find a new lease of life. He caught Graziano with a stinging right to the head and another heavy right to the midsection that drove Rocky back to the ropes. Both were looking tired by now, with the championship fight still in its infancy. In the fifth, Graziano connected with a solid right and Zale was swaying from side to side 'and looked as if he was going to go out', wrote Tony's biographers Clay Moyle and Thad

Zale, a nephew of the former champion, in *Tony Zale, The Man of Steel*.

Nat Fleischer of *Ring* magazine, who also acted as timekeeper for the fight, remarked to a ringside colleague at the end of round five: 'Too bad. It'll be all over in the next round. Zale can't stand that type of punishment much longer. He even went to the wrong corner that time.' Damon Runyon, writing for the *New York American*, scribbled a note to a companion: 'It's no bet. Zale's legs have gone. It's almost all over.'

When Zale got back to his corner at the end of the fifth round, his trainer Ray Arcel worked feverishly on him – and he had a lot of work to do. Tony had a badly bleeding lip, red welts over both eyes, a buzzing head and a chipped bone in his right thumb. Arcel said to him: 'Tony, don't let this guy take your title. This is your last chance. Hit this guy with your best punch. Just load one up and take your chance.'

Wit the crowd still on their feet for the sixth round, anticipation was running high. Rocky came out confidently, convinced that the title was his. Two smashing rights sunk into Zale's body and Rocky stood back to survey the damage. This was the golden moment Zale had been waiting for – and it was now or never. A smashing right to the body, thrown in desperation more than anything else, practically froze Graziano in his tracks. Quick as a flash, Zale followed through, the mark of a true champion, with a powerful left hook to the jaw with all his weight behind it and Rocky sank to the boards.

By the time Graziano realised he was on the floor, the count had reached eight. He reached for the top rope with his left hand and somehow managed to haul himself upright, but it was too late as the count had already reached ten. Graziano had been knocked out for the first time in his career, and he didn't like it one bit. When he struggled to his feet, he tried to break away from referee Goldstein and get at Zale. Police were immediately in the ring and pulling Rocky away, pushing him to his corner. 'The punch knocked the wind out of me,' he said to his cornermen. 'It straightened me up, tightened me all over, so it even clogged up my ears. I didn't hear the count until it reached eight, then nine, then out. It all came so fast. I'm sorry, boys.'

There were many at ringside who felt that Graziano was the victim of a short count. But that was not the case. Nat Fleischer, the timekeeper, said: 'I had two watches on the fight and they showed ten and three-tenth seconds, so Rocky lost by a fraction of a second. Tony himself was saved at the end of the second round when the bell rang early in the referee's count. He could scarcely get to his feet when aided by his seconds yet he showed amazing recuperative powers when he came out for the third round and stood up under withering punishment.'

Referee Goldstein recalled: 'There were no complaints from Rocky or his manager Irving Cohen that he had been given a short count. But since he had got up within a split second after the full count, there was, apparently, some bewilderment on the part of the spectators well back from the ring, who thought he may have beaten the count. Later that night, chatting to the boxing writer Lewis Burton, he told me that next time something like that happened, to give them a sign so that even the fans in the bleachers will know exactly what happened.'

In the dressing room, Zale looked more like a loser than a winner, with his cut and bruised face and a glaze in his eyes. He let his co-manager Art Winch do all the talking for him. 'Nobody would believe me when I said all along that Tony would retain his title and here he is, still middleweight champion of the world,' he said. 'He'll give Rocky a chance to regain it if that's what Rocky wants – and I'm sure he does.'

Over in Graziano's dressing room, the defeated challenger offered no excuses, saying the better man won. But 27 years later, he told writer Peter Heller: 'I was a wise guy going into that fight. I wasn't training that well. I thought I had a right hand that could knock anybody out but I didn't know how tough he was. He finally gave me a couple of good shots in the stomach and I started weakening and I lost.'

Radio sportscaster Don Dunphy, who later moved to television, recalled that the fight produced 'the greatest display of fistic fireworks I have ever seen. By the fifth round, Rocky was wearing his man down and I had the feeling that the sixth round would be the last. It was, but not the way I expected. Graziano was pounding Zale and it seemed that Tony would soon be knocked out. Then it happened.

'Eager to end it with a series of head shots, Rocky left his midsection unprotected. Zale saw the opening and landed a solar plexus punch that not only floored Rocky but paralysed him momentarily. Rocky was on the canvas, gasping for breath. He wasn't out and he knew what was going on, but he couldn't move. He was counted out and Tony Zale was still middleweight champion of the world.'

Gene Tunney, the former world heavyweight champion, said Zale's comeback from what looked like a certain defeat was 'the greatest exhibition of heart I have ever seen. Not only that, it was one of the best fights I've ever seen'.

A return fight between these two great warriors was inevitable. They met again, ten months later, on 16 July 1947. The venue was the Chicago Stadium and a crowd of 18,547 paid $422,918, a new record for an indoor boxing show that would last for 14 years. The magic figure was finally broken when Floyd Patterson knocked out Ingemar Johansson in six rounds at the Miami Beach Convention Hall on 13 March 1961, when receipts reached $485,000.

On an evening when the barometer reached 105 degrees, Zale immediately took the fight to Graziano, punishing him with a steady barrage of body punches and closing his left eye by the end of round one.

Zale was in trouble himself in the second round when, following a strong attack from the challenger, he went to the wrong corner. Tony split Graziano's right eye in the third and put him on the canvas for a no-count with a right to the head.

Zale looked like he had a lead going into the sixth round when Graziano connected with two rights to the jaw that sent Tony reeling across the ring. Rocky immediately followed up and sent Zale down for three. When he got to his feet, Graziano swarmed in and, draping Zale over the middle strand of the ropes, pounded the champion at will before referee Johnny Behr moved in and stopped the fight. The time was 2:10 of round six. Rocky Graziano, the kid from the slums of Brooklyn, was middleweight champion of the world.

Eleven months later, they were back in the ring for the rubber match. They clashed at Ruppert Stadium in Newark, New Jersey on 10 June 1948 before a crowd of 20,255, who paid a gross of $306,100 to witness what was the final act of the trilogy and the only one to be filmed. Graziano climbed into the ring as a prohibitive 12/5 favourite, but it was all Zale from the outset. With less than a minute gone in the first round, Rocky was on the canvas for a count of three from a fast left-right combination.

Zale dominated the second round except for a brief flurry from the champion, but Tony stormed back in the third and dropped his man for the second time. Using the ropes as a crutch, Graziano pulled himself up and, reeling and groggy, tried to fight back but was caught with a solid right to the ribs and a hard left hook to the jaw which stretched him out on his back, where he was counted out by referee Paul Cavalier. The time was 1:08 of the third round.

With his great victory, Zale became the first man to regain the middleweight championship of the world since Stanley Ketchel won back his title by knocking out Billy Papke in the 11th round of their fight in San Francisco on 26 November 1908. In many ways, Zale's win was even more significant as he was 34 years of age. Ketchel was a mere 22 when he beat Papke.

Neither Zale nor Graziano were ever as good again. Zale lost his title when he was beaten by the French-Moroccan, Marcel Cerdan, at Jersey City on 21 September 1948. He announced his retirement after the fight with a 67-18-2 record and settled down in his old hometown of Gary, where he was a respected member of the community. Zale was also a member of his local church and was involved in the Polish Boys' Club. He maintained his interest in the sport that made him famous and was often introduced at big fights. He died on 21 March 1997, two months short of his 84th birthday.

After the third fight with Zale, Graziano continued for another four years and had some impressive performances, including knockout wins over Charlie Fusari in ten rounds, Henry Brimm in four, Cecil Hudson in three and Tony Janiro in ten. Rocky got a world middleweight title fight with Sugar Ray Robinson in April 1952. He managed to knock down the Sugar Man in the third round but Robinson got straight up and knocked Rocky out before the round was finished. After losing his next fight, against the promising Chuck Davey on a decision over ten rounds, he hung up his gloves.

During his retirement, Graziano wrote a successful autobiography *Somebody Up There Likes Me,* which became a hit movie in 1956 starring Paul Newman. He also had a lengthy and successful career as a TV actor. Rocky died on 22 May 1990, aged 68. His record read 67-10-6.

Chapter 10

From triumph to tragedy

Randolph Turpin v Carl Bobo Olson, Madison Square Garden, 21 October 1953

ONE of the strangest scenarios for a fight in the history of the 160lb weight class dating back to 1886 came when 'Nonpareil' Jack Dempsey, not to be confused with the later heavyweight champion, faced Jack Fogarty in the first generally accepted middleweight championship bout. In an age of illegal prize-fighting, the Dempsey–Fogarty fight was staged at the Clarendon Hall on 13th Street in New York, supposedly away from the eyes of the police, and Dempsey, an Irishman from Co Kildare, won on a knockout in 27 rounds.

Now, 67 years later in the same city, Randolph Turpin was in town to challenge the Hawaiian Carl Bobo Olson for the vacant world middleweight championship that Sugar Ray Robinson had relinquished almost a year earlier to pursue a new career as a dancer. The venue was Madison Square Garden.

Turpin, from Leamington Spa in Warwickshire, England, was a very troubled man going into the fight. There were allegations of rape and assault hanging over him and he was missing training days, often refusing to meet boxing writers who turned up at his camp in the Catskills in Upper New York State only to find 'No

Admittance' signs at the gate. There were also stories that he was homesick, and reports that he was at loggerheads with his manager George Middleton and his brother Dick, who had travelled with him as trainer.

In a dispatch to the *Daily Mirror*, Peter Wilson reported: 'I am beginning to wonder if Turpin is 100 per cent fit. Physically, I believe he is as rugged as he's always been but in all my years of following the fights I have never come across a boxer in a mental condition like Turpin's.'

George Whiting of the *Evening Standard* said he was handed a letter by Turpin in which Randolph said he was going to quit boxing after the fight, win, lose or draw – hardly the right frame of mind for a world title fight.

Certainly Turpin had begun his career in highly impressive fashion, winning his first 15 fights, six by straight knockout, five on stoppage and four on points. Boxing writers predicted a bright future for the former sailor born on 7 June 1928, weighing in at 9lbs 7ozs.

The boy's mother, Beatrice Whitehouse, was white, a local woman whose father Tommy had been a bare-knuckle fighter. Turpin's father Lionel came from British Guyana. Three months after Randolph's birth, Lionel died from ill health as a result of being gassed in the Somme in the First World War, having never fully recovered from his experiences in the trenches.

Beatrice now had five children, including three boys, and she was forced to scrub floors and doorsteps to bring them up as best she could. She often had help from her mother and an aunt. Clothes for her children came from the stalls in the local market and a substantial meal was the rule rather than the exception. Discrimination was also rife in Britain at the time and she had to face jibes, sneers and insults about 'a n***** marrying a white girl'. But she was tough and many a neighbour felt the power of her fists whenever remarks were made about her. Turpin would later say that the three boys got their fighting spirit from their mother, who could exchange punches with any man. Adding to her problems was the fact she was half blind.

When he was three years old Randolph contracted double pneumonia, from which he nearly died. Around this time, too, his mother got married again, this time to a friend named Ernest Manley, a local white man. Meanwhile, Turpin, the youngest of the three boys, was doing well at West Gate Council School, both academically and at sports. He soon developed into an all-round athlete and was particularly good at swimming.

One evening after school hours, he was swimming in a nearby river when he was trapped underwater by some weeds. He managed to wrench himself free but he was held underwater for so long that he suffered a damaged eardrum. This made him partially deaf for the rest of his life and made it difficult for him to mix freely. Many, including sportswriters, would often accuse him of being anti-social, not realising his hearing problem.

It was Randolph's elder brother Dick who introduced him to boxing. Dick remembered: 'Grandad used to say that a boy would never get anywhere unless he could use his fists, so he'd better learn to fight his own battles. It was good advice and I never forgot it. I joined the boxing section of a newly formed Leamington Boys' Club and met a boxing man there named George Middleton, a local greengrocer, and picked up a few tips about the game. I had about seven contests, winning five, and George persuaded me to turn professional and get some money in my pocket. I turned to the pro game with George as my manager.'

Randolph and his other brother Jackie joined the club, the boxing section of which was run by John 'Gerry' Gibbs, a police inspector who soon saw the potential in the boy. Randolph began to box competitively at 12 and by 1943, at the age of 15, he was the British junior 112lbs champion. A year later, he won the 133lbs title and the following year, 1945, he won the British ABA welterweight championship at 147lbs.

Winning 95 of his 100 amateur contests, Randolph was encouraged by the success of Dick as a professional. The elder Turpin would go on to become the first black boxer to become a champion of Britain under British Boxing Board of Control rules and also win the Empire title, now Commonwealth. Dick was a cool, classy and scientific boxer with a good defence but faced criticism for being a little too cautious and careful. Jackie, who boxed at featherweight, had a reasonably successful career without reaching championship standard. It was Randolph who scaled the dizzy heights.

Boxing people were beginning to take notice of the hard-hitting Randolph Turpin, who had acquired the nickname 'Leamington Licker' even as an amateur. He turned to the paid ranks under manager George Middleton on 17 September 1946 with an impressive win after two minutes of the first round against Gordon Griffiths at Harringay Arena, London. The fight was one of the supporting bouts to the heavyweight headliner between British heavyweight champion Bruce Woodcock of Doncaster and the American Gus Lesnevich, the reigning world light-heavyweight champion. Woodcock won on a knockout in eight rounds.

'The way Turpin leapt on Griffiths was like a bronze tiger devouring a tethered kid,' wrote Peter Wilson, then with the *Daily Express*, 'battering him halfway through the ropes until the referee intervened in the first round. It was enough to prove that a new middleweight menace had already arrived.'

In his first 12 months Turpin had 15 bouts, all wins, before being held to a draw over eight rounds by the experienced Mark Hart, who he had previously outpointed, in London at the end of 1947. He had a less successful 1948, winning four but being outpointed by the cagey Albert Finch and retiring in five rounds against Jean Stock, a tough Frenchman who had been around the block. Stock floored Turpin four times. Learning from his defeats, Randolph would not be in the loser's corner for the next three years and 22 fights.

Nevertheless, Turpin had serious domestic problems on his mind. Following a row with Mary Stack, his childhood sweetheart from Leamington, he took a drug overdose and threatened suicide. They patched things up and eventually married. But within a year of the marriage, they separated after she accused her husband of assault. In court, she claimed he kicked her in the stomach while she was pregnant and hit her with a broomstick. Turpin strenuously denied the charges and the case was dismissed, though he did admit he 'slapped her around a bit'.

Turpin would later be seen around Leamington and neighbouring areas with different women and he was gaining a reputation as a ladies' man. His manager George Middleton warned him on one occasion: 'I can't get involved in your private life but as far as your boxing career is concerned, I can. You've got to dedicate your life to boxing. You have the talent to become champion of the world. A boxer's life at the top is short. Don't waste it.'

Turpin was philosophical about the situation. 'Don't worry, George,' he said. 'I'll be OK. I still train hard despite outside matters. I'll be fine.' Yet, as events turned out, it would be women who helped bring about his ultimate downfall.

In a return fight with Albert Finch on 17 October 1950, which was a particularly good year for him, Turpin avenged his first defeat by knocking out the Surrey boxer, now the British middleweight champion, in five rounds at Harringay Arena in London. A smashing left hook, with Turpin's full power behind it, ended Finch's interest in the fight. Turpin was really on the way now.

Less than a month later, Turpin knocked out the Spaniard Jose Alamo in two rounds in Wales and followed it up with an impressive eight-round win at Harringay over the classy American Tommy Yarosz, who was disqualified for persistent holding. 'Giving a fine exhibition of class box-fighting, Turpin was well on the way to gaining a decisive victory up to the disqualification,' reported *Boxing News*. 'Brimful of confidence and energy, Turpin tore into his man as soon as the opening bell sounded and was determined not to let his man get his machine-like boxing working.' The headline read: 'Turpin's best to date.'

Nat Fleischer, publisher of *Ring* magazine, thought so highly of the Warwickshire fighter that he had him as No 4 contender for Jake La Motta's world middleweight title. Things were certainly looking good for the one-time amateur star. Two fights later, on 27 February 1951, Turpin won the European middleweight title by knocking out the experienced Dutchman Luc Van Damn in just 48 seconds. A powerful right hand to the chin did the trick. Straight away, the enterprising London promoter Jack Solomons started negotiations for Turpin to face Sugar Ray Robinson for the world middleweight title, which the classy American had won from Jake La Motta 13 days earlier in Chicago.

Turpin continued his impressive form with four wins, all inside the distance, including a stoppage in five over Jean Stock, the Frenchman who had beaten him nearly three years earlier. The 'Leamington Licker' had now avenged his only two previous defeats and announced he was ready to bring the world 160lbs title back to Britain for the first time since the freckle-faced Cornishman Bob Fitzsimmons held it back in the late 1890s.

The Robinson–Turpin bout was held at the Earls Court Arena, London before a capacity crowd of 18,200 on 10 July 1951. It was Britain's biggest fight of the post-war years and the two boxers' arrival in London for the weigh-in at Solomons' gym in the West End caused traffic jams. By fight night the odds were 6/1 against Turpin, but in one of the biggest boxing upsets of the 20th century the Englishman outboxed and outpunched the champion to win a decision after 15 rounds. There were claims that Robinson was already tired when he climbed into the ring that night, having come straight from a successful six-fight continental tour. As Harry Carpenter, the future BBC commentator, later wrote in the *Sporting Record*: 'Robinson did most of his training on a soft mattress for the Turpin fight.' Be that as it may, Turpin was in superb form that famous sweltering summer night in 1951.

Besides Robinson, the real losers that night were the millions of radio listeners who tuned into the BBC Light Programme. Unfortunately, the two commentators, Raymond Glendenning and W Barrington Dalby, saw the fight differently from anybody else. Such was the power of Robinson's reputation that they began describing what they expected to see rather than what was actually happening. Glendenning gave the impression that the wily Robinson had matters in hand while Dalby suggested that Turpin was putting up a creditable show but that Sugar Ray's class would tell in the end. Listeners who half suspected that Turpin had been given a hometown decision were surprised to read in the papers the next day that Turpin had won easily.

Under contract for a return fight, this time set for New York, Robinson and Turpin faced each other again on 12 September at the Polo Grounds in New York. This time, a fitter Robinson regained the title on a stoppage in the tenth round before a crowd of 61,370 paying $767,630, a record up to then for a fight outside the heavyweight division. Referee Ruby Goldstein and the two judges had Sugar Ray marginally ahead after nine rounds when, in the tenth, Robinson emerged from a clinch with blood streaming down his face from a cut left eyebrow, apparently caused by a clash of heads.

This was a signal for an enraged Robinson to finish off Turpin as soon as possible. Having preserved his energy for a 15-rounder, the American launched an attack with every legitimate punch in the book. Turpin was dropped for a count of seven and, on rising on shaky legs, was driven with his back to the ropes as punches rained in from all angles. He was about to slump forward when Goldstein moved in and called it off. 'When Goldstein grabbed

Turpin in his arms,' wrote A J Liebling of *The New Yorker* in his brilliant book *The Sweet Science*, 'I thought I'd never seen a man so game or so beaten.' Turpin had been champion for only 64 days.

There was further trouble ahead in Turpin's private life. Before leaving for England, he was arrested for the alleged rape and assault of 24-year-old Adele Daniels, an Afro-American, in New York, a charge he strenuously denied. In court, Ms Daniels, who was suing for $100,000, said Turpin was 'a charming Englishman and he told me I was everything he longed for'. But one night back at her apartment, she claimed he put a pillow over her head and raped her. On the fifth day of the trial, before Turpin could be called to the stand, Daniels and her lawyer Ronald Sala accepted $3,500 in settlement, though Sala claimed they should have gotten 20 times as much. Turpin, through his lawyer Sol Strauss, also had to pay costs, which were considerable.

Turpin took a break of five months before resuming his career and won the British and Empire light-heavyweight titles, the Empire middleweight championship and the European title at the same weight. By now, Turpin's private life was starting to come apart. He invested heavily in a 29-bedroom hotel standing in 15 acres in Wales, but it flopped and Turpin lost around £7,000, triggering bouts of depression. To make matters worse, he was cited in a divorce case by a policeman who claimed the boxer raped his wife on a train.

To nobody's great surprise, Turpin's second marriage finally crumbled when his wife Mary Stack was granted a divorce over allegations of adultery, particularly after she discovered he was already hanging around with a young Welsh girl, Gwen Price, a farmer's daughter, and that they had planned to marry. Turpin had first met her when she asked him for an autograph at a training session and they dated soon afterwards, even though Gwen knew that her lover was a married man at the time.

On 18 December 1952, Robinson gave up his world middleweight championship title to embark on a showbusiness career as a dancer. Europe's number one would now meet America's best for the vacant title, and the two main men were Randolph Turpin and Carl Bobo Olson.

Olson was born in Honolulu on 11 July 1928 to a Portuguese mother and a Swedish father. Olson senior would immigrate to the US and settle in Oklahoma. At the outbreak of the First World

War, he was stationed in Hawaii, where he would meet his future wife and raise a family. Carl remembered the Japanese attack on Pearl Harbor in December 1941. 'I was 13 at the time and I remember coming out of the house and hearing those bombs going off,' he told Peter Heller for his book *In This Corner*. 'My mother thought it was the real thing but my father said no, they were just practising. Finally, she turned on the radio and discovered that we were being attacked. We were living on a mountainside and we could see all those ships burning in the water.'

Olson's parents split up some time later and Carl was brought up by his mother. By the time he was 15, Olson had found work on a dairy farm, where he did all kinds of jobs. 'Anything that needed to be done on the farm, I was the lad they called on,' he would remember in later years. 'Jobs were not all that plentiful in Honolulu but farm work was usually available. It was tough work but I enjoyed it. I think the toughness stood me well in my boxing career later on.'

Some of his pals would while away their infrequent leisure hours by sparring with others at the local gym. They encouraged the young Bobo to join them and he spent most of his free time whaling away at the heavy bag and doing his best to hit the speedball. One day, a sailor with too much to drink came into the gym and asked Bobo why he was not doing army service. Bobo said he was too young but his tormentor ignored that comment and started pushing the youngster around. Suddenly Bobo lashed out with his right and knocked the bully off his feet. He never bothered the kid again.

Olson returned to the gym as often as possible. One day, while working out on the heavy bag, Sid Flaherty was there. Flaherty was a boxing manager back in the US and he was serving in Honolulu as an army sergeant. His job was to put on boxing tournaments. He liked the look of the teenager and was impressed by his enthusiasm. Afterwards, they got talking and Flaherty recommended that the youngster should take boxing seriously. 'Give it a go,' he said, 'and we'll see how you get on.'

Under Flaherty's tuition, Olson participated in some amateur bouts and bootleg fights, and picked up valuable tips from American boxers, amateur and professional, who were stationed in Hawaii. With some impressive wins, Olson was anxious to go it alone and turn professional, even though he was only 16, legally under the age to obtain a licence. To make himself look older, he had two tattoos put on his arm, 'Mother' on one arm and a dragon on the other. Lying about his age and using a fake ID card he had four paid fights, all wins, before the Hawaiian Commission was tipped off and withdrew his licence. Discouraged by the sudden halt in his boxing ambitions, even though only temporary, Olson made up his mind to leave the island and head for San Francisco, a thriving fight town.

His career really took off there and he had ten fights, all victories, before the Californian State Athletic Commission discovered that he was not yet 18, the minimum age for a professional in the state. His licence withdrawn for the second time, he returned to Hawaii to contemplate his ring future, vowing never to return to the US again. With Sid Flaherty having returned to the US with his Hawaiian service completed, Olson joined up with local manager Herbert Campos and with an official licence spent the next four years competing in rings in Honolulu, Manila and Australia. He amassed a very impressive record against all-comers, including wins over the likes of Tommy Yarosz, Anton Raadik, Earl Turner, Flashy Sebastian and Henry Brimm, all tough cookies.

By the close of 1950, and now under the guidance of Flaherty, who had come back into the picture, Olson's only defeats in six years, with the exception of two early points losses, were against the talented Dave Sands, the best Australian middleweight since the legendary Les Darcy in the early 1900s, and Sugar Ray Robinson, the No 1 contender for Jake La Motta's world middleweight title, both in 1950. The Sands loss was on points but against Robinson, Olson was knocked out in the 12th round with a fast combination that ended with a left hook to the body. In both fights against top opposition, Olson nevertheless put up creditable performances.

To qualify for the vacant world title, Turpin was matched with Charles Humez of France to decide Europe's number one and Olson took on Paddy Young to find America's best. Turpin and Olson emerged victorious and set the scene for the undisputed middleweight championship of the world, scheduled for Madison Square Garden on 25 August 1953.

But the fight was postponed when the promoters, the International Boxing Club, announced that Turpin was injured in a car accident and would need several weeks to recover. No further details were released but it transpired that Randolph had nearly lost his life when losing control of his speeding saloon on the way to Leamington. The car skidded and overturned after hitting several oncoming cars, creating a big pile-up. His companions in the car were his Welsh girlfriend Gwen Price and another girl. All three escaped with minor injuries but were very badly shaken.

Why full details were never released to the media remained a mystery, but Turpin's biographer Peter McInnes recalled that it was one of several bad car crashes in which Randolph was involved, though they did nothing to persuade him to drive and lead his life at a more moderate pace.

The new date for the Olson fight was 21 October at the same venue. When Turpin arrived in New York to begin preparations, boxing writers found him surly, distant and uncooperative. Peter Wilson cabled back to the *Daily Mirror* in London that Turpin was 'a very moody man who barely answered questions put to him'. Wilson was left to wonder if the boxer was serious about taking part in a world championship fight.

'I am beginning to doubt that Turpin is a 100 per cent fit man,' said Wilson. 'Physically, I believe he is as rugged as he has always been but in all my years of following the fights I have never come across a boxer in a mental state like Turpin's. When I went to his training camp in the hills of the Catskills in Upper New York State, I was told by his manager George Middleton that Turpin had boxed only 20 rounds in 16 days, hardly the right preparation for a world championship fight.'

Middleton told Wilson and other writers that Turpin had said to him that he didn't want anybody near him. On a couple of occasions, after doing seven miles of roadwork in the hills, Turpin apparently went straight into the gym to spar a few rounds without relaxing or taking time out for breakfast. It was clear that Middleton was feeling the strain of the whole situation as much as anybody else.

There was another shock when Turpin gave the British scribe George Whiting of the *Evening Standard* a letter in which he said he intended to retire after the Olson fight. 'I've had enough,' he wrote, 'and I'm ready to call it a day. I am telling you these things now so that, win lose or draw, you will know the result of this fight had nothing to do with my decision. I've done British boxing what justice I could. The Olson fight will be my last.' Hardly the right attitude for a boxer on the verge of a world championship fight.

American newspapers had a field day, with their cartoonists lampooning the Britisher at every opportunity. The *New York Post* caricatured Turpin being outpaced by a turtle, with the caption saying 'Road work'. Another cartoon showed him 'doing four rounds by reading his mail'. He was becoming the laughing stock of the boxing world.

Meanwhile, Olson was working hard for what would be his second crack at the title. Over a year and a half earlier, in a San Francisco ring, he had given Sugar Ray Robinson some uncomfortable moments before losing a decision over 15 rounds. This time, he promised he would make up for that loss by winning the championship. 'I lacked confidence going in with such a great fighter as Robinson,' he told newspapermen. 'I also lacked experience. Now things are different. I respect Turpin as a fighter, sure I do, but this is one fight I'm going to win.'

The Hawaiian set up his training quarters at Asbury Park on the Atlantic coast in New Jersey, with its miles of golden sands and gentle breezes. He did miles of roadwork in the early mornings and worked out in the gym in the afternoons. He used both middleweights and light-heavyweights as sparring partners. While writers may have questioned his skill, there was little doubt about his reserves of stamina, which would be crucial in a long fight.

When asked about his chances against Turpin, he said: 'This is a very, very important fight for me, the most crucial of my career. I know of Turpin's reputation and conquering the great Sugar Robinson in London, but I'm going all out to win this fight and keep the title in US possession. Staying power? You'll see as the fight progresses who has the staying power, and it won't be Turpin.'

Asked about reports that Turpin was skipping several training sessions, he replied: 'I don't know anything about these stories and they could be a trick to lure me in a trap. I don't really know but we'll find out on fight night as to who is the better man and rightful middleweight champion of the world. That's the important thing.'

A week before the fight, Turpin was several pounds over the 160lbs middleweight limit so he would have to get that down. By literally starving himself, he stepped on to the scales at the official weigh-in at Madison Square Garden on the afternoon of the fight and weighed 157lbs, three pounds under the limit. Dr Vincent Nardiello of the New York State Athletic Commission said he was surprised that Randolph was so light. 'He could have made 160lbs naturally,' he said. 'Taking those extra pounds off at such a late stage could well weaken him. As it is, he looks somewhat withdrawn.'

It was the lightest Turpin had scaled for nearly three years. He had weighed 159lbs against the Frenchman Charles Humez for the European title four months earlier, and for his Empire defence against South Africa's George Angelo in October 1952 he was 158lbs. Olson tipped the scales at 159lbs. Both boxers posed for photographs for a battery of American and foreign cameramen. Olson was presented with a Hawaiian garland of pink flowers by a fan and Turpin was handed a red leather-bound album signed by 2,000 members of the Cunard White Star Line which brought the Brits across the Atlantic on the *Queen Mary*.

The most disappointed men in town were the crew of the liner who had hoped to be at the fight cheering Randolph on, only to find that the ship was sailing just six hours before the bout was due to start. In those days, before television, they would have to be content with picking up a five-minute broadcast of the action on the BBC Home Service at 7.10am the following day and repeated an hour later.

A capacity crowd of 18,862 filed into Madison Square Garden on fight night, with Olson favoured at 11/5 to repel the challenge of the Warwickshire warrior. Their records were not too dissimilar: Olson was 53-5-0 and Turpin 49-3-1. There were the usual introductions of ex-champions and a few reigning title-holders followed by the formal announcements and the final instructions by referee Al Berle. Then the bell clanged and the two combatants were on their way. It was make or break time.

Turpin started off with complete annihilation on his mind, driving Olson back under a hail of leather. The American looked like a novice, staggering and holding on tightly as referee Berle ordered 'break'. One punch, a smashing left hook to the jaw, jarred Olson, who held on to clear his head. George Whiting of the *Evening Standard* turned to his ringside companion Joseph C Nichols of the *New York Times* and said: 'This will be over soon, Joseph.' Nichols replied: 'Don't be too sure, George. It's early yet. Our boy has lots of stamina. He'll keep going.'

It was much the same in the second and third rounds, with Turpin on the attack and Olson in the firing line. Olson was having trouble solving Turpin's unorthodox style, which saw him throw looping punches often with his feet well apart and his head held high. It was the same style that baffled Robinson in their first fight.

By the fourth round, Olson was beginning to come into the fight. Though most of his punches were mere cuffs, he was connecting and he was beginning to get under Turpin's long left jabs and slam away to the body. Olson was now taking some liberties with renewed confidence, concentrating on left hooks to the head and midriff. Turpin emerged from a clinch with a slight cut under his right eye that seemed to bother him.

By the fifth, the Englishman was beginning to slow down and was not showing the fire of earlier, particularly in that first round. His injured eye did not trouble him, thanks to good corner work, but it was clear that Olson was now forcing the pace, trapping Turpin in the corner and whaling away with lefts and rights.

'It made us wonder if Randolph had the strength and stamina to keep Olson at bay,' reported *Boxing News*. 'No matter what Turpin did, the nimble Bobo was able to get to grips, driving his man to the ropes and then plastering him from all angles. We also saw the strange spectacle of Turpin claiming his rival rather than pushing him off and making him stand off and box. Turpin hadn't a clue in this direction. He poked a feeble left at the Hawaiian, or slung over a right that missed more often than it landed. There was no confident Turpin going forward with a planned and determined attack.'

By the seventh, Olson had a good points lead. He was continually pressing Turpin and while his punches lacked real power, the consistency of his attacks was beginning to wear the Britisher out. With little expression on his face, he simply banged away at every opportunity, often missing but landing enough to make the difference. The eighth was a good one for Turpin. He caught the American with a long right to the jaw and caused his legs to wobble like jelly on a plate, but again Olson weathered the storm and punched back or held on until the bell.

The real turning point, the moment of truth, came in the ninth. Olson, clearly the better conditioned of the two, dropped Turpin with a solid right to the body. He went down on his knees, then on all fours. A second later, the bell sounded but Berle either did not hear it or simply ignored it and counted to five before Turpin, looking dazed, got up off his knees and walked to his corner. Would he have made it had the bell not sounded?

In the tenth, Turpin tried to get Olson with a long right but missed and the Hawaiian was soon back on the attack, culminating in a burst of punches to head and body that sent the 'Leamington Licker' to the canvas for the second time. He was a little late getting to his knees but was up at nine and managed to keep out of trouble for the rest of the round. But at this stage it seemed that courage, and courage alone, was holding him up.

It was much the same in the 11th, with the grimly determined Olson on the attack and Turpin spending most his time lying back on the ropes or covering up, all the time doing his best to avoid the bombardment of leather. Randolph raised British hopes in the 12th when he fought off the Hawaiian with some good shots to the head. It was short-lived, though, and a long, hard right to the chin from Olson caused Turpin's knees to bend. But he straightened up soon after. It was noticeable that whenever Randolph did score, particularly with body blows, the fitter Olson was able to shake them off and come back stronger.

The Hawaiian took the 13th and 14th on aggression alone and Turpin looked tired and old as he absorbed a fusilade of blows from both hands. 'Observers felt that had Olson packed a heavier punch, he would most likely have knocked out the Warwickshire fighter,' noted *Boxing News*. 'Olson took our champion's best efforts unperturbed, and even when shaken made a quick recovery.'

In the 15th, Turpin had his best round since the early stages when he let loose with big punches and drove Olson back across the ring. But it was all too late. The Hawaiian was able to take everything the jaded Turpin had to offer and fire straight back. Randolph had put up a very plucky stand but gameness alone does not win world titles. He seemed relieved when the final bell rang but was sporting enough to follow Olson to the corner and shake his hand. He knew he had lost.

There was a hush as the scorecards were collected by Johnny Addie, the MC. Pulling down the microphone, he announced that judge Charlie Shortell made it 11-4 for Olson, judge Arthur Suskind had it 8-7 for Olson and referee Berle called it Olson 9-4 with two even. 'The winner and new middleweight champion of the world by a unanimous decision, Carl Bobo Olson,' he announced loud and clear as he held up the Hawaiian's right hand and the new champion wiped away tears with his other hand. Turpin lowered his head, his chances at an end of being champion of the world again.

Back in the dressing room, the Britisher had his injured left eye attended to by Dr Vicente Nardiello of the New York State Athletic Commission. 'If I'd been in the right physical and mental condition I would have stopped him in eight rounds,' he said. 'He's not in the same class as Sugar Ray Robinson. When Olson dropped me, I was dazed but not hurt. Yes, of course I'd fight him again. I'd fight anyone, even Rocky Marciano, the world heavyweight champion. Why was I caught by so many punches? Well, you can't go out in the rain and expect to dodge all the drops, can you?'

Olson said he always felt he could beat Turpin and now his dream had come true by winning the world title. He said the only punch he really felt was a left hook in the fourth round. Asked if he would give Turpin a return fight, he said: 'I don't think there would be a big demand for us to meet again after this result.'

Seventeen years later, he told Pete Heller, the writer and author of his book *In This Corner*: 'Turpin was such an awkward fighter that I kept on the outside at the outset and while he threw some terrific punches, I was in terrific shape. Later on, my trainer said I had better get inside because I was being hit with long right hands and left hooks. He was a long-range fighter and that's how he beat Robinson the first time. So I kept punching inside. In the last rounds I saw he was so tired and I kept on throwing punches.'

Press coverage of the fight showed that Olson had won well. 'Turpin was a disappointment,' said *Boxing News*. 'For the first three rounds we, in the English section of pressmen, were filled with hope and made to think that all our fears had been unnecessary and that Randy knew what he was doing. But after that our hearts sank lower and lower as, round by round, Turpin put up a pathetically futile display against a fast-punching fighter who crowded him against the ropes and overwhelmed him with a persistent battery of light blows. All the misgivings about Turpin's approach to this, the most important fight of his career, were justified. Turpin was not just the man he should have been. No fighter could possibly deteriorate to such an extent unless he was mentally unequipped for the job.'

Nat Fleischer of *Ring* magazine said: 'As I saw it, Olson took nine rounds, Turpin five and one even. Olson won because he was in prime physical condition, took the Briton's strong wallops in the first three rounds without flinching and came back with his own two-fisted attack in the remainder of the fight to turn the tide and clinch victory by a wide margin. As for Turpin, he said he was beaten by a mental hazard. He blamed his failure on personal affairs that kept him worried. But that's no excuse. He knew what he was in for. He realised his responsibility to himself, the British public and the people who enabled him to take home a huge payday envelope. He was beaten fairly, decisively.'

Peter Wilson in the *Daily Mirror* wrote: 'It was easy to summarise this fight and explain Turpin's failure. His courage was not enough. Olson's stamina was too much. Slapping, cuffing, laying on and wrestling, plus the single-minded will to win, overcame the science of boxing.'

Boxing and Wrestling magazine reported: 'On tricky manoeuvres and ring generalship, Turpin was vastly superior to his rugged and sometimes crude opponent but it was not getting results. Bobo was far from discouraged by his missing but increased the volume of attack while Randy was content to flash occasional rallies. In the closing rounds Turpin was mighty tired and it seemed as if his legs would collapse under him, but through superhuman effort he called upon every ounce of strength at his command to turn the tide. It was a hopeless gesture.'

Joseph Nicholls of the *New York Times* said: 'Olson's stamina was the deciding factor. Moving along inexorably after spotting his rival the first five rounds, Olson scored two knockdowns in gaining the unanimous decision. Turpin was hardly the performer he was two years ago in the Robinson fights. There were some fans who thought he could pull off the victory with one punch but it was not to be. Seasoned gladiator that he was, Turpin was woefully inadequate with his back against the ropes, and it was by forcing the Englishman to the strands that Olson was able to do his greatest damage.'

Turpin took a break of five months before returning to the ring to resume what would become an erratic and hugely disappointing finish to his career. After outpointing the moderate Swede Olle Bengtsson at Earls Court Arena in London, he went to Italy to defend his European title against Tiberio Mitri and was stopped in 65 seconds. His subsequent career had its ups and downs and he finally called it a day after being counted out in the second round of his fight with Yolande Pompey of Trinidad in Birmingham on 9 September 1958. It was all over for the man who was once king of the world's middleweights.

Turpin turned to professional wrestling, a last resort, to keep him off the breadline but early in 1962 he was hit by a £17,126 bill from the Inland Revenue for back taxes. He made occasional personal appearances at boxing tournaments to earn money but it was never enough. Later that year, a seven-page article appeared in *Boxing Illustrated* in which he claimed he was sucked dry by 'the greedy tappers, the phony pals, the loud-mouth slobs and worst of all, the legal pickpockets. I'm broke, I'm bitter and I've been bled to bankruptcy.'

Under the heading, 'Hate In My Heart', Turpin said: 'The records said I was paid $180,000 for the second Robinson fight. I got no more than $75,000. I don't remember even seeing a contract for that fight. Sure, I spent a lot during my career – cars, houses, a hotel but even so, that could not account for the fantastic spending fees recorded in my bank statements. Broke as I am, though, I wouldn't sell my Lonsdale Belt. I've given it and all my other trophies to my wife Gwen.'

Turpin's manager George Middleton, who always claimed he looked after Randolph's money properly and supplied him with full receipts, gave him a job in his scrapyard. The ex-champion rented a small roadside cafe over which he lived with his wife and four daughters. However, in 1964, a compulsory purchase order was served on the cafe, which the local council said was to be converted into a car park.

With tax demands still coming in, it was all too much. On the morning of 17 May 1966, Turpin took his 17-month old daughter up to his bedroom, shot her and then shot himself. The child, Carmen, survived. Randolph was three weeks short of his 38th birthday.

Olson, meanwhile, retained his world title with three successful defences in 1954 before coming up against his old foe Sugar Ray Robinson in Chicago shortly before Christmas 1955. Robinson had abandoned his dancing career by now and was on the comeback trail, culminating in a two-round knockout of Olson to win the title for the third time.

Around this time, Bobo's private life came under intense scrutiny when *Confidential,* the scandal magazine, revealed that he had two wives, Helen and Jane, and ten children between them. Both women knew about the situation and naturally were not happy with it. Helen sued for divorce, delivering a severe financial blow to Olson, though it allowed him to marry Jane. In later years, he would marry for a third time. Olson retired in November 1966 and did recreational and public relations work for labour unions. He later suffered from Alzheimer's disease and died in his native Honolulu on 16 January 2002, aged 73.

Chapter 11

Going for the impossible dream

**Rocky Marciano v Ezzard Charles,
Yankee Stadium, 17 June 1954**

THIS one had the makings of a battle royal. In one corner was
Rocky Marciano, the indestructible 'Brockton Blockbuster',
unbeaten in 45 professional fights and undisputed king of
the heavyweights. Limited in skill and decidedly lacking in height
for boxing's premier division, he made up for any deficiencies with
power-packed punches from both gloves and true grit. Directly
opposite him on the far side of the ring was Ezzard Charles,
the 'Cincinnati Cobra', a clever ring strategist and sharp hitter
determined to win back boxing's greatest prize, the heavyweight
championship of the world. Nobody had ever regained the title
after losing it, but Charles was sure he would be the first to pull
off what was regarded as the impossible dream.

One of the most underrated heavyweight champions since
the gaslight era of John L Sullivan and James J Corbett, Charles
rarely received full credit for his career achievements, certainly as
a heavyweight. Yet he beat most of the best middleweights, light-
heavyweights and heavyweights of his day. Most boxing experts
consider him the best light-heavyweight of all time even though he
was sidetracked out of a title fight in that division. *Ring* magazine
rated Charles the best light-heavyweight ever and *Boxing News*

had him at No 26 in their 100 Best Boxers of All Time list, in front of heavyweight champions such as Evander Holyfield, George Foreman, Joe Frazier, Mike Tyson, Michael Spinks, Sonny Liston and Cornwall's Bob Fitzsimmons.

In 1954, Charles was attempting to win back the heavyweight title he surprisingly lost to the veteran Jersey Joe Walcott, a 6/1 underdog, in seven rounds in Pittsburgh three years earlier. He had failed to regain it in a return with Walcott in June 1952, losing a points decision, and now he was making a second bid, this time against the formidable Marciano, who had swept all before him on the way to the title. 'The Rock' had knocked out Walcott in 13 rounds and later in one, and felt he could turn back the challenge of Charles no matter what the confident challenger threw at him. It added up to an intriguing battle – and the boxing world was ready for it.

Charles was born in a shack in Gwinnett County, Lawrenceville, Georgia on 7 July 1921 to William Charles and his wife Alberta. His father was a truck driver for a local cotton mill. The future world champion got his first name from the doctor, Webster Pierce Ezzard, who brought him into the world. Charles was known around Lawrenceville as 'Mack' or 'Snookie', nicknames whose origins are unknown. He would answer to these names on visits back home later in life. Ezzard's parents split up when the boy was five and his mother took him up north to Cincinnati, Ohio, where he was brought up by his grandmother Maude Foster and great-grandmother Belle Russell, a former slave. Alberta knew that her son would not make anything of himself in the troubled Deep South. She herself headed for New York.

Ezzard's new guardians were humble, church-going people and Charles spent his formative years in this environment, living alongside seven of Maude's own children. 'Great grandma kept after me about the Bible and grandma kept after me about praying, so I guess I had no time to go wrong,' Ezzard recalled in later years. 'It was a lovely environment and I was always grateful to them for bringing me up the way they did. Lovely people, and I couldn't say enough about them.'

Like many another youngsters at the time, including Sugar Ray Robinson, Charles was an admirer of Joe Louis and vowed that he would be a champion like Louis, never imagining that he would one day fight and beat his idol. In his backyard, Ezzard set up a homemade ring and invited local kids 'to spar around and have a bit of fun, but always mindful of grandma and great-grandma to take care of ourselves and not to get hurt,' as he remembered.

Charles' schooling in Georgia had been minimal but in Cincinnati he was enrolled in Woodward High School to continue his education. After graduation, he joined the local amateur boxing club and spent hours practising how to jab, hook, uppercut, cross, feint and move around, always remembering to protect his chin. He also used to meet well-known boxers who occasionally dropped into the gym, but mostly it was veteran fighters who hung around the place.

'They would talk about great fighters who brought great credit to the state of Ohio, like the featherweight champion Johnny Kilbane from Cleveland, the heavyweight champion James J Jeffries from Carroll and Freddie Miller, the featherweight champion from Cincinnati,' he recalled. 'I used to say I wanted to be a champion, too, like them and my idol Joe Louis and they'd say to keep working hard, learn all I could and I'd get there.'

While attending Woodward High School and after graduation, Charles became an accomplished amateur boxer, winning all his 42 bouts, including an impressive collection of local Golden Gloves and Diamond Belt competitions, as well as his most important championship, the National Amateur Athletic Union middleweight title, in 1939. It was a natural progression to turn professional and he made the switch on 15 March 1940 in a scheduled six-rounder against Medley Johnson at the Armory in Middleton, Ohio. Charles won on a stoppage in the fifth. Aged 18, he was on his way.

A sharp hitter with both hands, and often photographed with a scowl on the advice of a local newspaperman 'to frighten your opponent', Charles ran up an impressive record of 33 wins, four defeats and a draw in his first four years before being called up for active service in the US Army in early 1943. He served as a GI in Europe, based in Italy and North Africa, for the remainder of the Second World War. Two of his most impressive wins before donning his uniform came against Charlie Burley, one of a number of outstanding boxers to come out of Pittsburgh in the late 1930s and early 1940s.

Despite his success, or perhaps because of it, Burley, an African American, had great difficulty getting matches with the top fighters because of the colour bar. Normally a middleweight, he often had to face heavyweights who outweighed him by as much as 50lbs. Denied a deserved world title fight, the best Burley could do was to fight for and win the 'coloured welterweight championship' in 1938 and the 'coloured middleweight championship' in 1943, two titles that meant nothing. The only legitimate belt he won was the Californian middleweight title in 1943.

'You must understand that Burley was the best fighter I ever saw who not only ever won a world title but never got any glory,' said Ray Arcel, Charles' trainer at the time, who had worked with many world champions, including Benny Leonard, Barney Ross, Ceferino Garcia, Tony Zale, James J Braddock and Jack 'Kid' Berg. 'In those days if you were a good black fighter, nobody wanted to fight you. To get fights, Burley fought anybody who would take him on, and he didn't care if the other guy weighed 180lbs.

'When Charles fought Burley the first time, in May 1942, Burley was a 3/1 favourite, and in Charley's hometown Pittsburgh at that. Burley was on a long winning streak, 20 fights as I recall, but Charles, who was a late substitute, handled him with ease over the ten rounds, winning eight of them. Burley felt he could do better so they had a return fight, four weeks later, and in Pittsburgh again. Burley was 3/1 favourite once more, and what happens? Charles wins another clear decision over ten rounds. That will give you an idea of how good Ezzard was.'

By now, Charles had acquired an influential manager named Jake Mintz, who knew his way around the fight game. Ezzard had also compiled an impressive record. Besides his two wins over the feared Burley, he had beaten two former world champions, finishing off light-heavyweight Anton Christoforidis in three rounds – the first time the Greek had been stopped – and outpointing Teddy Yarosz over ten. Two points wins over the future world light-heavyweight champion Joey Maxim followed. By the end of 1942, Charles' record read 33-2-1, his two losses coming against middleweights Ken Overlin, an ex-world champion, and Kid Tunero, a slick Cuban ranked No 6 in *Ring* magazine's ratings.

If 1942 was a good year, 1943 certainly was not. Ezzard lost his only two fights that year. He dropped a ten-round decision to the talented heavyweight contender Jimmy Bivins and was stopped in eight rounds by the power-punching Lloyd Marshall, who would come to London in the summer of 1947 and knock out future world light-heavyweight champion Freddie Mills in five rounds at Harringay Arena. Shortly after Ezzard's loss to Marshall, he received his call-up papers for the US Army.

By 1946, with the war over, Charles resumed his career and started campaigning for a world light-heavyweight title fight, but the reigning champion Gus Lesnevich and his manager Joe Vella did not seem to be in any great hurry to accommodate him. In any event, Ezzard knew he had to overcome his earlier setbacks by seeking return fights with Bivins and Marshall. 'I'd never be able to call myself a legitimate contender as long as those two losses were there and I had to avenge them,' he recalled. Meanwhile, another contender was claiming he was also being denied a title chance, Archie Moore. A former middleweight contender who reached No 4 in the division's rankings, he had moved up to light-heavyweight and repeatedly challenged champion Lesnevich, but to no avail.

On 20 May 1946, Ezzard's manager Jake Mintz, who was also a promoter, had the idea of matching Moore with Charles to prove who was the No 1 contender. Moore entered the ring as 10/8 favourite but it was Charles who left the ring as winner after ten rounds. They would meet subsequently twice more, with Charles winning a decision and later knocking out Moore in eight rounds. Meanwhile, before 1946 ended, Charles beat his two conquerors of 1943, Jimmy Bivins on points and Lloyd Marshall twice by knockout, in the sixth and second rounds respectively.

With Ezzard's chances of a deserved and long-overdue world light-heavyweight title fight receding by the day, Mintz laid out a plan to campaign for a world heavyweight title shot, even though Charles could have made the 175lbs light-heavyweight limit comfortably. But the heavyweight division was where the big money lay – and the glory. Few fans could name the reigning light-heavyweight champion but everybody knew who the heavyweight king was. Joe Louis had been champion since knocking out James J Braddock in eight rounds in June 1937 and was running out of legitimate contenders. Perhaps Ezzard Charles could be the one who could make it to the No 1 challenger's position.

A rugged puncher named Elmer 'Violent' Ray, who claimed Louis refused to fight him, upset Charles in July 1947 by winning a disputed split decision over ten rounds, prompting *Ring* magazine to report: 'Ray was the aggressor most of the way but Charles was faster, the better boxer and the sharper hitter.' Ezzard would not lose again for another five years. In a return ten months later, he knocked out Ray in nine rounds with a fast left-right combination.

In the fight that preceded the second Ray match, Charles went to Chicago on 20 February 1948 to meet Sam Baroudi from Akron, Ohio. Ezzard was in complete control throughout. After 47 seconds of the tenth round, he landed a thudding left hook and Baroudi went down to be counted out – and stayed down. Baroudi was rushed to hospital, where doctors diagnosed a cerebral haemorrhage, or brain bleed. He died five hours later.

Charles was heartbroken. A win is a win but he never wanted this kind of thing to happen and considered quitting the ring before a local clergyman persuaded him to continue. 'It is an occupational hazard, and these things can happen,' the man of the cloth said. Charles donated $5,000 of his purse from his next fight, the return with Elmer Ray, to the Baroudi family.

There is a common fallacy in boxing that the death of Baroudi turned Charles from an aggressive puncher into a more cautious boxer unwilling to finish off a beaten rival, but the records do not bear this out. In later fights, when he was on the attack against heavier opponents than himself – which happened more often than not – Charles would depend on his skill and versatility to win.

For instance, when matched against the rugged Pennsylvanian ex-coal miner Joe Baksi in his last fight of 1948, Charles was outweighed by 32lbs yet managed to outbox and outfight Baksi to defeat in the 11th round. Baksi had previously trounced Britain's hopes, Bruce Woodcock in seven rounds and Freddie Mills in six. The defeat by Charles was the first time Baksi had been beaten inside the distance in 63 fights and the win pushed Ezzard to the forefront of challengers for Louis' world title.

When somebody put it to Ezzard, a modest and self-effacing man outside the ropes, that he should challenge the 'Brown Bomber' outright, he exclaimed: 'My goodness, not yet!' But he would get the chance to fight for the heavyweight title sooner than expected. Although it had been rumoured that Louis would retire after knocking out Jersey Joe Walcott in 11 rounds on 25 June 1948, it still came as a surprise the following March when he announced he was stepping down as undefeated champion after 11 years at the top. The National Boxing Association quickly stepped in and matched the two leading contenders, Charles and Walcott, for the vacant title, with Charles winning on points over 15 rounds.

Britain, determined to have a say in the destiny of boxing's most lucrative championship, refused to recognise the Charles–Walcott fight as being for the title. Backed by the European authorities, London promoter Jack Solomons paired Doncaster's Bruce Woodcock with the American Lee Savold for their version of the title at the White City Stadium, which Savold won on a retirement in four rounds. As it happened, nobody outside Europe took Savold's claims seriously and his 'title' soon faded into obscurity. Charles was No 1 even if the New York State Athletic Commission, continually at loggerheads with the NBA, refused to recognise him as champion.

It was not until Ezzard fought Louis, who had decided to make a comeback, that he earned worldwide recognition as champion. Louis, with his finances at a low ebb and owing a considerable amount in back taxes, was matched with Charles in a title fight over 15 rounds at the Yankee Stadium on 27 September 1950. Louis had climbed into the ring as a 2/1 favourite and, of the 48 writers polled for their forecasts, 30 went for the old ex-champion to win back the title. One of those who confidently tipped Charles was Frank Graham in the *New York Journal-American*. 'The notion here is that Charles will beat Louis and thereby make very clear his title as heavyweight champion,' he wrote. 'He is the best fighter in the world today... and I must believe that he will win.'

It was pathetically one-sided, with Charles winning an easy decision. There were times when Louis looked on the verge of going down under Charles' heavy and persistent attacks, but Ezzard eased up on his punches. 'I just couldn't, wouldn't, attempt to stop him or knock him out,' Charles would reminisce in later years. 'Joe Louis was always my idol, since I was a kid. He was the best of all time.'

Now universally recognised as world champion, Charles made four successful defences of his title before walking into a stunning left hook from Jersey Joe Walcott in the seventh round of their fight in Pittsburgh on 18 July 1951 and was counted out. In the return 11 months later, Walcott won again, this time on points over 15 rounds in Philadelphia. Charles remained in the title picture over the next two years, with 11 wins and three defeats, when Rocky Marciano, who had taken the title from Walcott, consented to give him a championship fight. The match was scheduled for 17 June 1954 at the Yankee Stadium.

Marciano, the eldest of six children born to an Italian emigrant family in Brockton, Massachusetts, would develop into one of the all-time great hitters in ring history despite a reach of only 68 inches, with both arms outstretched fingertip to fingertip. Compare this with the reaches of other heavyweight champions: Jack Dempsey and Gene Tunney 77 inches, Joe Louis 76, Primo Carnera 85, Jersey Joe Walcott 74, Joe Frazier 73, Muhammad Ali 82, George Foreman 78, Lennox Lewis 84, Mike Tyson 71 and Riddick Bowe 81. But Rocky's powerful punch from both gloves, plus his ruggedness and iron determination, would carry him through.

After his first and only bout as a professional in 1947, Marciano made it 11-0-0, all inside three rounds, in 1948. In 1949 it was 13-0-0, with just one going the full ten rounds. Roland LaStarza, a university graduate from New York and unbeaten in 37 fights, pushed him all the way on 24 March 1950, with a close decision going to Marciano. He had LaStarza on the canvas in the fourth round but lost the eighth for low blows. By now, Rocky was ranked No 10 in *Ring* magazine's annual ratings. Boxing writers were beginning to take notice of the tough kid from Brockton with the big wallop and his ability to take a sock on the chin and remain perpendicular.

A knockout in six rounds over the Utah contender Rex Layne in New York on 12 July 1951 was the turning point. Behind after four rounds and a 9/5 underdog, Rocky turned it on in round five by putting Layne under a sustained attack, finishing him off with a tremendous right that sheared off several of Rex's teeth at the gums. It was the first time that Layne had ever been knocked out. Three months later, Marciano took on the veteran former world heavyweight champion Joe Louis at Madison Square Garden and the fight was stopped in eight rounds, with Marciano a convincing winner.

After four more early wins, three inside three rounds, Marciano fought world heavyweight champion Jersey Joe Walcott on 23 September 1952 in Philadelphia and knocked him out in the 13th round with a pulverising right to the chin after being well behind on points. Suzy Q, Rocky's pet name for his piston-like right, had done her job. Eight months later, Marciano repeated his knockout victory, only this time after 2.25 of round one. A fast left hook followed by what Rocky described as 'a good right uppercut' did the trick. It was one of the swiftest endings ever in a heavyweight championship fight. Walcott claimed he didn't hear the count because he 'blacked out' after seven. 'When I jumped up, I couldn't believe I was counted out,' he said. Jersey Joe never fought again.

The Marciano one-man demolition machine rolled on. Next stop was the Polo Grounds, New York on 24 September 1953, when Rocky stopped his old foe Roland LaStarza in 11 rounds. Trailing on points after six rounds, Marciano subjected the local, who had taken him the full ten rounds over three years earlier, to a systematic battering before finally spraying him with his leather bullets as referee Ruby Goldstein called 'That's enough'. The next, and only, logical opponent now seemed to be the former champion of the big boys, Ezzard Charles.

James D Norris, millionaire head of the promotional group the International Boxing Club, set the date of 17 June 1954 at the Yankee Stadium. It would be Marciano's third defence of his title and Charles' 12th championship fight. It added up to an intriguing battle – the thunderous hitter that was the 'Brockton Blockbuster' against the slick, skilful 'Cincinnati Cobra'. Charles set up his training camp at Kutscher's Country Club, the inspiration for the 1987 hit movie *Dirty Dancing*, in the Catskill mountains in Upper New York State. Marciano set up his quarters 14 miles away at Grossingers Country Club.

When Charles was asked about his chances, he said: 'I plan to bring the fight to him. I'll be more aggressive than ever and I feel I can beat him at his own game, aggression. Remember, he hasn't fought since last September, when he beat Roland La Starza, while I've had two fights since then, knocking out Coley Wallace and Bob Satterfield. Marciano is easy to hit and we all know that. I can nail him more than he can nail me. Nobody has really gone after him. They've let him force the fight. Don't forget I can punch, too. I'll keep him so busy that he won't be able to stalk and get set to throw his big punches.'

When Marciano was asked if he planned a long or a short fight, he told newspapermen: 'I'm not going to forecast how long or how short this fight will be. That's for you guys to speculate. Naturally, I would like it to be quick and get him out of there and that's my aim, but you never know. I hear Ezzard is in fine shape and is expecting the fight of his life and that's understandable. He wants to be the first fighter in ring history to win back the heavyweight title and that's understandable, too. Let's just wait until fight night and see how it goes. All I will say is that I don't intend to let go of the title. I fought too hard to get it and I intend to keep it. Tell Ezzard that when you see him, boys.'

At the weigh-in at Madison Square Garden on the day of the fight, which was presided over by Robert Christenberry, chairman of the New York State Athletic Commission, both champion and challenger arrived looking very relaxed. Marciano scaled 187lbs and Charles 185lbs. As the crowd of 47,585 filed into the ballpark, Rocky remained a 7/2 favourite. In a poll of boxing writers conducted a few days earlier, 28 of 33 picked Marciano so it looked like it was going to be an uphill battle for Charles, at 33 the older man by two years.

Former world lightweight and welterweight champion Barney Ross felt Marciano would stop Charles within four rounds. 'Look at the power that guy packs,' said Ross. Former heavyweight king Jersey Joe Walcott, twice a loser to Marciano and with two wins and two losses to Charles, tipped Ezzard 'to win easily'. Roland LaStarza, who in two fights with Marciano had built up early leads only to see them crumble under Rocky's incessant aggression and hitting power, said: 'Charles is a slashing fighter, a remarkably good fighter. Sure, he can outbox Marciano but for how long? Rocky looks easy to hit inside but he has that left arm up and his chin down. He hits terribly hard punches to the body and I don't think Charles can stand up under these. I know I couldn't.'

After referee Ruby Goldstein called the two boxers together for last-minute instructions and they returned to their corners, the big fight was on. It started fast, predictably with Marciano on the attack, but Charles was moving well, tying up the champion at every opportunity and using his left jabs. For the first four rounds, Marciano could do little but lunge and grab his opponent in an attempt to make him stand still and serve as a target for his heavy right, Rocky's favourite punch. A sharp right cut Marciano over the left eye and Charles followed up with a whiplash left hook that sent Marciano's head back with a snap. It was looking good for the underdog. Going out for the fifth round, Charles had a points lead but there was still a long way to go.

By now, Marciano was becoming frustrated, having hit the challenger after the bell to end the fourth round. But he shared the fifth with some spirited exchanges. Peter Wilson of the *Daily Mirror* described the sixth as follows: 'This was one of Marciano's big rounds. Most of the time he was fighting out of a crouch, bobbing and weaving ponderously like you've seen a big ape in a zoo bouncing up and down in a frustrated frenzy at the bars of his cage – only the bars here were the big black arms of Charles. Then suddenly Marciano got the challenger in his sights, adjusted the range and started bombing with his blockbusting rights. A right to the jaw nearly dropped him and another sent him back on his heels. Charles rallied near the end of the round but this was caveman stuff and Marciano, who landed after the bell, not for the first time, swaggered back to his corner.'

Carrying on his relentless attack in the seventh, Rocky found that Charles was willing to mix with him, so much so that the challenger had the better of several exchanges in which his left hook was the potent weapon. The great strength that Marciano possessed seemed to manifest itself at this point. He seemed to retain his freshness after every bitter exchange whereas Ezzard, for all his courage, was slower and slower getting his punches in. Marciano punched away with little concern for anything coming back in the eighth and evened the matter of cuts by opening a small one beside Charles' right eye.

Certainly everyone in the big arena was admiring the challenger's great courage in refusing to go down. It would turn out to be his greatest fight. Marciano was still pounding away by the tenth and he was in a commanding lead, with five more rounds to go. Charles was still fighting, and fighting well, in the 11th and 12th and was landing effective jabs, hooks and uppercuts on the advancing champion, but the punches were carrying less power than before. Marciano was constantly scoring, particularly with heavy rights, and just before the bell ended the 13th he shook up the game Charles with a savage left hook thrown from the floor.

In the 14th, Charles found himself almost defenceless after strong lefts and rights caused him to sway, go into a clinch and buy a little time. But amazingly, he opened up with a barrage of his own. He might not win this fight but he would give it his best shot and stay on his feet until the final bell. Charles tried, and how he tried, to stem the barrage from the immensely strong Marciano in the 15th. Charles fired an overarm right that crashed into Rocky's face but the rugged Brockton man simply ignored it and stormed back into the attack, trying desperately to put his persistent challenger on the canvas once and for all. They were still trading punches when the final bell rang. It was all over. The underdog had put up the fight of his life against one of boxing's great champions.

The result came as no surprise. Referee Goldstein gave it to Marciano 8-5 with two rounds even. Judge Artie Aidala made it 9-5-1 and judge Harold Barnes scored it 8-6-1. Several American writers felt Charles deserved the decision, as did ex-champion Joe Louis, who marked his card 7-6-2 for Ezzard. However, the general view was that Marciano was a deserving winner. Joseph C Nichols of the *New York Times* marked it 9-6 for Rocky. 'Although he was plainly defeated, Charles made one of the best showings of his career,' said Nichols. 'He gamely mixed it with the ponderous-punching Rocky, and dealt out considerable punishment with his left hook. Marciano's strong point was his right hand. Strong as it was, though, it failed to knock down the challenger, a surprise as his supporters expected him to score a knockout. Only the fact that Charles was in the best of condition permitted Ezzard to go through the gruelling 15 rounds without hitting the canvas.'

In the days before post-fight media conferences, boxers were interviewed in their dressing rooms. Marciano was high in his praise for Charles. 'What can I say? The guy's a terrific boxer and he can really punch,' he said. 'He was a lot tougher than expected, that's for sure, and he was certainly much harder to fight than Jersey Joe Walcott. Yes, I would like to fight him again but that's up to my manager Al Weill. He does the business outside the ring and I do it inside the ring.' In the loser's dressing room, traditionally the saddest place in the world for a defeated boxer, Charles said: 'I thought I won out there. I felt I had him beaten. I did all the boxing, all the fighting, and I just can't believe that I lost. I wouldn't think Marciano was the best fighter I ever fought. He's strong and throws a lot of punches but he didn't give me as tough a fight as did Walcott. Sure, I'll fight him again if it can be arranged, sure I will.'

The return fight was held exactly three months later, again at the Yankee Stadium, with Marciano winning on a knockout in the eighth round. As in the first bout, Rocky climbed into the ring as favourite, this time at 9/2. Charles put up a good showing as expected but Marciano was simply too strong. Rocky had him down in the second round with a right to the jaw and while he jumped up at the count of two he was a little unsteady. But Marciano, in his eagerness, missed his chance to apply the *coup de grace* and Charles slipped away to ring centre, peppering his man with jabs and hooks. A turn of fortune appeared to come Charles' way in the sixth when Marciano emerged from a clinch with a nasty cut on the tip of his nose.

Unfortunately for Charles, he was too tired to follow up his advantage due to Marciano's incessant bombardments and hitting after the bell, as well as using the heel of his glove, both infringements bringing warnings from referee Al Berle. By the eighth, Marciano was bleeding from his sliced nose and a cut over his left eye. It looked like now or never for Rocky. After taking a long right to the head, he countered with a cracking right of his own that sent Charles down. Up at four, Ezzard tried to hold but Marciano shook him off with a left and a right that sent Charles down again. This time he failed to beat the count. The time of the knockout was 2:36 of the eighth round.

Marciano defended his title on two more occasions, stopping Don Cockell of Battersea, south London in nine rounds in San Francisco on 16 May 1955 and knocking out Archie Moore, also in the ninth round, at the Yankee Stadium four months later. The Moore fight brought in a crowd of 61,574, the largest gathering to see Rocky in action, while hundreds of thousands watched it on closed circuit television across the US. Overall, the fight grossed $2,248,117, which at the time was second only to the Jack Dempsey–Gene Tunney return bout in Chicago in 1927. Marciano never boxed again, having compiled an unblemished 49-0-0 record, which included 43 either by knockouts or stoppages, giving him an 87 per cent record of early victories.

Rocky died on 31 August 1969 when his light plane, a Cessna, crashed in bad weather in Des Moines, Iowa. All three occupants, the pilot, Marciano and a friend, were killed instantly. Rocky was a day short of his 46th birthday.

Charles never got another opportunity to fight for the heavyweight title but he continued his career over the next five years, losing more than he won, including a disqualification defeat by the Welshman Dick Richardson in London. The 'Cincinnati Cobra' finally hung up his gloves after dropping a ten-round decision to Alvin Green in Oklahoma City on 1 September 1959. He had taken part in 122 professional fights, compiling a record of 96-25-1, with 58 wins inside the distance. It is still a record in terms of the number of contests for a heavyweight champion, with the majority of his defeats coming towards the end of his 19-year career. It is one that is unlikely to be beaten.

In his retirement years, Charles lived in Chicago and worked as a wine salesman, sold cemetery lots and was a doorman in a nightclub. He would say his most meaningful job was in Mayor Richard Daley's human resources department, where he worked with children. In 1966 Ezzard was diagnosed with multiple sclerosis of the spine, or MS as it is commonly known, leaving him paralysed from the waist down, though he remained mentally alert. He died on 27 May 1975, two months short of his 54th birthday, leaving his wife Gladys behind, along with three children. Charles has a school named after him in Chicago and a street bears his name in his adopted city of Cincinnati. He is also remembered in Gwinnet County, Lawrenceville, Georgia, where he was born and where there is a monument in his honour in the town square. Ezzard would have liked that.

Chapter 12

Quiet man in a business of violence

Floyd Patterson v Ingemar Johansson, Polo Grounds, 20 June 1960

THE Swinging 60s ushered in a decade of social, cultural and technological change. John F Kennedy became the youngest ever President of the United States and many African nations were emerging from colonialism to independence. Alfred Hitchcock pushed the thriller movie into the horror genre with *Psycho*, and America put two men on the moon. In the opening year of the new decade, a brash, young Cassius Clay burst on to the Olympic boxing scene and Floyd Patterson would attempt to make ring history by becoming the first world heavyweight champion to win back the title.

Floyd had lost the championship to Ingemar Johansson, a Swede who knew his onions, in a stunning upset a year earlier and now he was going for Mission Impossible on 20 June 1960. No heavyweight had ever succeeded in regaining the title, and no less than eight had tried over half a century. James J Corbett, known as 'Gentleman Jim', made the first bid to recapture the championship in 1900 and he tried again in 1903. Then came Bob Fitzsimmons in 1902 and James J Jeffries in 1910. Jack Dempsey had a go in 1927 and Max Schmeling in 1938. Joe Louis also failed in 1950, as did his immediate successor Ezzard Charles, who made three attempts, one in 1952 and two in 1954. Jersey Joe Walcott failed in 1953.

Was it any wonder that the odds weighed heavily against Patterson to smash the jinx, especially as he had been beaten so comprehensively and so brutally in three rounds by the Swedish warrior in their previous fight?

In many ways, Patterson was one of the strangest boxers to hold the sport's most prestigious title, the heavyweight championship of the world. He was probably best described by the American sportswriter and author John McCallum as a man of contradictions. 'Here was a prizefighter who brought immense natural skill and devout dedication to his craft,' said McCallum. 'Yet Floyd was the enigma of the essentially non-violent person who found the only identity he ever knew in a business of violence.'

Peter Wilson in the *Daily Mirror* recalled: 'Every time I interviewed Patterson, whom I called Freud because of the introspective side of his nature, I came away with the same impression – the quizzical smile which made him look as though he were having a private joke on the world. For he had a wry sense of humour. Indeed, I was never fully satisfied with a Patterson interview because I never felt that he really trusted any newspaperman, except one particular American. And if you have to cope with lack of frankness as well as the inevitable barriers of print and paper replacing gestures, expressions and tones of voice, the conversation comes out as a hollow semblance of the real thing. He wanted to be regarded as a great champion. Alas, boxing history has proven otherwise.'

There were suggestions by many people that Floyd was not really cut out to be a boxer, certainly not a world champion, because he lacked the mean streak which was, and is, to be truthful, one of the most essential assets of the perfect fighting man. Shy and retiring outside the ring, Patterson bled and suffered and apologised to opponents for hurting them. He compassionately picked up fighters he had knocked down, and told one he was sorry for breaking his nose.

Floyd once indicated to the referee to intervene after outclassing an opponent and another time he knocked out a rival's mouthpiece, only for him to retrieve it straight away. He would often drop his hands and give the other boxer a chance to recover after landing a heavy blow. Would other champions have been so kind? Unlikely.

Certainly not Rocky Marciano, who committed the most appalling fouls, including persistently punching below the belt and using his elbows, or Jack Dempsey, who hovered over opponents he knocked down, ready to strike again, as well as using the illegal rabbit punch, a blow to the back of the neck.

Perhaps Patterson's early life and environment had a lot to do with it. He was born on 4 January 1935 in Waco, North Carolina, where his father was a labourer for the railway company. The following year, the ever-expanding family moved to New York City, living in a succession of dark, dismal tenements in the notorious Bedford-Stuyvesant district of Brooklyn, where a future heavyweight champion, Mike Tyson, would spend his early years. Floyd slept top to bottom with brothers Frank and Billy, and grew up a deeply unstable and shy boy. He rarely went to school and often stayed out at night, hiding in deserted buildings or subways. He convinced himself that everybody was laughing at him, at his shabby, hand-me-down clothes, his speech, his poverty.

Child psychology did not rate highly on the list of priorities in Bedford-Stuyvesant, so Patterson's condition went unchecked until finally, after a succession of juvenile court appearances for truancy and petty theft, he was sent at the age of ten to the Wiltwyck School for Boys, a reform school set in 350 acres of farmland, 90 miles outside New York City. For a boy who had no experience of open fields or who had never handled an animal or walked in the woods, Wiltwyck was a revelation. He responded well to the environment, and sympathetic teachers coaxed him through his difficulties with reading and writing.

'Every time I think of Wiltwyck, the joy bubbles inside me and I can't think of anything else about the place,' Patterson recalled in later years. 'I can never withhold my love and respect for the fine people there who helped straighten me out. They taught me to read and write. They gave me a sense of belonging. I learned how to make friends and how to live with myself and others. I have gone back there several times. Once, I even trained at Wiltwyck for a fight. I would have to credit Wiltwyck for turning my life around. There was no question about that.'

When he was 11, Floyd put on the gloves for the first time at the instigation of the school's executive director Walter Johnson, winning his first three contests. The boy revelled in his new activity and seemed to be a natural. He had found something he could do well. The following year he left Wiltwyck and returned to Brooklyn, where he started accompanying his brothers Frank and Billy, both boxers, to the Grammercy Park gym. The trainer there was Cus D'Amato, an independent-minded, white-haired individual, who recognised a latent talent in the spindly youngster and was credited in later years with moulding Mike Tyson into a world champion.

D'Amato instructed Patterson to keep his hands higher than most boxers, in front of his face, before launching his attacks, prompting sportswriters to refer to Floyd's style as a 'peek-a-boo' stance. It was very successful, nevertheless, and he lost only four of his 44 amateur contests, winning 37 by either stoppage or knockout, including a gold medal as a middleweight in the 1952 Olympics in Helsinki.

It now seemed inevitable that Patterson would move into the professional ranks, with D'Amato as his manager and trainer. Floyd had his first paid fight on 12 September 1952, beating Eddie Gold in four rounds. Campaigning as a light-heavyweight, he ran up an impressive streak of 13 more wins before being outpointed by Joey Maxim, a crafty veteran of 104 fights. Maxim had been world light-heavyweight champion two years earlier and had been in with the likes of Archie Moore, Ezzard Charles, Sugar Ray Robinson, Jersey Joe Walcott and Freddie Mills.

The *New York Daily News* reported the next day that all 11 boxing writers polled at ringside felt that Patterson should have been given the decision on the strength of his sharper all-round work. D'Amato filed a formal protest to the New York State Athletic Commission but nothing came of it. He wanted Maxim to give Floyd a return but Joey's canny manager Jack 'Doc' Kearns, who had guided Jack Dempsey to the heavyweight championship of the world in 1919, would have none of it.

Patterson was mortified by the defeat and spent days hiding in his New York apartment in case anybody recognised him in the street. He hated to be a loser. A week or so later, he viewed the defeat more positively. 'Even if I officially lost, the fight convinced me that someday I would be a world champion,' he told a reporter. D'Amato did not allow him time to dwell on the setback and Floyd was back in the ring inside a month to continue his world title campaign, first as a light-heavyweight and then as a heavyweight, particularly following Rocky Marciano's shock retirement as undefeated world heavyweight champion on 27 April 1956.

The International Boxing Club matched Patterson with Archie Moore, the former world light-heavyweight champion, for the vacant heavyweight title in Chicago on 30 November 1956. Floyd won on a knockout in the fifth round, a notable achievement as it had taken Marciano nine rounds to beat Moore. Rocky had also had to climb off the canvas in the second round from a right to the chin. Patterson had now made history by becoming the first Olympic gold medallist to win the world heavyweight championship.

There was another piece of history, too, with his victory. At 21 years and ten months, he was the youngest man to win the heavyweight title. It was a record that would stand for 30 years, almost to the day, before Mike Tyson won the championship aged 20 years and four months. As Patterson left the ring, he was given the news that, four hours earlier, his wife Sandra had given birth to their first daughter, Seneca Elizabeth. All this, and a nice pay cheque for $114,257. Life was good.

The only problem was that D'Amato was having an ongoing row with James D Norris, the millionaire businessman who ran the powerful International Boxing Club. Norris was the leading promoter and, as a result, the IBC put on most of the title fights, as well as having almost all the champions under contract. D'Amato said he would never do business with an organisation that had such a tight monopoly on the sport. 'Boxers should be free,' he maintained. 'The IBC is an octopus and downright corrupt.' D'Amato naturally wanted Patterson to hang on to his title and earn big money, and if that meant ducking leading contenders like Zora Folley, Eddie Machen and Nino Valdez, who were obligated to the IBC, then that was the way it was going to be.

Patterson was quite happy to go along with D'Amato's decisions, with the result that while his bank balance increased considerably, his reputation sank like a stone tossed into a river. On 22 August 1957, he took on the balding former Olympic champion Pete Rademacher, who had never fought professionally in his life but put Floyd on the canvas before being knocked out in the sixth round. A year later, Patterson fought the former schoolteacher Roy Harris and again had to climb off the floor before the Texan retired in the 12th round. By now, the public were becoming sick and tired of Patterson's hand-picked title defences organised by the ultra-cautious D'Amato, and demanded that Floyd meet a genuine contender and prove himself once and for all.

D'Amato and his champion finally yielded to mounting public pressure and agreed to defend the title against Sweden's Ingemar Johansson, who had become the No 1 contender by flattening the formidable American Eddie Machen in the first round in Gothenburg on 14 September 1958. The unbeaten Johansson was also European champion and the big fight would take place at the Yankee Stadium on 26 June 1959. It would be staged not by the IBC but by an independent promoter named Bill Rosensohn, a young newcomer in the boxing promotion business. One month earlier, Patterson would have a warm-up bout against the former British champion Brian London, who was thrashed by Henry Cooper earlier in the year.

Not surprisingly, London was given little chance against Floyd. They met in Indianapolis on 1 May 1959 and the Blackpool battler lasted into the 11th round before succumbing. The British Boxing Board of Control had thought so little of London's chances that they refused even to recognise the fight, suspended London after the bout for six months and fined him £1,000, a hefty sum in those days.

Patterson was now facing a real foe at last in Johansson, though Ingemar was still lightly regarded in the US. European heavyweights were seldom accorded respect in America in any event and even Johansson's quick win over Machen was dismissed as a fluke. US boxing writers laughed off the big Swede's chances and dismissed him as a no-hoper. Jimmy Cannon, one of the most respected American scribes, wrote in his preview in the *New York Post*: 'The United Nations should step in and prevent Johansson being smashed to a pulp, as Ingemar seems a nice boy. I wish he could compete with Floyd in the Charleston on the dance floor instead of having to meet him in the boxing ring.'

Ingemar moved into Grossingers Country Club, a plush resort high in the Catskills in Upper New York State. This was where Rocky Marciano had prepared for his big fights, living as a solitary monk and who was so dedicated in getting his body into the best possible physical condition that he was even unwilling to watch TV. Rocky lived in a lonely cabin by an aircraft hangar, a cabin which, by army standards, would have been regarded as luxurious.

The place, however, was not to Johansson's taste and the promoter promptly moved him to another part of Grossingers and into the guest house of Max Ackerman, the multi-millionaire owner of a fleet of some 3,000 taxicabs.

As soon as he settled in, Johansson immediately brought along his father, mother, brother, sister, plus his beautiful fiancee Birgit Lundgren, even though girlfriends or wives were not normally allowed in training camps as it was considered that they would distract the boxer. Also with Ingemar was his physician Dr Gosta Karlson, a pensive gentleman who somewhat remarkably admitted that he did not fully approve of boxing and felt it should be banned. Nevertheless, he was part of the Johansson entourage and was constantly by Ingemar's side. American scribes were more than slightly aghast by it all, though it was no secret that they were more interested in looking at Birgit in her shocking pink ski pants and red sweater to match than at Johansson.

They could not take seriously a challenger who spent so much of his time with the delectable Birgit, either in the Olympic-sized swimming pool or on the dance floor. He even played a leisurely 18 holes of golf a few days before the most important fight of his career. The Swede appeared to have training methods entirely of his own conception, and seemed to eat what he liked rather than what was recommended. Boxing writers reported that he did very little exercising or ball punching and never showed his much-publicised right hand that had knocked out so many opponents. Did it exist at all? Really, was this the right kind of conditioning for a man about to box for the heavyweight championship of the world, boxing's premier title?

Pressmen shook their heads. Here was a challenger aiming to smash America's monopoly on boxing's most important title but one who could not possibly be dangerous, a flash-in-the-pan, no more. They went back to their offices, sat down at their typewriters and forecast a clear win for Patterson. How could they think otherwise? Unknown to the scribes, however, or to anybody else outside the Swede's inner circle, Johansson was taking part in secret training sessions, mainly at night, when he really let himself go.

Ingemar's running schedule was tougher than the norm, doing six miles a day, but no reporters were aware of this. He had told them that his right hand was named Thor, after the Scandinavian God of Thunder, but they had to take his word for it. It would subsequently be known as 'Ingo's Bingo'. In contrast to the plush surroundings of Grossingers, Patterson led his usual ascetic, spartan life which he had become used to. He was based in Summit, New Jersey, described by one observer as resembling a barn. As always, too, Floyd stayed completely away from Sandra throughout his training.

A rainy evening meant that only 18,125 turned out at the Yankee Stadium, though for the first time in ring history receipts from closed-circuit television grossed over $1 million. But what a sensation the fight turned out to be. After two rounds without much happening, the 4/1 European underdog landed his much-lauded right at the opening of the third round and Patterson went down on his back. Up at eight, he was so dazed that he walked to a neutral corner, bizarrely thinking that he had scored the knockdown rather than his opponent.

Ingemar actually ran after Floyd and put him down again, this time with a wicked left hook. Patterson was on the canvas five more times in that one-sided third round before referee Ruby Goldstein wisely intervened at 2:03. Boxing had a new world heavyweight champion. The big question now was: could Floyd regain the title? He would get the opportunity 12 months later, yet did he possess the equipment to smash the 64-year-old jinx which had defied heavyweights from calling themselves champions of the world again?

For a man who won the top title in the sport, Johansson's introduction to mainstream boxing was anything but auspicious. Born in Gothenburg on 22 September 1932 to a maintenance foreman and his wife, the young Ingemar followed the same course when he left school at 15. Two years earlier, he had become interested in amateur boxing. While walking home, his route took him past an old fire station which was used as the headquarters of the Redbergslid Boxing Club. The door was open and Ingemar stood there and watched, fascinated by the activity. He made enquiries and joined the club there and then.

At 13 and weighing 140lbs, Johansson was big for his age. By the time he reached 16, he had already grown into a heavyweight at around 200lbs. Starting his official amateur career in December 1947, within three months he was the Swedish junior champion. Inside two years, he had progressed to the senior title and became an international representative. Ingemar was on his way, and finished up winning 61 bouts, 32 inside the distance, with just ten losses.

Unfortunately, his amateur career was marred by shame when he was disqualified against America's Ed Sanders for not putting up a fight in the 1952 Olympic heavyweight final in Helsinki. This was the same Olympics where Patterson won a gold medal as a middleweight. The restless crowd started to boo and whistle during a listless first round, with both Sanders and Johansson warned by referee Roger Vaisberg to 'make a fight of it'.

Vaisberg admonished the Swede for his lack of initiative in the second round, but Sanders was equally to blame and got no warning, though he did attempt an attack. In the interval before the third round, Vaisberg conferred with ringside officials before going over to Sanders' corner and raising his right hand. The American was the winner and Johansson was disqualified for 'not trying'. Ingemar protested he was boxing on orders from his corner and explained that he was instructed to take it easy for the first two rounds and then snatch victory with a big finish in the last round, but the referee, ringside officials, the press and spectators were unconvinced.

The Swede returned home in disgrace to find an angry nation fuming at what had happened despite his claims that he was not the only one who was being over-cautious in such a vitally important contest. Screaming front-page headlines blasted his performance, calling him a coward and 'one who put a black mark on the proud banner of Swedish sport'. Officials too were scathing in their criticism.

'Johansson brought shame to the Swedish name,' said Oscar Soderlund, chairman of the Swedish Amateur Boxing Association. 'We are ashamed of such a boxer. He crept out of the hall to avoid the score when the jury quite rightly agreed to not let him have his silver medal and further not to hoist the Swedish flag at the prizegiving. We don't want points won by a sportsman who so little comes up to the conception of sportsmanship. He has brought shame to the whole of the Swedish Olympic team by his cowardice. For my part, I can find no mitigating circumstances.'

Looking back on the incident in later years, Johansson recalled: 'I certainly did not think I had done anything dishonourable. I was merely protecting myself in case Sanders launched a surprise attack. This was too important a contest to take unnecessary risks. I don't remember too much of the exact events and the uproar it caused, but I do recall an old man jumping up, shaking his clenched fist in my face and shouting: "You wouldn't dare to fight me, you coward" or something like that. I didn't take much notice of the public's anger or of the bitter words and the dislike. The fight was an Olympic final and I was merely protecting myself in the ring.'

It was not until 1982 that Johansson received his silver medal from the International Olympic Committee, by which time the whole incident had long been forgotten. Back in 1952, however, Ingemar had decided he'd had enough of amateur boxing and, giving up his job in maintenance, began fighting for kronas in exhibitions with a travelling circus. His formal professional career started with a knockout in four rounds against the French heavyweight Robert Masson in Gothenburg a few weeks before Christmas 1952. He had worried about the public's interest and while there were some boos among the crowd, the hall sold out, with 5,500 fans in attendance.

Ingemar won his first four fights before hanging up his gloves temporarily to serve a stint in the Swedish Navy. After his discharge, he returned to the ring in November 1954 and continued to compile victories, culminating in winning the European heavyweight title in 1956. He successfully defended the belt twice, finishing off two British challengers in impressive fashion, Henry Cooper in five rounds and Joe Erskine in 13. It was his sensational win over the favoured American Eddie Machen in one round on 14 September 1958 that clinched him his successful attempt on Floyd Patterson's world title nine months later.

In one interview after winning the championship, Johansson admitted that he was drawn to boxing in the same way that others were attracted to acting or painting. 'The only difference is that the theatre and painting are respectable occupations while boxing is regarded as brutality,' he explained. 'It is a strange profession but it suits me. It's the thing that I can do best. Many of the great ones in art have been wrecked in the conflict between their own greatness and the critics' smallness. Geniuses have been murdered and condemned to exile and destruction by ignorance and self-righteousness. Yet the ignorant and blunt critic is an accepted institution in spite of his cruelty and his attacks on unprotected people.

'A boxer has the chance to defend himself and has, moreover, defence as his profession. An artist is defenceless. It's his profession to leave himself open. In these days, many people go under who have a profession in which they leave themselves open to attack. I think people ought to remember this when they call boxing brutal. It is an easily understood form of acting. I maintain that far from brutalising the mind, it gives a symbolic or idealised picture of what is going on all around us. It is formally brutal but its idea is honour and obedience to the law. Most frequently, it is the opposite around us.'

For his return fight with Patterson, Johansson was back in Grossingers, again with his entourage that included Birgit. The match was scheduled for 20 June 1960, this time at the Polo Grounds in New York. The Swede expressed his view that he was happy to be boxing in such a famous ballpark for the very first time. As the name suggested, the original Polo Grounds was built in 1876 for polo matches, though of the four stadiums that carried its name over the years, the original structure was the only one used for polo. The fourth was the best known and was used mainly for baseball, football and boxing, though it had been underused since the departure of the New York Giants baseball team in 1957.

It was the scene of many famous fights, including Jack Dempsey's classic encounter with Luis Firpo in 1923, Billy Conn's near-upset of Joe Louis in 1941 and Sugar Ray Robinson's dramatic win over Randolph Turpin in 1951. The final reincarnation of the stadium would be demolished in April 1964 by the same wrecking ball, painted to look like a giant baseball, which had been used four years earlier to knock down another famous stadium, Ebbets Field in Brooklyn.

For Patterson, the 12 months following his shock loss to Johansson were dark days. A sensitive individual, he felt he had let down his own followers. The people who had called him a bum in the past were screaming: 'There you are, we told you so.' He locked himself away in his house at Rockville Centre, a suburb for New York businessmen, and refused to see anybody. He would not reply to his mail or talk to anybody except his wife Sandra and his immediate family. He watched television most of the time but could not bear to see re-runs of his disastrous defeat. He would not even read the sports pages of newspapers in case he saw any mentions of the first fight and certainly would not allow boxing magazines into the house.

For the fight itself, Patterson again trained in spartan conditions, this time in Newtown, Connecticut. It was a camp described by one New York columnist as 'an abandoned house buried in the woods, with paint peeling off the walls, the plaster all cracked, and neglect having taken over.' In any event, Floyd was being generally ignored by the media. He was yesterday's man, an ex-champion who didn't count. Johansson was the new kid on the block. The Swede trained hard in luxurious surroundings at Grossingers again, but he was also doing plenty of relaxing. His motto seemed to be, 'Never let training interfere with living,' a kind of variation on a remark made by the Dublin playwright Brendan Behan. 'That's the trouble with work, Thomas,' he said. 'It interferes with one's leisure.'

Once again, Patterson's family was not with him. Nor was his manager and mentor Cus D'Amato, who was under suspension by the New York State Athletic Commission for alleged connections with the underworld. D'Amato was still Patterson's legal manager but the barring order meant that he could no longer take any official part in his boxer's future plans. Nor was he allowed in the corner. For Patterson, it effectively meant that in addition to overcoming most of his depression since the first fight, Floyd was now more fully and personally in charge of his own professional life.

The ex-champion could well have severed all links with D'Amato but he refused to do so. 'Cus is still my friend,' he told reporters before leaving for camp. 'I'm not going to change my so-called peek-a-boo style, which Cus taught me. The style will be the same because it's the best style for me. When I drop my hands, I get hit. To discard it, I would have to pick off too many punches with my gloves. It's a style that brought me the championship in the first place when I beat Archie Moore and that's good enough proof for me.' Patterson also emphasised that he was now his own manager, at least for the present. Dan Florio was his chief trainer, with his attorney Julius November staying on in that capacity.

'During those lonely months after the Johansson fight, I had three problems which had to be faced directly,' he recalled in later years. 'The first and most important one was to prepare myself emotionally for what lay ahead of me. The second was to work up a defence for Ingemar's right hand, which did all the damage. The third was my own offence against him. The thing, it seemed to me, that made everything easier was the eventual appreciation that while I was champion I didn't feel like one. It was not until I lost the title did I begin to understand properly how much it was that I lost. It was less a belief in myself than the belief that others might have had in me.

'This is the thing that really hurt and as the months went on it became a real pain, driving me harder and harder towards the goal I was determined to achieve. As I say, I didn't read newspapers or boxing magazines, but on the television one night was something that caught me by surprise. Ingemar returned to America to receive an award as sportsman of the year, and there he was making a speech in which he went out of his way to disparage me. He even called me a gymnasium fighter. That was uncalled for, and it made me all the more determined to beat him and win back my title.'

Promoter Bill Rosensohn had promoted the first fight but the New York State Athletic Commission were not happy with the arrangements, amid rumours of underworld affiliations which had prompted them to suspend D'Amato. A new promotional team came in called Feature Sports Inc., headed by Humbert J Fugazy, a veteran boxing promoter fondly known as 'Hard Luck' Fugazy because it always rained on the nights he put on shows. A New Yorker from Greenwich Village who was said to have encouraged the great British lightweight Freddie Walsh, Fugazy was the figurehead in the organisation. But the real brains and energy behind it was his son William Fugazy and his partner, a bright young attorney named Roy Cohn.

Together, they got several former world heavyweight champions to visit Patterson's camp for publicity purposes. Joe Louis said he felt Floyd had been too flat-footed against Johansson the first time. 'Floyd must try to keep Johansson close, work on his body to bring his guard down and not let him get set in the middle of the ring,' he said. Pointing out how he himself had beaten Max Schmeling in the first round of their grudge fight in 1938, Louis went on: 'The only way to beat a puncher is to crowd him. If you give him punching room, he'll beat your brains out.' Louis predicted Patterson would win between the seventh and tenth rounds, though after visiting Johansson he stretched his forecast to '11 rounds but it's still Patterson for me.'

While Louis was very confident of an American victory, other ex-champions were not so sure. Schmeling declared curtly: 'Patterson was never a proper champion, Johansson is. I feel that only a miracle would give Patterson a chance for a knockout, a wild, lucky punch.' Jack Dempsey, who had been one of the very few to predict a Johansson win in the first fight, said: 'I'll have to go with the puncher again, and Ingemar has the power. His right is a helluva punch. As for Patterson, I think he's an amateur. Johansson can end this fight with one punch.' Gene Tunney, twice conqueror of Dempsey, commented: 'I always had a very dim view of Patterson and I have seen no reason to change my views. I am of the considered opinion that Patterson is a novice and I feel Johansson will win again, on an early knockout.'

Rocky Marciano, Patterson's immediate predecessor as champion, thought Johansson's right hand was the best he had ever seen. 'I think he will be too strong for Patterson, and I feel it will end early,' he said. A few, like Jack Sharkey and Primo Carnera, thought Patterson had been beaten by a lucky punch the first time and that he would have learned not to be so careless. Ezzard Charles was asked but said he had never seen Johansson fight and could not give an opinion, while James J Braddock commented: 'Patterson fought a foolish fight last time but if he stands in front of Johansson this time, it would be the end for Ingo soon.' The only former champion, aside from Louis, who was tipping Patterson without any ifs or buts was Jersey Joe Walcott. 'In their first fight Floyd looked stale and I think he beat himself,' said Walcott. 'I doubt if that will happen again, so I predict a Patterson victory.'

The majority of former champions were not alone in forecasting a repeat victory for the Swede. American boxing writers were freely tipping Johansson. Typical of the reviews was the *Pittsburgh Courier*'s Wendell Smith, a man who knew his boxers and his boxing. Smith told his readers: 'The way I see it is that Johansson is too big and too strong for the challenger. Of course Floyd has our best wishes but that won't help him much when the bell goes.' British writers, too, saw another Johansson victory. George Whiting in the *Evening Standard* wrote in his elegant style: 'Having misread last year's portents and potentials so badly that I picked Patterson, I now extend my neck from the safe side of the ropes and suggest that what Johansson has done once he can do again. But it may take him a little longer, say about ten rounds.'

In Johansson's final press conference before leaving for New York City, the Swede said: 'There is no doubt that what I did before I can do again. I am certain about that. Floyd says he is going to get me before I get him, but that is just speculation. Ever since I started boxing, my dream was to win the world title and now that I am champion, I don't intend to let it go. Outside of what the writers call the jinx in heavyweights failing to regain the title, the facts are that I am stronger, fitter and carry the heavier punch. The memory of the last fight must be terrible for Floyd and he has to live with it. I understand all that but that's what boxing is all about. You win, you lose. This time, I will win again and you can place your bets on me. I'm sure of that.'

After living like a hermit for a year, Patterson now wanted to come out of the shadows and show his true self beneath the arc lights blazing down on the white canvas. 'I will be heavier this time,' he told reporters. 'I plan to cut down on my speed but I think that will add to my punching power. Last time, I was fooled by Ingemar's training methods, the reports of his lack of a big punch and by the odds in his favour. I won't be fooled this time. I won't be afraid of him, or his right hand, when we come together in the ring.'

In private, however, Patterson outlined his plans with his team. Years later, he recalled: 'We talked of how the return fight was going to be entirely different. In the first fight, I boxed out of a crouch from which I could bob and weave better, but from that crouch I couldn't reach with a good punch unless I closed with him. So I reckoned that if I crouched less in the second fight, I could be right on target.'

There was a threat of rain on 20 June but it held off right through. The big fight attracted worldwide interest and for weeks beforehand the film of the first bout was shown on television many times. A crowd of 31,892 passed through the turnstiles at the Polo Grounds, among them 4,500 who paid $100 apiece for ringside seats, including, as one writer described them, 'the millionaires and the mink maidens'.

It was later revealed that an estimated 10,000 crashed the gates, pushing the attendance to over 41,000. The fight was blacked out in New York and 229 cinemas organised out-of-town showings, which would attract 484,894 fans. Gross receipts, including cinema, TV and radio, came to $2,251,162.

At ringside, not far from New York governor Nelson Rockefeller and former governor Thomas Dewey, were past ring greats like Jack Dempsey, Gene Tunney and Joe Louis. Patterson's former mentor Cus D'Amato was there too, but this time as a spectator instead of imparting his deep knowledge of the sport to the boxer he discovered all those years ago. D'Amato had secretly visited Floyd at his camp early on, however, and advised him on tactics: 'Take a good look at the film of the first fight, study it, run it through again and again. Locate your faults, determine how to avoid them, look for his defects and faults and if you have the brains I've always credited you with, then you can't lose.'

D'Amato may have been confident of a Patterson victory but few shared his views. The big questions hanging over the fight like a dark cloud were: Could Patterson wipe away the bitter memories of the last time? Had he fully recovered, physically and mentally, from those crushing seven knockdowns which must have felt like a recurring nightmare? Could he get close enough for his fast, flashing punches without being driven back by those stinging jabs before being destroyed again by that crashing right? Could he still take a punch and keep going?

The answers from the people who made the odds were all in the negative, as Johansson was the 7/5 favourite. Would this affect Floyd? The general feeling was that what Johansson had done before he could do again, and that Ingo's Bingo would get through once more. For the first time, too, D'Amato would not be in Patterson's corner. Would this have any effect on the somewhat sensitive former champion? Only time would tell.

Before the contestants climbed into the ring, with Patterson as the challenger due first by tradition, there was time to reflect on the statistics. Johansson weighed in at 194lbs, two pounds lighter than in the first fight, and Patterson tipped the scales at 190lbs, eight pounds heavier than before. Floyd's team were happy with that as it meant he would be stronger against such a heavy puncher. Johansson thought that his own lighter poundage would give him more manoeuvrability. Patterson, at 25, was two years younger than the champion and had a 37-2-0 record as against Johansson's clean slate of 22-0-0.

Interestingly, Floyd would get the higher purse even though he was the challenger. This was down to the shrewd negotiating skills of Julius November, who had looked after Patterson's legal and financial interests with D'Amato and now, with Cus on the sidelines, took over. Floyd's cut was $771,232, with Johansson picking up $643,107.

Patterson's only stipulation was that Ruby Goldstein, the referee in the first fight, would not be in charge this time. He had nothing personal against Goldstein, one of the world's most respected officials, but he felt that having Ruby again might bring back horrific memories, so Arthur Mercante was selected by the New York State Athletic Commission. Mercante had been a referee in main events for six years and while this would be his first world title fight, Patterson had every confidence in him to get a square deal. When Mercante retired in 2001 at the age of 81, he was still the premier referee in boxing, having officiated in a record 70 world title fights.

After Mercante called the two boxers together and explained the rules, there was a deep hush, like a graveyard at night. Then the bell. Both tried to find the range with their left jabs and when Patterson got through with a strong left hook, Johansson came in quickly to smother any follow-through attack. Floyd, looking brisk and confident, landed a succession of quick left hooks which made Ingemar hold on briefly. Floyd caught his man with a long right to the head. Johansson had his celebrated right hand cocked and ready for another demolition job, but he was not getting a chance to use it because of the American's greater speed. That is, until the closing seconds of the round but the punch missed Floyd's chin by a fraction.

Patterson's rights had already marked Johansson under the left eye but the Swede asserted himself in the second round with a three-punch burst, including that big right hand which caught Patterson on the side of the head. Floyd looked badly dazed and quickly retreated before going into a clinch, which brought a warning from Mercante. After breaking quickly, Patterson was quickly on to the attack and hurt Johansson with some hooks to the body. The Swede's pale face and body were becoming marked with red blotches, an indication of the challenger's power.

In the third it was noticeable that Johansson's left jabs, so dominant in the first fight, were nowhere near as effective this time. It appeared that his confidence was draining from him like sand from a bag slashed with a knife. This was clearly a much better Patterson than the one a year earlier almost to the day. This time there was no hesitancy and no evidence of the peek-a-boo style, although he often went into a slight crouch, bobbing and weaving. Patterson was jabbing his man consistently, forcing him back across the ring. Two left hooks made the champion miss. Floyd was looking smooth and sharp as he went after his opponent, keeping up the incessant pressure while still carefully watching Johansson's always-dangerous right.

Johansson's seconds applied the ice bag to his bruised eye between the third and fourth rounds, and Patterson was still able to push him back. Ingemar connected with long lefts and rights to the head but Patterson got under his guard with a short, solid right to the jaw. Ingemar tried a left-right combination but they were short and Floyd made him give ground. The Swede's body was reddening more now as a result of Patterson's constant attacks. They went into a maul, one of the few in a fight that was fast-paced, and Floyd smashed a short right to the head that made the champion visibly wince.

At the bell, it was agreed among the newspapermen that Patterson had won three of the four completed rounds, with Johansson winning one, the second. Judges Leo Birnbaum and Artie Aidala also had it 3-1, with referee Mercante marking it 2-1 with one even. The Swede and his seconds were looking decidedly worried. This was a rejuvenated Patterson, not the uncertain one of the first match.

Patterson opened the fifth round with a fast, stabbing left jab and two short hooks to the head. Suddenly, like a dam bursting, Patterson stepped in with an arcing left hook which landed high on Johansson's head and dropped him, his legs shooting up as he went down on his back. He managed to get to one knee as Mercante yelled 'nine'. On rising fully, Ingo tried desperately to cling on but Patterson elbowed him away and kept the punches pouring in. A final, crunching left hook, perhaps the best punch he had thrown in his career, swivelled Johansson's head around and he was unconscious before hitting the floor like a sack of potatoes, his arms and legs widespread, resembling some giant starfish. Mercante went through the formality of counting out the prostrate champion, now the ex-champion, who never moved a muscle.

The grinning Patterson leapt high in the air as the ring was invaded by an avalanche of fans who raised the new champion on their shoulders, with the big crowd roaring. As soon as Patterson got back on his feet, he pushed his way over to the stricken Swede, still stretched out on the canvas as the commission doctor tried to bring him round. Floyd waited until Johansson opened his eyes and then told him he could have a rubber meeting within 90 days, although he might as well have made the offer to the late John L Sullivan for all Johansson heard.

After being out for ten minutes, Ingemar finally managed to get to his feet with the help of his seconds and sat on his stool before being assisted from the ring and to his dressing room. Patterson recognised D'Amato down near the press bench and, on leaving the ring, they embraced. 'I always knew you could do it,' said his temporarily estranged mentor, who had a trace of tears in his eyes.

In the dressing room, Patterson agreed the left hook that finished the fight was the hardest he had ever thrown. 'That was because I was heavier than last time, and I felt much better too,' he said in a voice just above a whisper. What about the right hand that Johansson landed in the second round, the only session Floyd lost? 'Yes. It hurt but not as bad as some people may have thought.' A third fight? 'Yes, I told Ingemar in the ring that I would give him another chance, like he gave me,' he said. 'This was the most gratifying night of my life. I never thought for a moment of losing but to win this way, it's just perfect. For the first time, I feel I'm the real champion.'

When Johansson was asked why he didn't follow up his advantage when he landed his big right hand in the second round, he said: 'Even though I might have had him then, I didn't want to take any chances. I thought he might have been playacting. Anyhow, I had planned a long fight. I felt I would get him again and he would tire himself out.'

Ingemar's adviser Edwin Ahlquist said: 'We have no abilis. The better man won. Of course Ingemar is shocked. This is the first time in his life he has been knocked out but he will be back. We haven't seen the last of him yet.'

George Whiting in the *Evening Standard* said: 'Let there be no talk of a fluke or accident about Patterson's fever-packed revenge. The fighting Floyd was the aggressor from the start and only once, in the second round, did he seem to be in the slightest trouble from the vaunted right hand that had humbled him out of the championship last year. Patterson blinked, backed off for a full minute and swayed his way as Johansson sought, rather cumbersomely, to repeat the dose. From that point, we saw but little of Johansson's right hand. What we did see was a Patterson leaping out of harm's way, getting the inside berth in the clinches, avoiding the ropes that spelt disaster last time and diving in to deliver swift correction.'

Boxing Illustrated reported: 'Patterson got a big kick out of fooling practically all the experts. But Johansson did not live up to what is expected from the heavyweight champion of the world. And of course, his training methods made a mockery of the accepted time-tested routines. People were puzzled reading about Ingo's plush training quarters at Grossingers. They wondered if he really was a fighter when he said: 'I do not try to hurt my sparring partners.' But he gave Patterson the chance to make boxing history – the first heavyweight champion to win back the title. It is always gratifying to see a fighter pick himself off the floor. Patterson did that after taking the most devastating blow possible. For it wasn't merely Ingo's heavy right fist that knocked him out in 1959. It was the whole world. But Floyd came off the floor to hit back. When has there ever been a greater or more heartwarming victory?'

Referee Mercante remembered over 45 years later: 'The fight was one of the most memorable moments of my professional life. Frankly, I could not have inaugurated my big-time career with a more auspicious event. The fight was the most anticipated boxing event since the second Joe Louis–Billy Conn fight nearly a decade and a half earlier. It was one of the few big fights that lived up to its billing – exciting all the way and ending with a spectacular knockout. Last but not least, it had Patterson becoming the first man to regain the heavyweight title. A glorious and unprecedented moment in boxing history.'

Johansson suffered a further blow the day after the fight when he was served with a $14,590 demand for back taxes. Still, he would get his promised rubber meeting, on 13 March 1961, and this time Patterson won on a knockout in the sixth round, though he had to climb off the canvas twice to achieve victory.

Looking back in later years on the historic night he won back the title, Patterson recalled: 'When I put Johansson down in that fifth round and he lay motionless on the canvas, with blood trickling from the corner of his mouth and his left leg shaking like he was having a fit or something, I was really scared that I had seriously hurt him. I had knocked out men before but I'd never seen anybody shake like that. I remember hearing the broadcaster Howard Cosell hollering at Ingemar's trainer Whitey Bimstein: "Is he dead? Is he dead?" and Bimstein shouting back: "No, but the son-of-a-bitch should be. I told him to watch out for the left hook."Happily, Ingemar recovered and I was relieved to hear he was OK.'

Patterson would also remember leaving the Polo Grounds that balmy summer night in 1960 in a hired Cadillac and telling the driver to take him through Harlem. He wanted to show himself to his own people and they gave him a noisy and joyous reception. He remembered, too, the next morning when, after getting up early and reading all the papers, he held his first press conference and answered all the questions fired at him and how he was never at a loss for words. When it was over, he motioned to his lawyer Julius November that they go out for a walk into the New York streets for some fresh air. It was great to be 25 and to prove that as the underdog you could come back and win the heavyweight championship of the world for the second time. After a year in seclusion, boxing's quiet man had found himself.

Floyd lost his title to the menacing Sonny Liston on 25 September 1962 and while he was never a major force in boxing afterwards, he challenged four times for the heavyweight title before retiring in September 1972 with a 55-8-1 record. He remained active in boxing and served as chairman of the New York State Athletic Commission, overseeing boxing and wrestling in the state. He also managed and trained his son Tracey in the professional ranks and dabbled in movies. Patterson remained close friends with Johansson and they ran several marathons together in the 1980s, as well as visiting each other's homes. Patterson died of prostate cancer in New Paltz, New York on 11 May 2006, aged 71.

Johansson never again challenged for the world title but he was a successful European champion and was always a big attraction up to his retirement in April 1963 following a disappointing victory over Blackpool's Brian London. His record read 26-2-0. Outside the ring, Ingemar sang with legendary songstress Dinah Shore on television and made several movies. He also owned a fishing boat, a restaurant and a motel, as well as being involved in the construction business in Europe and the US. Johansson died of pneumonia in Kungsbacka, a principality 30 miles south of Gothenburg, on 30 January 2009. He was 76.

Chapter 13

Ring war that ended on the sidewalk

Harry Greb v Mickey Walker, Polo Grounds, 2 July 1925

WHEN promoter Humbert J Fugazy announced in the press that he had matched Harry Greb, the world middleweight champion, with Mickey Walker, the welterweight king, there was an immediate demand for tickets. This had to be a good one. Like Walker, Greb knew no fear. Known as 'the Pittsburgh Windmill' because of his boundless energy and non-stop aggression, they all came alike to Harry. He went in against the best fighters of his day through the 1910s and 1920s – middleweights, light-heavyweights and heavyweights – and beat most of them.

A compulsive drinker and prodigious womaniser like Walker, Greb usually scorned training, maintaining that regular fighting kept him fit. Moreover, Greb was also a master at dirty fighting and had no qualms about employing all manner of dubious tactics, such as spinning his opponent, using the heel and laces of his gloves and throwing in a few headbutts. He hated referees. 'God dammit, they interfere too much,' he would complain.

Greb often took as much as he gave and, unbeknown to the press, continued to fight for five years – five of his most productive years – blind in his right eye as a result of an injury received in a fight with the tough Kid Norfolk in 1921. But then, Greb was the most durable of fighters, suffering only two stoppage losses. When he finally hung up his worn gloves after 13 years, he had gone through 299 fights, losing three, drawing three and fighting 183 no-decision bouts at a time when the law forbade verdicts. Like Walker, Greb felt that fraternising with women well into the early hours before an important fight was the norm.

Not that Walker was any angel. Mickey fought hard, drank even harder and loved the ladies, making him the perfect figure for the Roaring 20s. A brawler who employed more than his share of illegal tactics, although not on the same massive scale as Greb, Mickey was billed as 'the Toy Bulldog' due to his stocky physique and doggedness. Though he was only 5ft 7in tall, he fought the best men of his day from welterweight up to heavyweight, and had the distinction of holding future world heavyweight champion Jack Sharkey to a draw. Mickey was a world champion for nine years, holding the welterweight and middleweight championships successfully.

Mickey was born of Irish immigrant parents in Elizabeth, New Jersey on 13 July 1901. Because of his aggressive nature, he built a reputation as a bit of a scrapper in Keighry, a rough and poor Irish section of the town. If there was a fight going, you could be sure that Walker was one of the participants. Mickey's father Mike, who worked on construction sites, was a close friend of John L Sullivan, the former heavyweight champion of the world, who also was of Irish extraction. Sullivan used to encourage Mike to become a professional boxer but Mike said he had a well-paid job as a bricklayer and was content to watch boxing and boxers from outside the ring.

'After I left school at 14, my uncle got me a job with an architectural firm and sent me to night school to brush up on my studies,' recalled the younger Walker. 'That pleased my dad no end as he always had an idea at the back of his head that I was really cut out to design buildings and he was thrilled to bits with my new occupation. If only I shared his enthusiasm. I hated the job. I wanted to quit several times but I stuck it out for his sake.

'I worked there until one day the draftsman handed me a milk bottle and asked me to get it filled with radium. When I went to the drug store, the guy laughed at me. Finally, a man at the drug store said somebody was playing a joke on me. When I got back to the job and the draftsman asked me where the radium was, I didn't say anything. I just shot a long, hard right to his jaw and he fell flat on his face. That was the end of my architectural job.

'World War One had just broken out and I wanted to enlist, but they told me down at the war office that at 5ft 7in I was too short, but I got jobs in the shipyards as an iron worker. There were always plenty of jobs in the shipyards. In Staten Island, I was working as a rivet heater. I hadn't drawn my first week's pay when I got into an argument with the foreman and I knocked him down with a right to the chin. But he was a good guy. He let me stay. I was making $90 a week but I was getting restless and when that happens you have to move on.'

When the war ended in 1918, Walker had still not found his true vocation. One day, somebody suggested he become a boxer and he went down to the local YMCA gym. Impressed with all the boxers shadowboxing, sparring, skipping, doing floor exercises and working out on punchbags and speedballs, he opted to become a member as a bantamweight, hitting the scales at around 118lbs. Club officials wanted him to enter amateur tournaments and get some experience, but Mickey was anxious to go straight into professional boxing and earn some money. The man who triggered it all off was Jack Dempsey.

On 4 July 1919, in Toledo, Ohio, Dempsey won the heavyweight championship of the world by stopping big Jess Willard in three one-sided rounds. Reading about the fight and seeing pictures of Dempsey in action impressed Walker so much that he decided there and then to become a professional boxer. 'I always admired Jack,' he would recall. 'I tried to follow his aggressive style in the ring and he had that never-say-die spirit. He was my idol.'

Walker made his professional debut at the age of 17 in his hometown of Elizabeth on 10 February 1919. He made a good start, winning his first seven fights by knockout, before walking into a big right hand from Phil Delmont in the very first round. 'Down and out, it was the best lesson I ever had,' he said in the dressing room. 'It proved that you can't win 'em all. There is somebody out there better than you. It was a lesson I never forgot.'

Walker was managed at the time by Johnny Anthes but when Anthes refused to give him time off to visit his grandmother in hospital as he had a fight coming up that night and wouldn't have time, they broke up. The next day, Mickey travelled to New York and met up with old Tom O'Rourke, a much-respected manager who had had a lot of good boxers on his books over the years.

It was when O'Rourke pitted Walker against the experienced Panama Joe Gans that they separated. 'The guy was trying to get me killed,' Mickey would recall. Walker's next manager was Jack Bulger, who matched him carefully to give the boxer a chance to learn something about the game. Because he had no formal boxing training, nor any amateur experience, Walker was a crude sort of fighter from the start, but he packed a punch and relied on sheer aggression to often overwhelm opponents.

Losing just twice in his first 40 contests, all fought in New Jersey over a two-year period, Walker secured himself a non-title fight with the reigning world welterweight champion Jack Britton at the Newark Sporting Club, New Jersey on 18 July 1921. Just five days past his 20th birthday, Walker put up a creditable performance against the more experienced champion. Britton forced the pace from the start, dropping the New Jersey-Irishman with a fast clip to the chin in the opening minute – 'Just to show the cocky kid who was boss,' Britton quipped afterwards.

Mickey took the world champion to a draw over the 12-round distance. Britton sportingly agreed to give Mickey a return fight, this time with the title on the line. The crafty old champion and the brash new contender met at Madison Square Garden on 1 November 1922 over 15 rounds before a capacity crowd of 15,000 excited fans. Tex Rickard was the promoter. They were not disappointed.

Walker knew he was in for a tough night as Britton was one of the top fighters of his day. More of a skilful boxer than a devastating hitter, the New Yorker of Irish extraction had been in with many of the greats and had a famous 21-fight rivalry with Ted 'Kid' Lewis, the fearless battler from London's East End, who was world welterweight champion when the 147lbs division was packed with great fighters.

'After 20 years in the ring, Britton was a poor match for the aggressive New Jersey man,' reported the Associated Press. 'Walker won all the way. Throughout the latter half of the battle, Britton was on the verge of a knockout. At one stage, his eyes were glassy but by a strategic retreat he managed to hold off his man until his brain cleared. The crowd howled as they watched the 21-year-old pummel Britton, and held their breath and applauded as each of the closing rounds ended with Britton, though reeling, still on the safe side of a knockout. The decision was unanimous for Walker, winner and new champion.'

'Jack was very cute and would box like the great Benny Leonard, the classy lightweight champion,' Walker would remember. 'But I always felt I could beat him. It's funny, you know. You didn't feel like a champion until you went out on the town and met the crowds along Broadway. Jack Kearns was my manager at the time. He was the guy who also managed Jack Dempsey, my idol, so I felt in good company. Moreover, he took me into all the top nightspots and I met all the girls, who fussed over me. It was terrific. This was the life.

'Kearns was a great guy. A big spender yes, but if he spent a buck he'd soon make another one. He was a big gambler. For 12 years, he took me all over the United States and into Europe, too. I fought whoever Jack found for me, big guys, little guys. It didn't matter. I was drinking, dancing, laughing but whenever I had a fight coming up, I'd get down to serious training, sure. Jack used to say, "Have fun, but don't neglect your training." It was good advice.'

It is an indication of how good Walker was in that he very often went into the ring drunk, having being on the booze earlier in the day, but it never affected his performance. 'It's true,' he said. 'Instead of swigging ammonia water between rounds, Doc would give me booze. To be honest, there were times I didn't know who I was fighting until the day after the fight when I read the newspaper reports. I'm not proud of that, and it's not the way a boxer should conduct himself. I lived hard and fast, and I got away with it. But what the hell. It's over now and I may as well tell it the way it was.'

Despite his wild lifestyle, and supported by his playboy manager, Walker successfully defended his welterweight title three times. By now, however, Mickey was getting ambitious. He wanted to move up a division and have a crack at Harry Greb's middleweight title. 'Greb's title is there for the taking,' he told Doc Kearns. 'I'm a better boxer than he is and I can handle his brawling tactics. What say, Doc?' Kearns thought for a moment before replying: 'Okay, but let's see what kind of money they are offering us. If it's what we want, then we'll sign.' The actual purse monies have never been revealed but Kearns would admit in later years that he had no problem accepting the terms. In any event, victory would bring Walker his second world title and then they could really call the shots. The championship fight for Greb's world middleweight title was set for the Polo Grounds. The date was 2 July 1925.

Let it be said that Greb was one of the greatest fighters of all time. He had a highly aggressive, very fast, swarming style of fighting and buried his opponents under a blizzard of punches. He was elusive with excellent footwork, jumping in and out of opponents' range. He was also a master at dirty fighting.

Contemporary writers would record that Greb was the kind of fighter who attacked life in the same way he went for opponents in the ring, as if he knew he would not live to celebrate his next birthday. He charged at life head on, as his dented nose proved. So why hold back? Why play it cool? Why not live every day as if it was your last? To Harry Greb, the world was a big nightclub overflowing with glamorous girls and bubbling champagne. He lived hard and had a total disregard for training, most of which he did in bars. 'Harry was a wild stallion who couldn't be tamed and I certainly didn't try to tame him,' said James 'Red' Mason, his first manager. 'Remarkably, he rarely lost, a tribute to his ability and staying power.'

Greb biographer Bill Paxton believes the many tales of the fighter's exploits with women were greatly exaggerated. 'He was married faithfully to a woman he loved for five years and was dating her for years before that,' Paxton wrote in *The Fearless Harry Greb*. 'After her death, he sowed some wild oats but eventually settled down a little. Greb then had two lengthy relationships with women he was engaged to. Many of the myths surrounding Greb's alleged womanising throughout his career are perpetuated by people's opinion of how they would expect a boxer like Greb to act.'

Harry was born on 6 June 1894 in Pittsburgh, Pennsylvania to a German father and an American mother. On leaving school at 16, he got a job as an electrician's apprentice in a local mining plant. Later on, he ran away from home 'to seek a life of adventure', only to return a little later when, by his own admission, he felt the pangs of loneliness but particularly missed his mother's cooking. Back at the mining plant, he discovered a local amateur boxing club, Waldemier Hall, about a mile of so from his home. On making enquiries, he was invited to join the club.

After several weeks, with Harry working out with the boxing coach everybody knew simply as Skipper Manning, the club announced it was about to stage a big boxing and wrestling tournament over three nights in which all club members, including their latest recruit, would participate. Greb would compete in the 147lbs division, welterweight. He won all three of his bouts and made up his mind to stick with boxing. While learning the rudiments of the fight business, Harry had just five fights over a three-month period before making up his mind to turn professional.

'First, I had to have a manager and after asking round I learned that a guy named James 'Red' Mason looked after a few local pros and I would approach him,' recalled Greb. 'The first thing Mason asked me was "Are you game?" I replied that I guess I was as I had fallen from the window of a three-storey house [and landed] on my head without being hurt. That convinced him and he took me under his wing. Mason was a good guy and he managed me for all of my career with the exception of a few months in 1921 and 1922. Any success I ever had would be down to Red, who got me the fights that mattered.'

Greb made his professional debut at the Exposition Hall, Pittsburgh on 29 May 1913 over six rounds against Frank Kirkwood. Even though it was a no-decision bout with no official verdict announced, the ringside newspapermen gave it to Greb on points. It was the beginning of a long and busy career which would take Harry to fistic greatness and a firm place in boxing history as one of the all-time immortals.

A quick glance at his record shows what a busy boxer he was. In his first year, 1913, he had nine fights. In 1914, he had 17 and the following year 23. In 1916, he fought 19 times and in 1917 he entered the ring an astonishing 37 times. They were all no-decision fights, as the rules demanded at the time, with ringside reporters deciding the winners, but Greb's record shows rare losses.

One of his defeats was in his seventh bout, when he was knocked out by Joe Chip in the Old City Hall, Pittsburgh on 29 November 1913. Chip was a younger brother of George Chip, the reigning world middleweight champion, and he was able to pick up many tips from his elder. With a 14lbs difference in the weights, Greb won the first round on his aggression but the crafty Chip saw an opening in the second round and caught Greb with a fast, hard right to the jaw that sent the Pittsburgher down and out. It would be the first and only time Greb was knocked out by a punch. In the future, there would be one loss by stoppage but the Chip fight was completely different. Harry and his manager 'Red' Mason put it down to inexperience.

Greb was now not only developing into a middleweight but was taking on light-heavyweights and heavyweights. In 1915, he went in against Billy Miske, a future opponent of heavyweight Jack Dempsey, and forced a draw. Later that year, he fought Tom Gibbons, who would take Dempsey the full 15 rounds in a championship fight several years later. Gibbons would be a bit too crafty for Greb on that occasion, with a similar result in two later fights. Harry would finally master the man from St Paul, Minnesota in their fourth and final meeting with a points win over 15 rounds at Madison Square Garden in March 1922.

Harry got his first chance at the world middleweight title on 30 April 1917 against Al McCoy in the Exposition Hall, Pittsburgh, but it was a no-decision bout. Under the existing rules at the time, a challenger would have to win by a knockout to claim the title. Cheered on by a crowd of 5,000 rooting for their local hero, Greb dominated the action throughout the ten fast rounds.

Describing the last two rounds, Greb biographer Bill Paxton wrote: 'When round nine started, Greb rushed after McCoy and got him against the ropes, where he bombarded him with constant punches until McCoy staggered. A normal fighter would have gone down under this barrage but McCoy was trying to stay on his feet to save his title. This was a massacre in which Greb was said to have thrown 500 punches to one. McCoy was barely on his feet when the round ended.

'The tenth and final round began and both fighters shook hands before continuing. The crowd was yelling for a knockout. Greb followed McCoy like a cat and drove him into a corner, then on to the ropes. McCoy made a last-ditch effort but Greb was throwing everything at McCoy, yet he was still staying on his feet, albeit barely. The champion was taking an immense amount of punishment when the final bell rang. Greb won every single round but he didn't get the knockout or the title. If Greb had knocked out McCoy, he may have reigned as middleweight champion for nine uninterrupted years.'

Greb would remember in later years: 'Sure, I was disappointed with what happened but there you go. I felt I would get another shot at the title later on because I believed in myself. If you don't believe in yourself, who will? My time would come. I was sure of that. There was a hell of a lot of competition around in those days and a guy had to be on his game to survive. I really wanted that middleweight title, or any title, and I would take on anybody to get that opportunity.'

Greb increased his ring activity in 1919 with 45 fights, topping the 37 two years earlier. He took on middleweights, light-heavyweights and heavyweights. It made no difference to the 'Pittsburgh Windmill'. When Jack Dempsey won the heavyweight title from Jess Willard that year, Greb sent off a telegram challenging him to a title fight. Dempsey's manager Jack 'Doc' Kearns replied: 'Put on some more pounds, kid, and you got yourself a title shot.'

Personally, Dempsey did not relish taking on the tearaway middleweight contender and they never shared a ring, except for several exhibition matches in 1920. Historians agree, though, that it would have been some fight, although the odds would have favoured the heavyweight champion. Ironically, when Greb fought Mickey Walker in 1925, Walker was managed by 'Doc' Kearns.

By the end of 1921, Greb had long since established himself as one of the most formidable fighters in the world. It was only his close friends and confidants who knew that he was now blind in his right eye as a result of a tough battle with Kid Norfolk, known as the 'Black Thunderbolt', in Forbes Field, Pittsburgh on 29 August 1921. Norfolk was one of many outstanding boxers denied a title shot because of the infamous colour bar. Outweighed by 17lbs, Greb waded into Norfolk straight away but was dropped in the third round for a quick count by a flashing right to the jaw. It was a no-decision bout but the newspapermen agreed that Harry won the verdict.

Greb complained after the fight of pain in his right eye and, following a private examination, it was discovered that he had suffered a retinal detachment. The trouble was aggravated in a fight a year later against Captain Jack Roper, which he also won. But the injuries were boxing's best-kept secret and would not be revealed until after Greb's death in October 1926, when his personal physician Dr Carl S McGivern, based in Atlantic City, gave the news to the *New York Times*. Questions were then asked, such as: 'How did Greb pass his medicals before his fights?' 'How did he fool the commissioners?' It seems he memorised the wall charts as well as having 'friends' in commission offices.

Harry beat his old rival Tom Gibbons over 15 rounds on 13 March 1922, a year before Gibbons would take heavyweight champion Jack Dempsey the full distance in a title fight. Gene Tunney, the classy New York light-heavyweight contender, fancied his chances against Greb and the match was set for Madison Square Garden on 23 May 1923. The American light-heavyweight title, which Tunney had won by outpointing Battling Levinsky over 12 rounds the previous year, would be on the line.

Tunney was a master technician with a solid defence who could use aggressive tactics when needed. A former US Marine, he was the son of a comfortably off Irish family in Greenwich Village, New York. Gene always aspired to the world heavyweight title and mapped out his campaign to that end. His career began in earnest on his return from First World War service in France. An unbeaten run of 22 contests qualified him for the Levinsky challenge and he was confident he would emerge the winner.

'Many people said I couldn't hit hard but that wasn't true,' he would recall. 'The point was that I didn't feel the need to go in for the kill against an opponent when I felt I could outbox him. That was my style – boxer not fighter. Normally I could hit hard enough, as anybody who studied my fights might have known. But the impression was that I was essentially defensive, the very reverse of a killer, the prizefighter who read books and mingled with literary figures like George Bernard Shaw and Thornton Wilder, and spent a lot of time reading Shakespeare. As a West Side kid fooling around with boxing gloves, I had been for some reason of temperament more interested in dodging a blow than in striking one.'

The Greb–Walker bout followed a four-week run of the Ringling Brothers Three-Ring Circus, billed as 'The Greatest Show On Earth'. But the 15,000 fans did not expect any clowning, fun or frolics on fight night. With the winner expected to get the next crack at the world light-heavyweight title held by the Frenchman, Georges Carpentier, Tunney was considered too inexperienced to handle the rough, tough middleweight contender and Harry climbed into the smoke-filled ring a 3/1 favourite over the younger, heavier champion. It was a fight in which, by now, official decisions were allowed in New York, on points or inside the distance.

What happened once the first bell sounded 'was something of a cross between a boxing contest and a back-alley mugging', said Bert Sugar in *The Great Fights: A History of Boxing's Greatest Bouts.* The pattern was set in the first round when Greb rushed at Tunney, butting him squarely in the face and breaking Gene's nose. Tunney, in great pain, fought timidly as Greb alternated between using his patented windmill attack and a manoeuvre which consisted of grabbing Tunney's head with one hand while punching with the other.

This tactic earned a warning from referee Kid McPartland, a former boxer and one of America's top officials, and infuriated the pro-Tunney crowd. After 15 brutal rounds, Tunney was a badly beaten man and would have been knocked out had Greb possessed a heavier punch. Interestingly, it was to be the only loss on Tunney's overall record of 63 fights – including one draw – to the day he retired as undefeated heavyweight champion of the world six years later.

Greb was the new champion but he lost many fans. 'Greb cares nothing at all for the rules and regulations,' commented the *New York Sun.* 'He has two active hands that fly in all sorts of weird motions but the top of his head is his most dangerous weapon. If the rules of boxing were strictly enforced, Greb wouldn't have lasted a round without being disqualified.'

Greb should have fought Carpentier for the world title but the Frenchman opted instead to defend in Paris against the West African Battling Siki in what he considered 'an easy one' – only to be sensationally knocked out in six rounds. When suggestions were made to Siki for a title defence against Greb, the Senegalese fighter instead put his title on the line against Mike McTigue in Dublin six months later and lost over 20 rounds. Among the many questions asked was: Did Siki consider it wise to risk his newly won championship against an Irishman in the Irish capital during a civil war on St Patrick's Day, the national holiday? Apparently not.

Meanwhile, Greb continued his career, defending his American light-heavyweight title against master boxer Tommy Loughran over 15 rounds at Madison Square Garden on 30 January 1923. He lost the title to his old rival Gene Tunney on a split decision over 15 rounds three weeks later. Though the newspapermen generally agreed with the verdict, Greb and his manager did not. 'Well, it can happen even in New York,' 'Red' Mason bawled in a packed dressing room. 'They say that crime is abating in the big cities and that Broadway is exempt from robbers. Perhaps Broadway is but

Madison Avenue and Madison Square Garden evidently are not.'
Greb and Walker fought each other three more times over the next
two years, with Tunney winning two and the second to last one
ending in a disputed draw. What a rivalry.

Greb finally got a shot at the 'real' world middleweight title
after having two tries in no-decision bouts several years previously.
This time, his opponent would be Johnny Wilson from New York's
Harlem. The fight took a long time to arrange, however. Wilson's
manager Marty Killelea knew that Greb would be a heavy favourite
and was reluctant to let his man share a ring with Greb, who was
the No 1 contender. Harry and 'Red' Mason devised a clever plan
to persuade Killelea to change his mind.

They let out stories that he wasn't training hard for the title
fight and that he was doing his 'workouts' in nightclubs and
speakeasies. They reportedly paid a few waiters in Pittsburgh
and New York to serve him water in coloured tumblers and then
proceeded to feign intoxication in a highly theatrical spectacle.
When Killelea witnessed one of these performances, he assumed
Greb was ripe for the taking and hurriedly arranged for the bout
to take place.

In reality, Greb had been training in secret at the Conneaut
Lake camp, around 90 miles from Pittsburgh, before moving to
Manhasset, Long Island to finish his preparations. 'This will be
a pushover,' said Wilson. 'The guy is taking me so lightly that he
isn't even training.'

On the night of the fight, 31 August 1923, at Madison Square
Garden, Greb looked in great shape to go the full 15 rounds or
less. Where was the flabby, unfit fighter Wilson had expected?
He was nowhere to be seen. The fight was nothing more than a
roughhouse brawl. Greb opened fast, setting the scene early on,
and simply overwhelmed the New Yorker with hooks, swings and
uppercuts to any exposed part of his anatomy. So what if most of
his punches landed below the belt? This wasn't a tea party.

In the sixth round, referee Jack O'Sullivan broke up the two
battlers from one of the many clinches and barked at Greb: 'What's
the idea? That's the tenth time you've thumbed Wilson's inflamed
eye. So what do you think you're doing?' Harry glared at the referee
and said: 'Gouging my thumb in his eye, ref. Hell, what does it
look like?' Greb went back to continuing his attacks, giving Wilson
little or no chance to retaliate. Mind you, Wilson was guilty of

fouls, too, but what could he do? Try to give as good as he got but he always came off second best. At the last bell, it was estimated that the Pittsburgher had won practically every round – and most importantly the world middleweight title.

The following morning's newspapers told the whole story. The *Pittsburgh Post* headline was: 'Harry Greb is new middleweight champion of the world', above a report saying that Wilson was 'puzzled by Harry's tactics'. The *Chicago Tribune* said: 'Greb won the world championship by fighting rings around Johnny Wilson.' The *New York Times* reported: 'The Pittsburger was elated with the new prominence he had won but, as characteristic of him, carried himself modestly. Interviewed by James P Dawson, the paper's boxing writer, Greb said: "I think I showed everybody who saw the bout that I am Wilson's master. Now, any middleweight in the world can have a crack at my title. I don't intend to remain idle. If Wilson wants a return bout and a promoter will arrange the match, that's fine."'

Greb kept to his word. After a successful defence against Bryan Downey three weeks before Christmas 1923, Greb tackled Wilson again on 18 January 1924, winning a 15-round decision. His third defence was against Fay Kaiser, and this one ended in a knockout for Greb in the 12th round. With persistent calls in the press from 'Doc' Kearns for Greb to put his title on the line against his boxer Mickey Walker, the world welterweight champion, to decide who was 'real' middleweight champion, the match was signed for 19 June 1925 at the Polo Grounds. It would soon be rescheduled for 2 July when the promoter Humbert J Fugazy announced that Walker had to go to hospital to have treatment on an ingrown toenail.

Greb started his build-up at an Atlantic City training camp before finalising his preparations at Philadelphia Jack O'Brien's gym in New York City. Harry was an 8/5 favourite and when people noted how fit he was in public workouts, the odds increased to 2/1. Still, he wanted to bet on himself and change the odds. Writer Stanley Weston recalled: 'Several gangsters were shooting the breeze in Lindy's restaurant when, at around 2am, a yellow cab rolled up to the kerb and Greb fell out. One of the mobsters Arnold Rothstein, who had bet a bundle on Greb, looked down at the guy who was going to carry his marbles and broke into a cold sweat.

'Two glamorous showgirls hopped out of the cab and helped Greb get back in before they sped off. The gamblers looked at each other and then, as if a tornado had struck, disappeared in different directions, heading for the nearest telephones. They called all over the country and hedged their bets off Greb and put them on to the well-conditioned Walker.'

Irrespective of such stories circulating, writer Damon Runyon had a feeling that Walker could present Greb with some problems because of his youth. In his preview in the *New York Journal-American*, Runyon said: 'It is difficult to concede a mere welterweight having a chance against Greb, but this particular welterweight happens to be an extraordinary fighter himself. And the Greb he is meeting probably is not the Greb of other years. Walker, on the other hand, has improved far more than the New York fans realise. The writer is inclined to believe that he has a great chance.'

On fight night, celebrities from all walks of life took their customary ringside seats expecting a thriller. Famed announcer Joe Humphries pulled down the overhead microphone and announced that at the morning weigh-in Greb had scaled 159lbs, one pound inside the middleweight limit, and Walker 152lbs. As referee Eddie Purdy called the two boxers together to explain the rules, there were several titters from some of the newspapermen. 'Greb or Walker in a clean fight?' said one. 'Neither of these guys don't know what rules means [sic], let alone abide by them.'

Missing from Walker's corner was his new manager Jack 'Doc' Kearns. 'Doc' did not have his licence renewed by the New York State Athletic Commission because of a row with commission officials over his refusal to allow his fighter Jack Dempsey to defend his title against the No 1 heavyweight contender Harry Wills, an African American from New Orleans. Dempsey himself was willing to meet Wills but Kearns, supported by promoter Tex Rickard, always came up with the colour bar issue. Teddy Hayes, a long-time member of the Walker camp, took over proceedings. Greb's manager 'Red' Mason was in charge of Harry's corner. Greb was now 31, with his best days probably behind him after a great many tough fights. Walker was 24. Would youth be served? Almost 65,000 fans in the ballpark awaited the answer.

Both boxers started fast, exchanging hooks and uppercuts almost before the sound of the bell had died away. There was no easing off, as if both men wanted to get rid of the other in the shortest possible time. In the early rounds, it looked like the older man would be making his exit. 'For five rounds Greb, old and slow, took one of the most frightful beatings any man has ever had to take,' wrote one of Greb's early biographers, James R Fair. 'He was fighting back but his attempts were feeble, and Walker was strong and contemptuous. You winced as you contemplated what Walker would do in the next round, the sixth.'

Greb came out of his corner with a grim look on his face. Meeting Walker halfway across the ring, he drove the challenger back under a hail of punches from all angles, finishing his assault with four stiff hooks to the body. Walker held on tightly but the Pittsburgher shook him off and resumed his attack to win the round easily. Walker knew he would have to pull off something special to hold off and conquer this rampaging battler – and the sooner the better.

Matters improved for Walker in the seventh when he matched Greb punch for punch, repeatedly catching the middleweight champion with sharp right crosses. But Greb was a human tank, impervious to punishment, and he simply roared back into the fray. The eighth was another thriller, but it did seem that Greb was moving ahead with steady bombardments from both gloves. Walker was so dazed by a heavy right to the chin that he walked to the wrong corner at the bell before realising his mistake.

The ninth, tenth and 11th rounds followed much the same pattern, with both men punching away at each other and the big crowd on their feet. Referee Purdy had trouble separating the fighters from the many clinches that were marring the bout. Greb won the 12th round when he staggered the New Jersey battler, who had to grab the top rope for support. The 13th also went to Greb on his sharper punching, and in the 14th Walker complained to the referee that Greb had thumbed him in the eye but Purdy waved them on, apparently on the grounds that he hadn't seen the alleged foul in the fast action that ensued. In the 15th, Greb made sure he would stage a grandstand finish and swamped Walker with every punch in the book, and many that were not in any book. Walker was practically out on his feet in the final minute of the round but gamely fought on.

'I saw his right hand coming,' Walker would recall in his retirement years, 'but I was too tired to avoid it. It looked as big as a balloon shooting towards me. I raised my left shoulder to protect my chin, confident I could block the blow. But somehow it slipped past me and landed high on my jaw. I was not knocked off my feet but I felt silly. You know, like a man walking in a dream. It nearly tore off my roof.'

Finally, the last bell rang and there could be only one winner – a unanimous decision for Greb, who was still the middleweight champion of the world. It had been a classic contest, one of the greatest of all time, and *Ring* magazine would name it Fight of the Year.

'Let me say that Mickey is a hell of a fighter, and I want all you guys to remember that,' said Greb in his dressing room. 'I let him have it with everything I'd got and he still came forward. I reckon it's his fighting Irish spirit. In the end though, my strategy and punching power made all the difference. I think you will all agree on that.'

In Walker's quarters, Mickey paid full tribute to Greb and readily admitted that Harry was the best man he ever fought. 'It would have been great to have taken his middleweight title to add to my welterweight belt but maybe my day will come,' he said. Nearly 50 years later, Walker told Pete Heller for his book *In This Corner*: 'Harry Greb was the greatest fighter I ever fought. You've got to put him in the class of Stanley Ketchel and Jack Dempsey. I was the world welterweight champion when I fought Greb, who was middleweight champion, and he gave me a good shellacking. It was one of the greatest fights New York had ever seen, and there's no question about that.'

Greb and Walker fought each other again, but this time it never made the record books. It was an unofficial battle on the sidewalk outside a speakeasy run by the entrepreneur and ex-showgirl Mary Louise Guinan, known as 'Texas Guinan'. Born in Waco, Texas of Irish and Canadian heritage, she ran the 300 Club on West 54th Street, an exclusive club which became famous for its troupe of 40 scantily clad fan dancers and for Guinan's distinctive aplomb, which made her a celebrity. At this hangout of the wealthy, composer George Gershwin often played impromptu piano for famous guests such as Mae West, George Raft and Ruby Keeler, as well as top society figures and leading politicians.

'I had a date at the 300 Club and so had Harry,' Walker remembered. 'When we spotted each other, we forget about the girls and we got drinking champagne, as we were thirsty after our 15-rounder. "Texas" was sitting with us. We never talked about the fight. It was around 2am when we got outside. I said to Greb: "You know Harry, you'd have never licked me if you hadn't stuck your thumb in my eye." He looked at me and said, "Why you bum, I could have licked you anywhere, anytime, even if I had no hands." I said: "You think so? Then why don't you prove it?" He started to take his coat off and when it was down around his elbows and he couldn't move his arms, I wound up my best punch, a left hook, and let him have it, straight to the chin.

'He flew about four feet in the air, fell against the door of the club and slid to the ground. I might not have been able to put him down in the fight itself, but I made sure this time. As he was struggling to take his coat off and get to his feet, a burly Irish cop I knew named Pat Casey was on his beat. He came along, helped Greb to his feet, called a yellow cab, pushed both of us into the back seat and told the driver to take us straight home and let us sleep it off. Only a few onlookers witnessed that unofficial bout but I could say afterwards that while Greb won the official fight, I won the unofficial one.'

Greb continued his career, by now winding down, and retained his title by outpointing Tony 'Young' Marullo over 15 rounds at the Coliseum Arena, New Orleans on 13 November 1925. Tiger Flowers, a southpaw contender from Georgia, was moving up the ratings around this time with some impressive performances and Greb's manager 'Red' Mason agreed that they should give Flowers a title shot. They were also helping to break the colour barrier by allowing Flowers to become the first African American to fight for the title in almost 20 years. Not since Jack Johnson won the heavyweight title had a non-white boxer captured a world championship.

Flowers and Greb clashed at Madison Square Garden on 26 February 1926 before a crowd of 16,311 fans. Harry climbed into the ring a solid 3/1 favourite, even though he had trouble getting inside the 160lbs limit. Years of hard fighting, fast life and soft living were gradually catching up with him. In addition, his right eye had been giving him severe pain. Flowers, on the other hand, was boxing's 'Quiet Man'. Before entering the ring, he would always quote a passage from Psalm 144: 'Blessed be the Lord my strength, which reaches my hands to war, and my fingers to fight.'

Flowers took the initiative in the early rounds but Greb dominated the middle rounds. Flowers won a split decision, a verdict very unpopular with the crowd. Several newspapermen felt Greb deserved the verdict or at least a draw. Hype Igoe of the *New York World* wrote: 'I made it 7-5 for Greb and three even.' Frank Getty of *United News* reported: 'The worst the former champion should have had was a draw.'

They fought again six months later at Madison Square Garden and this time Flowers, an 8/5 favourite, was awarded another split decision, which brought a storm of booing from the crowd. It was Greb's last fight. In October, he was involved in a car accident in Pittsburgh when he swerved to avoid two farmers and finished up plunging down an embankment.

Several weeks later, he went into hospital to undergo surgery to repair facial damage caused by the accident and boxing, and to have treatment on his eyes, as he now only had partial vision. He never left the hospital alive. 'Following the operation, Greb fell into a state of coma from which he failed to rally,' reported the *New York Times*. 'Death was attributed to heart failure induced by the shock of the operation combined with the injuries received in the accident.' He was 32.

Meanwhile, Walker continued to dominate his welterweight title challengers before losing to Pete Latzo at the Watres Armoury, Scranton, Pennsylvania on 20 May 1926. 'Latzo won simply because he was a better boxer than Walker,' wrote James P Dawson of the *New York Times*. 'He stood up under the terrific body punishment the champion inflicted and despite this attack was able to come back with a counter-offensive that invariably swept Walker before it and not infrequently had the defending champion stung and staggering. Both judges awarded the fight to Latzo while the referee, who was therefore not required under Pennsylvania law, called it a draw.'

Walker blamed his weight-making ordeal in trying to get down to 147lbs as his undoing. On 3 December 1926, he challenged Greb's two-time conqueror Tiger Flowers at the Chicago Coliseum and won a very unpopular verdict after ten rounds of hard action, with boos and angry shouts greeting the decision of referee Benny Yanger, the sole official under Illinois rules. Reports of the fight the following day showed that all the newspapermen, including three from the *Chicago Tribune*, felt Flowers had been robbed. The Illinois Commission carried out an investigation but could find no evidence of a fix.

Early in the New Year, Walker's manager 'Doc' Kearns received a telegram from the London impresario Charles B Cochran for a title defence against Scotland's Tommy Milligan, the British middleweight champion. 'There's good money in it for you both,' promised Cochran. Kearns accepted but insisted that the guarantee, $125,000, was delivered to him in New York before the Walker party sailed for England. Kearns got his money, took his percentage and handed the rest to Walker. Before a 10,000 crowd at London's Olympia on 30 June 1927, Milligan was outclassed and took the count in the tenth following a left hook to the body and a right to the jaw, just as the towel came fluttering in.

In the meantime, Flowers and his handlers were seeking a rematch with Walker but Tiger had to go into hospital to have surgery to remove scar tissue from around his eyes. Complications from the surgery resulted in his death on 16 November 1927, reminiscent of the circumstances that caused the death of his old rival Harry Greb the year before.

Walker was alternating between his own division and light-heavyweight with success, and before the end of the year he had beaten two former world light-heavyweight champions, knocking out Mike McTigue in four rounds and outpointing Paul Berlenbach over ten. By 1929, he was campaigning successfully in the heavyweight division, with his eyes fixed on the world title. Incredibly, he boxed a draw over 15 rounds with Jack Sharkey less than a year before Sharkey won the world heavyweight title, and outpunched one of the top heavyweight contenders in King Levinsky over ten rounds.

Walker also outpointed the formidable Bearcat Wright, who outweighed him by 100lbs. Mickey's heavyweight ambitions came to a sudden end when Max Schmeling knocked him out in eight rounds three months after the German lost a controversial decision, and the heavyweight title, to Sharkey.

Walker retired, aged 34, just before Christmas 1935 following a defeat in seven rounds by the German, Eric Seelig. It was time to get out, having compiled a 93-19-4 record and 46 no-decision bouts. He ran a popular New York bar on Eighth Avenue and 49th Street, across the street from Madison Square Garden, made a brief excursion into movies and wrote a column for the *National Police Gazette*. Walker also took up painting as a hobby after seeing the movie *The Moon and Sixpence* starring George Sanders and based on a novel by W Somerset Maugham. 'I couldn't forget that movie,' he remembered. 'It was all about a French businessman who went to the South Seas and painted pictures.

'It was a true story and it showed how this successful man sacrificed his home and family to discover true satisfaction. I was drinking and running around at the time and I forgot my worries when I picked up a dab of paint and smeared it on a canvas. An artist friend gave me a few tips and I was up and running. I had my paintings on display in art galleries in New York and made a good living at it. I had found a new way of life which I enjoyed.'

The former world champion at two weights would often say he found his new hobby less painful – putting paint rather than opponents on the canvas. Walker also maintained his interest in the sport that made him famous and was often introduced from the ring at big fights. He died on 28 April 1981, aged 79.

Chapter 14

Night of the
record breakers

**Lennox Lewis v Michael Grant,
Madison Square Garden,
29 April 2000**

WHEN England's Lennox Lewis and America's Michael Grant climbed through the ropes to contest the destination of the heavyweight championship of the world at boxing's most famous arena, they smashed a long-standing record.

Lewis, at 247lbs, and Grant, at 250lbs, were the heaviest pair for 67 years to fight for boxing's most prestigious title, at a combined 497lbs. The biggest previous aggregate was in October 1933 when the 259lbs Italian Primo Carnera faced the 30lbs lighter Paulino Uzcudun of Spain in Rome. The Lewis–Grant record would stand for seven years before the giant Russian Nikolay Valuev, all 7ft of him, finished off the American challenger Jameel McCline, a mere 6ft 6in, in round three of their scheduled 12-rounder in Basel, Switzerland in January 2007.

Known as 'The Lion', Lewis has been in retirement for 13 years and now lives in Jamaica, but he remains one of Britain's most popular former world champions. There is never a shortage of autograph hunters, with books and pieces of paper at the ready, when Lewis makes a public appearance. *Boxing News* listed him at No 35 in their 100 Best Boxers list, ahead of fighters like Mike Tyson, Floyd Mayweather, Bob Fitzsimmons, Benny Lynch, Ted 'Kid' Lewis, Billy Conn, Bob Foster, Kid Gavilan, Barney Ross and many others. He was unquestionably the greatest of Britain's modern heavyweights, with many experts calling him the best big man ever to come from these islands. The first Briton to be universally recognised as world heavyweight champion for over 100 years, Lewis was inducted into the International Boxing Hall of Fame in Canastota, New York in 2009 – the supreme honour.

Back in the spring of 2000, he was the reigning heavyweight champion of the world and when the offer came to put his title up against the American contender Michael Grant at Madison Square Garden on 29 April 2000, he had no intention of refusing. A wealthy man, Lewis did not need the big purse running into millions but wanted to prove he was the best heavyweight in the world. Grant was the No 3 contender and had been going around saying that Lewis was a 'cheese champion' and would not stand up to heavy bombardment. Lewis wanted to set the record straight with a decisive victory, but he knew it could be tough.

In 31 fights, Grant had won all of them, 22 by either straight knockout or stoppage, as compared with Lewis' 35 wins in 37 fights, 27 inside the scheduled distance, with one loss and a draw. But there was still enough evidence to suggest that the quality of opponents Lewis had faced was stronger than those who fought Grant. Nevertheless, the American felt he had the leather tools to topple the Englishman. Now he had the chance to prove it.

Boxing people used to disparage Lewis as 'the mammy's boy', but there is no doubt that he has always credited his mother with all his success. Violet Lewis was brought up in the small shanty town of Port Antonio on Jamaica's north-east tip, where blue breakers pound in over the great sweeps of white sand and a fast-flowing green river, the Rio Grande, tumbles through gorges and great tunnels of bamboo. San Antonio was once the major banana port where many of the island's first tourists arrived on makeshift boats.

Violet's father was a casual labourer, her mother a big, strong washerwoman, and there were 12 children in the family. They lived in a little shack near the harbour. When little Violet was out of nappies, she was farmed out to live with her Aunt Gee, a vegetable hawker, and later, when Gee married, to another aunt, Lou. Farming out children to available relatives was more than just a custom. It was very often a necessity and a way of life Violet knew and accepted.

Violet still dreamed about a different life, a better life, far away from the hand-to-mouth Jamaican world, and the solution seemed to travel. She had been brought up to regard England as the mother country where she had been told 'the streets were paved with gold and money grew on trees', Lennox once recalled. In any event, Aunt Gee had already left Jamaica to set up home with her husband in London's East End. It was 1956 and Britain was enjoying the post-war economic boom under a Conservative government led by Anthony Eden.

Violet wrote to Aunt Gee and back came a one-way ticket to London, then known as 'The Big Smoke'. She started off by living with Aunt Gee but over the next few years rented rooms in a number of Victorian tenement houses converted into flats. All were close to West Ham United Football Club, which later on her two sons would grow to support. She became a nursing auxiliary and worked at several hospitals. Meanwhile, she had developed a relationship with a fellow Jamaican, Rupert Daries, whom she met at a party. She bore him a child but never loved him because of his jealousies.

Violet soon found the real love of her life when she met another Jamaican, Carlton Brooks, at a party. They socialised a lot before discovering he was already married. 'I'd never known,' she remembered. 'In those days men would leave their wives at home in Jamaica while they came to England to make a better life for themselves. When I told him I was pregnant with Lennox, he said: "I'm sorry Vi, I can't marry you because I'm already married." It was sad as he was the only man I ever truly loved. I would have married him but there you go.'

Lennox Claudius Lewis weighed in at 10lbs 10ozs at Queen Mary's Hospital, Stratford, in London's East End, on 2 September 1965. He got his first name from the doctor who brought him into the world by Caesarean section. Violet chose the second because it had an imperious ring about it. The remaining space on the birth certificate stayed blank. It was where the father's name would usually go. She decided to leave Carlton's name off and put down her own surname, Lewis.

When Lennox was 11 and his brother Dennis (named after Dennis the Menace) was 14, Violet made a decision that was to change all their lives. The daily drudgery of working several shifts a week at the hospital and looking after two children, as well as doing the shopping and household chores, was becoming too strenuous. Farming out the children to Aunt Gee and the two men, Rupert and Carlton, as well as often having to pay childminders when the others were not available, was not really working, so Violet decided to leave England for Canada on the advice of some Jamaican friends.

They told her there were good jobs in Kitchener, Ontario, 60 miles from Toronto. It was a 150-year-old German-Canadian town with a population of around 18,000. She would take Lennox with her and bring Dennis over when they settled in. 'I got a lot of abuse at school in England because I was black,' Lennox recalled. 'As a result, I got into lots of fights. Ok, I was hyperactive and real aggressive. If you called me names, I would walk up and punch you. I would want to fight. I'm not the verbal guy. I got myself into trouble with the authorities and I was sent to different schools, but not reform schools because I never fell foul of the law. When my mother told me she was taking me to Canada, I reckoned it would be nice to go to a different country and start afresh. I looked forward to it, very much so.'

Violet got in touch with some acquaintances in London who were flying to Canada and they agreed to look after Lennox on the plane. He was now 12, and 6ft tall. In Kitchener, he attended Cameron Heights Collegiate Institute, where he excelled in basketball, as well as Canadian and English football. Once again, as in England, Lennox got into plenty of fights. This time, it was whenever schoolmates made fun of his 'strange' Cockney accent. Typical remarks would be along the lines of 'You can't be a Jamaican with a voice like that' and 'Go back to England where you belong.'

After one particular punch-up a pal, Andrew Powis, suggested to the bullies that they should all come along to the local gym run by the Waterloo Regional Police Boxing Association and settle their arguments in the boxing ring. Arrangements were made to meet outside the gym but when the troublemakers did not show up, Lennox and Andrew decided to go in anyway and see what the place looked like. 'We had nothing to lose,' Lennox would remember.

The gym was presided over by Jerome 'Hook' McComb, a craggy sergeant in the local police force. McComb had both

Lennox and Andrew do lots of floor exercises. 'We went back again the next week and it was still the same, exercises, exercises, exercises,' Lewis remembered. 'Finally, I went to McComb and said to him that I thought all this exercise was a bit tiresome and when was he going to put me in the ring with somebody. He told me it would be shortly and, sure enough, the next week he had me in the ring with a big guy and I think I acquitted myself well.'

In his first official amateur bout, Lennox knocked out Junior Lindsay in two rounds. He would go undefeated for three years before dropping a narrow decision to Donovan 'Razor' Ruddock, whom he would subsequently defeat in a Commonwealth title fight as a professional. Adding more wins to an already impressive record, Lewis was now beginning to run out of opposition. His reputation had spread and potential rivals steered clear of him. By the time he was 15, in 1980, he was Ontario Golden Gloves champion.

The first major international title Lewis won was in November 1983, when he picked up a gold medal at super-heavyweight in the World Junior Championships at Santo Domingo in the Dominican Republic. His scheduled opponent in the final, Pedro Nemicio of Cuba, had broken his right hand in the semi-finals and given Lewis a walkover to the final. On his return to Kitchener, Lennox was voted Canada's Junior Male Athlete of the Year. By the time the 1984 Olympics in Los Angeles came around, Lennox felt it was time to test his abilities among the big men and make a bid for selection. He got his place on the Canadian team. Lewis progressed through the first round with a 5-0 win over Pakistan's Mohammad Yousef but lost out in the quarter-finals 0-5 to America's Tyrell Biggs, who went on to win the gold medal. He would later defeat Biggs decisively as a professional.

Disappointed, he returned home and despite offers from Canada, the US and Britain to turn to the paid ranks, Lennox decided to stay around and try to win more international honours. He was back in the US in 1986 when he qualified for the World Championships in Reno, Nevada but lost in the preliminaries to Peter Stoymenov of Bulgaria. Several other titles would follow before he was selected by the Canadian authorities to represent his country in the 1988 Olympics set for Seoul, South Korea. 'It was my dream come true,' he said in later years. 'Everything I sought to win as an amateur. I trained as if my life depended on it and I wasn't going to let myself or anybody else down. I would do my very best to win the gold medal. I had my heart set on it.'

Lewis got a bye in the first round and progressed into the second session with a stoppage of Kenya's Chris Odera in two rounds. This win put him into the quarter-finals, where he knocked out Ulli Kaden of the German Democratic Republic in 30 seconds. Now into the semi-finals, he received a walkover when his opponent, Janusz Zarenkiewicz of Poland, pulled out with an injured hand. Lewis had now qualified for the finals, where he would face the American Riddick Bowe, who had beaten him in a previous international tournament.

With the Games already riddled with allegations of drug-enhanced performances, the Lewis–Bowe decider would immediately follow the light-middleweight final between America's Roy Jones and Korea's Park Si-hun, which ended in bitter controversy. There was prolonged booing and shouts of 'robbery' and 'shame' when the Korean was awarded a 3-2 decision. 'It was a ringside disgrace,' said Lewis' biographer Gavin Evans. 'While Bowe was the face of the US boxing team, it was Jones who delivered in the ring with his scintillating combination of speed, skill and power. It was not one of those fights where you could mount an argument either way. Jones won every minute of every round.'

The Soviet and Hungarian judges made Jones a 60-56 winner but the other three – from Uganda, Uruguay and Morocco – called it for the local boxer. While the decision remained unchanged, a completely embarrassed International Amateur Boxing Association decided the judges could not be trusted and introduced a new 'computer' scoring system, where the judges had to punch the right buttons for the right punches. The system would be adopted worldwide. To make matters worse, the Val Barker Trophy awarded to the outstanding boxer of the tournament went to the 'loser', Jones, an admission that the decision was a travesty of justice. Jones, from Pensacola, Florida, would go on to win world titles at four different weights and is considered one of boxing's true greats. Sadly, he left Korea with just a silver medal instead of a deserved gold.

When Lewis and his team left the dressing room for their final, the crowd were still booing and there was general unrest in the arena. Lennox was told by his coach Adrian Teodorescu when they got into the ring: 'We can't take any chances with the judges. Get out there and finish him as quickly as you can. The judges may have sympathy after the Jones decision but we can't take that chance. They could well rob us if it goes to a decision, so let him have it.'

When the bell rang, Lewis advanced cautiously to the centre of the ring but Bowe was first to score, a stiff jab that drew blood from Lennox's nose. Lewis fought back with his big shots and seemed to be the stronger of the two. Bowe received a warning for illegal use of his head, which resulted in a one-point deduction. This meant that Lewis shaded the round but back in the corner at the interval Teodorescu warned him: 'You're not doing enough, for God's sake. Get out there and break up his attacks with your left jab. Hurt him.' Lewis nodded.

Going out fast for round two, a grimly determined Lewis went on the attack with a fine five-punch combination that sent the American back on the ropes, gasping for air like a beached whale, and the East German referee Gustav Baumgardt gave him a standing count. On resuming, Lewis found Bowe's chin with a hard right hook followed by a powerful left hook. Riddick was given another eight count but was on wobbly legs and Baumgardt intervened. It was all over after 43 seconds of round two and Lennox Lewis had achieved his amateur goal, to become Olympic super-heavyweight champion. Bowe protested that the stoppage was premature and that he could have carried on, but he was out on his feet at the finish.

'I really tagged him,' remembered Lewis. 'I wish I'd knocked him cold because he's complained ever since he was robbed. But he was gone. I'd hit him with some good shots. He was walking around trying to waste time so that he could get his senses back. His eyes weren't there, so the referee gave him the count. One more punch and he would have been out of it and he'd have had no grounds for complaining about anything.'

Flag bearer for Canada at the closing ceremony, Lennox was the country's first Olympic gold medallist for 56 years since Horace Gwynn won the bantamweight title at the 1932 Games. His mind was now made up, however. He would turn professional. The offers were coming in fast and he opted to return to the UK and sign with Frank Maloney, a manager/promoter with many connections in the fight trade. Maloney caused a sensation in the summer of

2014 when he announced, at the age of 61, that he had had a sex change and was now living as a woman, Kellie. But that's another story for another day.

Born in Peckham, London to Irish parents, Maloney was one of boxing's most colourful characters. He once harboured thoughts of becoming a priest, tried his hand at being a jockey, became a street trader, chef, pub landlord, taxi driver and greengrocer. He also liked sports. As a footballer, he had a trial with Wimbledon FC as a winger. He problem was his size, 5ft 3in. In later years, rival promoter Don King would call Maloney the 'mental midget' and the 'pugilistic pygmy'. Yet Frank's stature did not prevent him from having 64 bouts as an amateur boxer. 'I contemplated turning professional at one time and went to the gym, but my heart wasn't in it,' he explained. 'I learned how boxers were manipulated and regarded as merely raw meat by all kinds of guys and I felt that this was not for me. If I ever became a manager, I would treat boxers with the respect they deserved. After all, they are putting their lives at stake when they get into the ring.'

Maloney became an assistant to leading boxing promoters. He was a trainer in Frank Warren's stable and a matchmaker for Mickey Duff, and was well respected in the game. Fighters knew they would get a square deal from him. 'You have to have trust, otherwise you can forget it,' he explained. 'You find me a boxer who has had a bad word to say about me and I'll show you a living dinosaur.'

Lewis was criticised by Canadians for opting to go back to England to box for pay instead of staying in the Maple Leaf country, but he always claimed he considered himself British. But many British fans regarded him as 'a Canadian at heart and a Briton for convenience'. In an interview in 2014, he said: 'This controversy has been going on for years. When I decided to turn professional, I opted to return to England, the land of my birth and where my parents lived, to pursue my career.

'The infrastructure to develop boxers was not in Canada at the time. It was as simple as that. I felt, and rightly so as it happened, that England was essentially a boxing country and that is where it would be best to start off, and with Frank Maloney as my manager. After all, boxing was the birthplace of the sport going back centuries and where the original Queensberry Rules were formed. It made sense to me.'

Immediately after the contract with Maloney was signed in London, they left for New York to announce the deal to the sceptical American media, who laughed at the prospect of this little Cockney guy etc managing the Olympic super-heavyweight champion. 'Lewis is making a big mistake in signing with an unknown Londoner,' claimed the *New York Times*. 'Surely there are enough influential managers over here to take him over – and the offers are there for all to see.' After New York, they left for another press conference, this time in Toronto, where it was gently broken to the Canadians that Lewis was not their man any longer.

Maloney considered several American trainers rather than British to coach Lewis as he wanted his boxer to get used to US tactics and styles. Several established names were considered, including Angelo Dundee, who had guided Muhammad Ali, then known as Cassius Clay, to the world heavyweight championship. But Dundee was ruled out when he wanted too big a percentage and because of his reluctance to base himself in Britain for long periods. Teddy Atlas was another name which came up. An assistant to legendary trainer/manager Cus D'Amato, he once pulled a gun on a young Mike Tyson following an altercation.

Maloney heard the scar-faced Atlas was 'troublesome' and decided not to go with him. Eventually, Maloney opted for an ex-US Marine and boxing man named John Davenport on the recommendation and advice of some businessmen. Davenport would subsequently be succeeded by a trainer forever associated with Lewis, Emanuel Steward, who founded and ran the famous Kronk Gym in Detroit. Stewart was America's No 1 coach.

Lewis made his professional debut on 27 June 1989, two months before his 24th birthday and after six weeks of preparation. At the Royal Albert Hall, London, he knocked out Al Malcolm, the 215lbs English Midlands Area heavyweight champion, in the second round after a powerful left jab sent his opponent sprawling to the canvas for the full count. It would be the start of a run of 14 wins that would take Lewis to his first title as a professional, the European heavyweight championship, when he stopped the veteran Frenchman Jean-Maurice Chanet in six rounds at the National Sports Centre, Crystal Palace on 31 October 1990.

In his next fight five months later, against the world-rated and undefeated Gary Mason at Wembley, Lewis sent the Londoner into retirement in seven rounds and picked up the British title in the process, as well as defending his European belt. It is worth noting that the referee that night was Larry O'Connell, who boxed for London's Fitzroy Lodge ABC as an amateur in the 1960s and who, as a judge, would feature in the most controversial fight of Lewis' career in later years, the draw with Evander Holyfield in March 1999.

Following Lennox's impressive win over Mason, Maloney decided their next step would be an attempt to conquer America and campaign for a world heavyweight title fight while, at the same time, not forgetting the UK, where both were born and where Lewis got his start as a pro.

Lennox had already made his American debut in his second fight when he stopped the Ohio journeyman Bruce Johnson in two rounds in Atlantic City on 22 July 1989, but this second trip would be more meaningful. Up against Mike Weaver at Caesars in Tahoe, California on 12 July 1991, Lewis knocked out the local, a former World Boxing Association heavyweight champion, in round six with a smashing right hand to the chin. Six more wins got him into No 1 spot for Riddick Bowe's World Boxing Council title when he destroyed Donovan 'Razor' Ruddock, the Canadian regarded by many as the most dangerous heavyweight in the world.

A title fight with his old amateur rival Bowe was arranged. At a specially convened media conference in St James's Court Hotel in London to announce the fight, Riddick dramatically proclaimed that he was pulling out on the grounds that he considered the WBC a crooked organisation and that the acronym stood for Will Be Corrupt. He said the organisation consistently favoured Don King's boxers and he did not want any more to do with them. To many observers and the general boxing public, it seemed that Bowe was simply backing out of a risky confrontation with Lewis and was using the WBC as an excuse to do so. 'I looked into Riddick's eyes and I saw fear,' Lewis would say later. 'I knew then that he would sidestep me.'

On the way out of the hotel by a back door and followed by a horde of photographers, Bowe dumped a replica of the WBC belt in a rubbish bin, but went back when the snappers had left and retrieved it. The WBC subsequently proclaimed Lewis as their new champion retrospectively on the basis of his quick win over Ruddock in an official final eliminator. Bowe, meanwhile, held on to his WBA and IBF titles but regrettably he and Lewis would never met in the ring as professionals.

Lewis made three successful defences of his title before losing it to the Chicago contender Oliver McCall, a recovering drug addict, at Wembley Arena on 25 September 1994 in one of the biggest upsets of the decade. It ended in the second round when Lewis was floored by a tremendous right hook. He managed to beat the count but was in no condition to defend himself and Mexican referee Jose Guadalupe intervened 31 seconds into the round. McCall was the new WBC heavyweight champion of the world. Lewis had no excuses following his first loss as a professional. 'Oliver just caught me cold,' he said. 'The only consolation was that many of the great champions came back after a defeat – Sugar Ray Robinson, Joe Louis, Sugar Ray Leonard, lots more. I'll be back.'

Eight months later, Lewis was back in the ring. Overcoming a nervous start, he stopped the dangerous Lionel Butler from Louisiana in Sacramento, California in five rounds in a WBC eliminator. A return with McCall in Las Vegas on 7 February won him back the WBC title when Oliver was stopped in the fifth round of a bizarre fight. After being behind for three rounds, McCall suddenly turned his back on Lewis near the end of the fourth and walked forlornly around the perimeter of the ring 'weeping buckets of tears', as the *Los Angeles Times* reported. When referee Mills Lane promptly asked him if he wanted to fight, he said: 'I do! I do!' At the bell, Lane pushed him back to his corner. In the fifth, McCall was putting up no resistance as Lewis landed a barrage of unanswered punches. Lane had seen enough and stopped the fight after 55 seconds of the round.

Lewis made four further successful defences of his WBC title before meeting Evander Holyfield at Madison Square Garden on 13 March 1999. This was a unification title fight recognised by the World Boxing Association, the International Boxing Federation, the International Boxing Organisation and the WBC. It ended in a controversial draw. Eight months later they met again, this time at the Thomas and Mack Center, Las Vegas, with Lewis winning on points.

The WBA ordered Lewis to defend his title against John Ruiz, at the time a somewhat obscure Puerto Rican heavyweight billed as 'The Quiet Man'. He was managed by promoter Don King, who had manoeuvred Ruiz into their No 1 spot. When the WBC ordered Lewis to defend his title against their mandatory contender Michael Grant or forfeit the belt, the WBA gave permission for a Lewis–Grant fight as long as Lennox agreed to meet Ruiz next, always assuming Lewis defeated Grant. King objected to this and challenged the move in court on the basis that there was a clause in the Lewis–Holyfield contract stipulating that Lewis' first defence would have to be against Ruiz.

Lewis went ahead and signed to meet Grant in a title fight scheduled for Madison Square Garden on 29 April 2000, with the result that the WBA stripped Lennox of his title. The other three belts would be on the line. Lewis was philosophical about the situation. 'Four heavyweight belts, three heavyweight belts, I don't think it makes any difference really,' he said. 'People still regard me as the real heavyweight champion of the world and that's the important thing.'

It was convenient for Don King to have Lewis stripped of his WBA title and to rubbish the Lewis–Grant match. The promoter had acted quickly and paired John Ruiz with Evander Holyfield in Las Vegas on 12 August for the vacant WBA championship, even though Ruiz did not even make it into the top 15 in one ratings list. 'The Holyfield–Ruiz fight, too, will be more exciting than Lewis–Grant,' shouted King. For the record, Ruiz lost on points. It was quite clear that Lewis was the legitimate champion, and the Lewis–Grant bout for the 'real' championship. In any event, Lewis' team was already looking past the Grant fight and Lennox's next engagement had already been booked for London on 15 July against either the South African Frans Botha or Ukraine's European champion Wladimir Klitschko.

Negotiations had already opened, too, for an autumn match between Lewis and the hard-hitting David Tua from Western Samoa. Tua was ranked the No 1 contender by the International Boxing Federation and held a one-round win over John Ruiz. Lewis wanted to be a fighting champion despite the interferences of the various boxing organisations, known as the Alphabet Boys, such as the WBA, the WBO, the IBF and the WBC. In the meantime, however, there was the not inconsequential matter of dealing with Grant.

Michael Anthony Grant was born in Chicago on 4 August 1972 and while in college showed much promise at baseball, football and basketball. He was offered the opportunity of a professional career in football before opting for boxing at the age of 20. He had 12 amateur bouts, with just one defeat, before turning professional on 21 July 1994 with a stoppage win in one round against Ernest English at Hasbrouck Heights, New Jersey. Big at 6ft 7in as well as being powerful and enthusiastic, he made good progress in the paid ranks.

Wins over opponents in the various Top 20 ratings took Grant to the Lewis title fight, particularly a ten-round victory over the powerful but erratic Pole Andrew Golota in New Jersey on 20 November 1999. Knocked down twice in the opening round, Grant finally caught up with his man in the tenth, battered him around the ring and knocked him down heavily before the fight was stopped. With his confidence and resilience broken, Golota had nothing left. The result went down as a technical knockout, or in American eyes, a knockout. *Ring* magazine and *Boxing News* ranked Grant No 3 in the world, though some other sources had him at No 1. The real test would now come against Lewis.

At his training camp in Pimlico County, North Carolina, Grant looked very impressive in workouts and was confident of upsetting the favoured Lewis. The American had proven, particularly against Golota, that he could be dangerous in the later rounds, something that Lewis would have to be wary of. His respected trainer Don Turner, a former light-heavyweight boxer, said Grant had the equipment to beat Lewis. He felt he had the determination and confidence of Evander Holyfield and the height of Henry Akinwande, the British heavyweight, two former Lewis opponents. 'I'm fully confident there will be a new champion,' he forecast. 'Lewis has no heart and my man will be too strong for him. He will be unable to cope with Michael's workrate.'

Grant also had a supporter in the former IBF cruiserweight champion Glenn McCrory, a friend, admirer and former victim of Lewis. McCrory, from County Durham, visited both camps and came away impressed by the sheer effort, conditioning and confidence of the challenger, whose preparations lasted ten weeks and exceeded 70 rounds of sparring.

'Nothing is being taken for granted in the Grant camp,' he told *Boxing News*. 'Grant is extremely down to earth and they all realise how good Lewis is. If this goes past six rounds, I'm going for Grant. I watched as Grant went a complete six rounds on the heavy bag, the final three minutes consisting of 267 punches thrown, a considerable amount for a big man.'

Over at Lewis' camp at Mount Pocono deep in the hills of Pennsylvania, Lewis was sparring, running, doing his workouts in the gym and was reported to be ready for 'the fight of his life'. One major advantage for Lewis was that he would have Emanuel Steward in his corner once again. Steward had worked with many of the greats. Operating out of the Kronk Gym, his most notable achievement was with Thomas Hearns. It was Emanuel, or Manny as he was known, who transformed Hearns from a comparatively light hitter into one of the most destructive punchers in boxing history.

Hearns became the first boxer to win world titles at five weights, from welterweight to light-heavyweight.

With Steward in his corner, most observers felt that Lewis would be able to handle Grant without too much trouble. Manny had an invaluable ability to 'read' a fight better than most and would be able to pick out any flaws in the Chicago boxer's defence in the opening round and advise Lewis of the direction he needed to take. But lurking behind the fight was the belief among American boxing observers that they wanted a home boxer to remove this 'foreigner' from the heavyweight scene. 'Let's keep it American' seemed to be their motto. 'There was always this thing that Lewis wasn't an American,' recalled Lennox's manager Frank Maloney, 'and I had this strong sense that Home Box Office wanted Grant to beat him.'

Gavin Evans, the British writer and author, said: 'If you ignore questions of loyalty, you can see why an American network selling fights primarily to American buyers might want a big, popular, good-looking, clean-living, unbeaten young American as champion in preference to an older, more enigmatic Englishman. Grant fitted the profile of the perfect imaginary heavyweight champion in every superficial category. He really looked the part – 6ft 7in, powerfully built, usually weighing around 255lbs, with an 86-inch wingspan – and he was handsome to boot.

'He was also intelligent, articulate and, naturally, a born-again Christian. He played the piano, sang in the church choir and wore spectacles outside the ring. There was a good deal of Clark Kent about his image, gentle and urbane-looking in his suit, huge and imposing when he stripped down. Home Box Office executives, salivating over his potential, called him "the anti-Tyson".'

At the final media conference in New York, Lewis' last words were: 'They tell me Grant has been going through a super-human training regime but you can't put muscles on your chin. If you take the right sock on your chin, you are in trouble, right?' Grant's retort was: 'Don't forget Oliver McCall once finished out Lewis in two rounds, so he can be hit and hurt and put on the floor. Why can't I repeat that performance? He's vulnerable and his team know that. Don't forget, too, that he's 35 while I'm only 28. Fighters don't improve when they reach their mid-30s.'

When referee Arthur Mercante Jr called the two boxers to the centre of the ring for their final instructions, Grant said to Lewis: 'God bless you.' The crowd of 17,324 were expecting a good fight between two top heavyweights. Grant came out fast, connected with a long left jab followed by a fast left-right combination which made Lewis blink. This looked like being a tough night for the Briton as Lennox liked to have his man feel him out for a few rounds. But the follow-through punches from Grant were wild swings and smacked of over-eagerness. Was the American looking for a short fight before Lewis got into his stride? It certainly seemed that way.

Lewis was looking for an opening for his big right but Grant caught him with a hard left jab. Suddenly, the Londoner saw an opening and caught Grant with a hard left hook followed by a stiff right uppercut under the chin, which sent him to the floor. He pulled himself up at seven for the mandatory eight count but appeared unsteady and looked to his corner as if to ask for assistance. Lewis moved in fast for the finish as Grant attempted to grab and hold, but Lennox pulled himself free and landed four clubbing blows to the head that sent the challenger staggering into a neutral corner. The ring post broke his fall but Mercante applied the standing count and Lewis' momentum was broken.

When the referee waved them on, Lewis connected with a powerful left hook followed by a right cross which Grant took, although he was beginning to look in bad shape. Claude Abrams of *Boxing News* reported: 'It looked as if Grant might somehow survive the opening-round onslaught but Lewis – far more experienced at the top level, going back to his 1988 Olympic gold medal days – stood off and took a good look before following a range-finding left with a terrific right hand that sent Michael crashing to the canvas. This time, it seemed all over but Grant dragged himself up at eight and the bell went straight away to end his Calvary.'

This could and should have been the end, with either the referee calling a halt or the challenger's corner recognising their man had taken enough. Grant's trainer Don Turner wanted to stop it but the challenger said: 'I'm fine. This is a world heavyweight title fight, probably the only shot I'll ever get at the big title, so don't intervene. I have a feeling that Lewis has used up his best efforts. Let's give it one more round.' Turner nodded: 'One more round, that's it.'

When the bell sounded for round two, Lewis came out with a determined look on his face. He was anxious to find that one punch that would bring the fight to an end. He couldn't find it, at least not yet. Grant was still full of fight even as Lewis' punches came winging in. He held when he could and fought when he could. Nobody but nobody could criticise his gameness and his courage but in the cut and thrust of big-time boxing, gameness and courage are rarely enough on their own. A hard right cross caught Lewis full in the face but Lennox seemed unmoved. Grant was still taking the fight to the champion despite that disastrous first round. There was still a chance, albeit a slim one, that he could pull it off.

Lewis was continuing his attacks, always looking for that one opening that could end it all. A powerful right to the head rocked Grant and he held tightly. Lennox pulled himself free and connected with four solid smashes to the head and body that made Michael's knees buckle. He held on as if his life depended on it but the Londoner shook him off. 'How long can this last?' queried one writer. Grant, still full of fight, connected with a stiff right but Lewis found the opening he was looking for and whipped in a powerful right uppercut that broke through the American's guard and sent him crashing to the canvas, his arms and legs spread-eagled. There was very little chance he would beat the count and Mercante tolled off the fateful ten seconds, with the time of the knockout 2:53 of round two.

In the dressing room, Lewis complimented his gallant challenger: 'Michael's still a fine prospect and his second chance may well come. He should definitely keep on boxing. Me? I did my job and that's it. Styles make fights and Grant had the perfect style to suit me. Any guy who steps in front of me gets knocked out and that's it. If the fight had moved into the later rounds I would have showed a little more but I don't get paid for overtime. I just come to conquer and I feel I improve with every fight. As far as I'm concerned, I'm still the unified champion. I've always said I'm like fine wine. I'm getting better with age. Every time I step into the ring, I want to improve. My next fight is in England shortly against Frans Botha, so it's back to camp now and keep in good shape.'

Grant told the waiting media: 'I guess I got my tactics all wrong but in the end, I just got caught, that's all. Lennox is champion for a reason. He'd fought the best out there and I've no excuses. He caught me in the first round and it pretty much stunned me thereafter. I'm glad I came out for the second round because the intensity and determination stayed in me. But this fight was a great experience for me. I took the wrong mentality into this fight, for selfish reasons. Lennox showed me openings and I just wanted to take his head off when I should have respected the game plan worked out between Don and I. He dropped his hands and said "Come on", which was a smart move on his part. His power wasn't tremendous but it was enough to knock me down. But I'll be back.'

Paul Hayward of the *Daily Telegraph* wrote from ringside: 'Lewis' merciless demolition of Grant in less than two rounds confirmed the suspicions of the preceding week. Britain's first real world heavyweight champion for 102 years cherishes the title and the gravitas it confers. The reality of the Grant fight was that the American turned out to be hopelessly out of his depth. But let nobody say that Grant's spirit fled. Three times he rejected the safe haven of the canvas. The final punch showed how naive he was. A more experienced fighter would have seen Lewis' uppercut coming and jerked his head out of the position it was in, the bull's-eye zone. Grant was an off-Broadway fighter rushed up the line to give him a lucrative payday before a lesser opponent knocked him out and destroyed his mystique.'

Lewis had taken a major step in his slow journey into the affections of the American boxing public, whose boxing writers, somewhat jarringly, had voted him 'Fighter of the Year' the previous week.

Next stop was the New London Arena in Millwall on 15 July, when Lennox scored another two-round victory by stopping Frans Botha, summoned from the plains of South Africa and known as 'The White Buffalo'. Lewis' three titles were on the line and the win was 14 seconds faster than the Grant victory. On 11 November, it was back to Las Vegas, where he handed a one-sided boxing lesson to David Tua. Born in Western Samoa and raised in New Zealand,

Tua was a bronze medallist at the 1992 Barcelona Olympics but at 5ft 10in he was simply too small to make any kind of impression on Lewis. He had a powerful left hook but Lennox easily outboxed and outfought him to stroll to victory by scores of 119-109, 118-110 and 117-111. By now, Lewis was 35 and his hair was flecked with grey, but like so many before and since he failed to see the warning signs and the menacing shadow of Old Father Time.

Still, he carried on, feeling that he had a few more good fights left. Suddenly, disaster struck in South Africa. It happened at the Carnival City Arena, Brakpan against the American Hasim Rahman on 17 November 2001, with all three titles at stake. As Bob Mee wrote in his book *The Heavyweights*: 'After making a movie in Las Vegas, Lewis went to South Africa far too late. He was jet-lagged, under-prepared, arrogantly over-confident.

'Rahman's skills were ordinary but he trained ferociously hard in Johannesburg, went in fit and sharp and in the fifth round knocked out Lewis with a right hand to the jaw. At first, the beaten champion refused to believe it had happened – "He can't knock me out," he said in confusion, almost outrage. Seven months later a fit, fully motivated and to some extent repentant Lewis took out Rahman in the fourth round with one right hand in Las Vegas.'

There were calls for Lewis to retire then but he had some unfinished business to deal with. 'I want Mike Tyson,' he said. When they were both in their primes, the fight the world wanted never happened and you can take your pick as to why – contractual problems, promoters' squabbles, Tyson's out-of-control private life and a myriad of other issues. But a match was finally arranged, even though both boxers were past their best. They met on 8 June 2002 at the Pyramid in Memphis, Tennessee and while many had wished for a classic, it turned out to be as one-sided as a bull fight. Lewis used his considerably longer reach and superior jab to control Tyson and scored a knockout in the eighth round with a powerful right hook.

After the fight, the former world heavyweight champion George Foreman said: 'Lewis has proven without doubt that he's the best heavyweight champion of all time. What he's done clearly puts him on top of the heap.' The fight was the highest-grossing event in pay-per-view history, generating $106.9 million from 1.95 million buys in the US until it was surpassed by the Oscar De La Hoya–Floyd Mayweather fight in 2007.

Lewis' final fight was at the Staples Center, Los Angeles on 21 June 2003, when he defended his WBC and IBO titles against the Ukrainian Vitali Klitschko. Lewis should have boxed Kirk Johnson and trained lightly as he was fully expected to defeat the Canadian without breaking sweat. Johnson, however, pulled out and Klitschko was brought in. In the poorest condition of his career at 256lbs, Lewis struggled throughout and was rocked as early as the second round by a smashing left-right combination.

The Londoner opened a cut over Klitschko's right eye in the third round but before the start of the seventh, with a severe cut over the Ukrainian's left eye, the ringside doctor advised that the fight should be stopped and Lewis' right hand was raised by referee Lou Moret for a technical knockout win. At the time, Klitschko was ahead by 58-56 on all three judges' scorecards. A return was set for December but Lewis declined and announced his retirement in a London hotel two months later. His record read 41-2-1, with 32 wins by the short route.

Whatever happened to Michael Grant after the Lewis loss? He continued his career and went on to win the vacant North American Boxing Association heavyweight championship in 2008 and the vacant World Boxing Federation title in 2011. He hung up his gloves after two losses, in France in 2013 and Moscow the following year, with a 48-6-0 record, including 36 victories by knockout or stoppage. 'I had a good run and I've no regrets,' he says today. 'And I got to fight for boxing's most important title, the heavyweight championship of the world. What more can you ask?'

Bibliography

Birtley, Jack, *The Tragedy of Randolph Turpin*, New English Library, 1975

Curl, James, *Jack Sharkey*, Win by KO Publications, 2015

Dundee, Angelo, Sugar, Bert Randolph, *My View from the Corner*, McGraw-Hill, 2008

Evans, Gavin, *Mama's Boy*, Highdown, 2004

Graziano, Rocky, Barber, Rowland, *Somebody Up There Likes Me*, Simon and Schuster, 1955

Heller, Peter, *In This Corner*, Dell Publishing, 1973

Holyfield, Evander, Gruenfeld, Lee, *Becoming Holyfield*, Simon and Schuster, 2008

Jarrett, John, *Toy Bulldog*, McFarland, 2013

Johansson, Ingemar, Stanley Paul, 1960

Johnston, J J, Beck, Nick, *Babyface and Pop*, Bustout Books, 2011

Kent, Graeme, *A Welshman in the Bronx*, Gomer Press, 2009

Lawton, James, *Mission Impossible*, Mainstream, 2000

Lonkhurst, Bob, *Man of Courage*, The Book Guild, 1997

McInnes, Peter, *Randy*, Caesus Books, 1996

Mee, Bob, *The Heavyweights*, Tempus Publishing, 2006

Mullan, Harry, Mee, Bob, *The Ultimate Encyclopaedia of Boxing*, Carlton Boos, 2010

Myler, Patrick, *Gentleman Jim Corbett*, Robson Books, 1998

Myler, Thomas, *Ringside with the Celtic Warriors*, Currach Press, 2012

Paxton, Bill, *The Fearless Harry Greb*, McFarland, 2009

Roberts, James B, Skutt, Alexander G, *The Boxing Register*, McBooks Press, 2006

Taub, Michael, *Fighting For Love*, Stanley Paul, 1990

Tyson, Mike, Sloman, Larry, *Mike Tyson, Undisputed Truth*, HarperSport, 2014

Zale, Tony, Moyle, Clay, *Tony Zale, The Man of Steel*, Win by KO Publications, 2014